AMERICAN INDIANS AND THE
AMERICAN IMAGINARY

AMERICAN INDIANS AND THE AMERICAN IMAGINARY

CULTURAL REPRESENTATION ACROSS THE CENTURIES

PAULINE TURNER STRONG

Paradigm Publishers
Boulder • London

Copyright © 2013 Paradigm Publishers

Published in the United States by Paradigm Publishers, 5589 Arapahoe Avenue, Boulder, CO 80303 USA.

Paradigm Publishers is the trade name of Birkenkamp & Company, LLC, Dean Birkenkamp, President and Publisher.

Library of Congress Cataloging-in-Publication Data
  Strong, Pauline Turner, 1953–
  American Indians and the American imaginary : cultural representation across the centuries/ Pauline Turner Strong.
    p. cm.
  Includes bibliographical references and index.
  ISBN 978-1-61205-048-5 (pbk. : alk. paper)
  1. Indians of North America—Public opinion. 2. Indians of North America—Historiography. 3. Indian captivities—Historiography. 4. Ethnohistory—North America. 5. Indians in popular culture. 6. Indians in literature. 7. Indians in motion pictures. 8. Public opinion—North America. I. Title.
  E98.P99S77 2012
  970.004'97—dc23

                                                                    2012018339

Printed and bound in the United States of America on acid-free paper that meets the standards of the American National Standard for Permanence of Paper for Printed Library Materials.

Designed and Typeset by Straight Creek Bookmakers.

17 16 15 14 13   1 2 3 4 5

For Katie and Tina Van Winkle,
who know well that "girls grow quicker than books"

CONTENTS

LIST OF ILLUSTRATIONS

ACKNOWLEDGMENTS

This volume is the culmination of many years of research, and it has benefited immensely from the vision, expertise, and generosity of numerous colleagues. Art Pettit and Alfonso Ortiz first inspired my interest in representations of American Indians. Don Brenneis and Dan Segal proposed that I write this volume and encouraged me to make it accessible to a broad public. Faculty and students at the University of Texas at Austin, the University of Missouri at St. Louis, the University of Chicago, the Newberry Library, and Colorado College have provided supportive and stimulating environments in which to work. My students in Representation, Indigenous Cultural Politics, and Native American Ethnography classes have challenged and inspired me, as have audiences at countless lectures, conferences, and seminars. Hilary Davis, Gary Garufi, Kortney Kloppe, Patricia Lynn, Mercedes Martinez, Katie Van Winkle, and Tina Van Winkle provided invaluable research assistance. Hilary Davis, Suzanne McEndree, Suloni Robertson, and Chris Gilette assisted with the illustrations.

Dozens of colleagues facilitated my work through extending invitations and commenting on portions of the manuscript. These include Daryl Adair, Kamran Asdar Ali, Ana Alonso, Lee Baker, Elazar Barkan, Cora Bender, Tom Biolsi, John Bodinger de Uriarte, Don Brenneis, Evan Carton, Eric Cheyfitz, D. Anthony Tyeeme Clark, Raymond Fogelson, Sarah Franklin, Bruce Grant, Richard Handler, Sandya Hewamanne, Jean Jackson, Sergei Kan, Jennifer Karson, C. Richard King, Dana Klar, Klára Kolinská, Annette Kolodny, Mark Leone, Susan McKinnon, Mario Montano, Nancy Munn, Mark Nuttall, John E. O'Connor, Laurie Posner, Martina Rieker, Peter Rollins, Dan Segal, Joel Sherzer, Neil Asher Silberman, George Stocking, Michael Trujillo, Greg Urban, Barrik Van Winkle, Geoffrey White, Sam Wilson, and Norman Yetman. Barrik

CHAPTER ONE

THE ETHNOGRAPHY OF
REPRESENTATIONAL PRACTICES

> Manifestly, the *indian* is an occidental misnomer, an overseas enactment
> that has no referent to real native cultures or communities.
>
> —*Gerald Vizenor*

The Anishinaabe scholar Gerald Vizenor (1999) has written astutely that the *indian* is a "simulation and ruse of colonial dominance" (vii). Departing from Vizenor's insight, this book explores how various practices associated with this simulation—including calculating "Indian blood," adopting "Indian" mascots, assuming "Indian" names, and "playing Indian"—work to establish and maintain colonial dominance. Just as importantly, though, we will consider oppositional representations that challenge dominant power structures—as Vizenor does himself in promoting the powerful notion of "postindian survivance" (1999).

This first chapter, which sets the stage for the more concrete case studies that follow, surveys the main scholarly approaches to the study of representation as a context for the approach used in this book, which I call the ethnography of representational practices. Following Vizenor's lead, I try to reserve the misnomer *Indian* for representations, and use tribal designations (*Anishinaabe, Lakota, Osage*) or the collective terms *Native, Native American,* and *indigenous* to refer to "real cultures or communities" (vii) (although this notion, dealing as it does with concepts of authenticity, is itself problematic). There will be many necessary exceptions, however, including quotations, the titles of publications, the names of organizations, and certain conventional phrases such as "Indian tribe,"

"Indian treaty," "Indian reservation," "Indian policy," and "Indian Country." Indeed, as we will see, there is an argument to be made for preserving phrases such as these precisely because of the legal rights they entail, regardless of the misnaming involved.

"The Indian's Image-Maker": Scholarship on Representational Practices

The study of representations of American Indians first emerged in the fields of literary and intellectual history, notably with the publication in 1953 of Roy Harvey Pearce's *The Savages of America* (better known under its 1965 title, *Savagism and Civilization: A Study of the Indian and the American Mind*). In speaking of "the American mind" in the singular, Pearce assumed a degree of cultural homogeneity and consensus that is unconvincing today (Abu-Lughod 1991; Jackson 1995; Brightman 2006). Nevertheless, he anticipated contemporary approaches to the construction of identity and otherness in his analysis of the Indian as a figure who "became important for the English [colonial] mind, not for what he was in and of himself, but for what he [presumably] showed civilized men they were not and must not be" (Pearce 1965, 5). *Presumably*, I add, because the construction of "savagery" and "civilized" were, as Vizenor puts it, the most basic "ruse of colonial dominance."

Pearce is known primarily for his interpretation of literary representations, but *Savagism and Civilization* also considers the work of such nineteenth-century scholars as Henry Rowe Schoolcraft and Lewis Henry Morgan. For Pearce (1965), the "idea of savagism" as a "morally inferior and historically anterior" state of hunting and warfare (105) culminated in the studies of these scholars. This is true in two senses: although the idea of savagery (which we would now, more precisely, call an *ideology, discourse,* or *paradigm*) generated Schoolcraft's and Morgan's systematic investigations of Native American cultures (the first sense), the complexity and diversity their research revealed ultimately undermined the idea of savagery itself (the second sense). This led to the development of new interpretive frameworks centered on the concept of the *primitive*—a concept that, in turn, would be questioned and dismantled by subsequent scholars. There is, in other words, a tendency for representations of otherness (the *savage*, the *primitive*, the *tribal*) to develop and then implode (Strong 1986), only to be replaced by other representations that repeat the interpretive cycle.

Pearce opened up a productive area of inquiry that has been developed in major works in a variety of fields. Of several historical studies published in the wake of *Savagism and Civilization*, Brian Dippie's *The Vanishing American: White Attitudes and U.S. Indian Policy* (1982) is particularly worthy of mention.

Dippie traces the relationship between US policy and popular attitudes, showing the connection between nineteenth-century removal and reservation policies on the one hand, and the widespread belief that Native Americans were doomed to vanish on the other. The trope of the *vanishing Indian,* most familiar in James Earle Fraser's widely reproduced sculpture, *The End of the Trail* (see Figure 1), is central to the pervasive practice that Johannes Fabian (1983) has called "allochronism," that is, the representation of contemporary peoples as mere "survivals" or "remnants" of a more authentic past.

Until fairly recently, the search for exoticism and "authenticity" has led anthropologists and others to ignore or disdain significant contemporary or hybrid aspects of indigenous life. For example, Mick Gidley (1998) and others have shown how the photographer Edward Curtis erased clocks and other signs of modern life in his widely distributed photographs of Native individuals. Similarly, as David Samuels (1999, 2004) reveals, scholars' fascination with traditional Apache music has led to an underappreciation of the importance of mainstream popular music in Apache life. Jean O'Brien's *Firsting and Lasting: Writing Indians Out of Existence in New England* (2010) and Philip Deloria's *Indians in Unexpected Places* (2004) address the tropes of Indians vanishing or frozen in time with analyses that probe the relationship among colonialism, modernity, and primitivism.

Robert Berkhofer's aptly named *The White Man's Indian: Images of the American Indian from Columbus to the Present* is a more general work that connects popular and scholarly representations to the history of US Indian policy. Over the many periods and multiple cultural domains he surveyed, Berkhofer perceived a basic coherence and persistence in what he called "the image of the Indian." Like Pearce, Berkhofer

Figure 1. James Earle Fraser, American, 1876–1953, *The End of the Trail.* Widely reproduced image of the "vanishing Indian." Earlier versions of this sculpture were displayed at the 1893 World Columbian Exposition in Chicago and the 1915 Panama-Pacific International Exposition in San Francisco. 1918, bronze, height: 111.8 cm (44 in.), bequest of Arthur Rubloff Trust, 1991.325, The Art Institute of Chicago. Photography © The Art Institute of Chicago.

presented the "White man's Indian" as a negation of features associated with what today would be called White masculinity. The same image of savagery might be evaluated as "noble" or "ignoble," according to Berkhofer, depending on whether it is used to validate or critique Euro-American "civilization."

Berkhofer's (1978) genealogy of scholarship ends with the warning that contemporary anthropologists' "cultural conception of the Indian" might come to "appear as biased and mythical" as the more overtly objectionable imagery of nineteenth-century social evolutionism and scientific racism (68–69). Berkhofer was prescient in this regard (if unaware that in its emphasis on coherence and persistence his own analysis of the "White man's Indian" uses a monolithic concept of culture that would itself come to appear mythical). Even before the publication of *The White Man's Indian,* critical questions had been raised about the anthropological concept of culture and the discipline's methodology of fieldwork. Most influentially, the Lakota scholar Vine Deloria, in *Custer Died for Your Sins* (1969), castigated "anthropologists and other friends" for their arrogance, intrusiveness, and lack of accountability to Native American communities. Internal critiques emerged at this time as well. For example, soon after *Custer* appeared, Dell Hymes (1972) published an influential collection that aimed to "reinvent anthropology" as a more critical, reflexive, and politically transformative discipline. Such critiques prompted the development, over the next four decades, of more collaborative and activist research methods (Biolsi and Zimmerman 1997; Field 2004; Lassiter 2005).

During the same period, the Lakota anthropologist Beatrice Medicine and her Tewa Pueblo colleagues Edward Dozier and Alfonso Ortiz played important roles in convening the First Convocation of American Indian Scholars, a landmark event held at Ortiz's institution, Princeton University, in 1970. D'Arcy McNickle, the Flathead novelist and chair of the anthropology department at the University of Saskatchewan, also participated in the convocation. As the Osage scholar Robert Warrior (1998) argues, together with Deloria's book and the award of the 1969 Pulitzer Prize to the Kiowa novelist N. Scott Momaday, the convocation marked "the emergence of Native American voices into contemporary public and academic life" (116).

Anthropologists were well represented in this emergence. Among the issues discussed at the conference was the need to abandon the discipline's "litany of Indian exotica and assorted trivia" in order to consider the "philosophical and spiritual values" of Native Americans and their relevance for solving their communities' and the larger world's "pressing and immediate problems," as Ortiz put it (1970, 22–28). Similarly, in a collection published soon after the convocation, Medicine (1972) questioned the role of anthropology as "the Indian's

other scholars. Vine Deloria continued to be particularly influential in this regard: for example, he analyzed a scholarly treatment of the concept of Mother Earth as part of an ongoing "struggle for authority and the control of definitions" (1998, 68, 75–78). And in an important debate for the discipline of anthropology, the authority of William Fenton and other ethnohistorians has been questioned by traditionalist Iroquois in the context of disputes over the repatriation of wampum belts, the influence of the League of the Iroquois on the US Constitution, and the content of social studies curricula in New York State. These debates are the subject of several penetrating articles on the politics of representation in the academy (Landsman and Cikorski 1992; Landsman 1997; McCarthy 2008).

Certain indigenous critiques of representation have shown that laughter is at least as effective as argumentation in contesting outsiders' ethnographic authority. Zuni artist Phil Hughte (1994) has produced a hilarious series of cartoons about Cushing as ethnographer, collector, initiate, advocate, traitor, and buffoon. The Cherokee scholar Rayna Green (1996) has explored Mickey Mouse kachinas, parodies of tourists, and other humorous Southwestern representations of "whitemen" (206; see also 1988a, 1988b, 1992). And Gerald Vizenor has published a series of works that, as Karl Kroeber (1990) notes, show "how the modern term 'culture' itself imposes boundaries, restricts freedom, is the ideological equivalent of a reservation." While Vizenor's position on culture is congruent with postmodern criticism within the discipline, his critique is distinctive. Writing as a trickster or "postindian warrior," Vizenor (1999, 1–44) challenges "academic power and control over tribal images." He imagines a "tribal striptease" in which "captured images" (2005, 181, 45)—especially those of anthropology and photography—are cast off so that "postindian survivance" (1999) may be achieved.

As James Clifford (1988d) has pointed out in a review of Said's *Orientalism*, those who critique representation—ethnographic or otherwise—are faced with a dilemma: "Should criticism work to counter sets of culturally produced images such as those of Orientalism with more 'authentic' or more 'human' representations? Or if criticism must struggle against the procedures of representation itself, how is it to begin?" (258). Vizenor's work, situated within what he calls the "ruins of representation" (1993), would appear to be engaged in precisely this struggle against representation itself.

Toward an Ethnography of Representational Practices

Whether they view representation as a crisis, a social relation, a struggle, a ruin, or a set of technologies and strategies, contemporary scholars employ a practice-based approach to the study of representation. After an initial focus on reflexive critiques of ethnographic representation, anthropologists are increasingly studying representations and self-representations of indigenous peoples in contemporary public culture. Increasingly strict tribal controls on ethnographic research in the United States and Canada have encouraged a turn toward studies of representation, as has the growth in publication venues oriented toward the topic. Ethnographic studies of the representation of American Indians in public culture have also been inspired by historical events, such as the commemoration of the US bicentennial in 1976 (Chiapelli, Allen, and Benson 1976) and the contested Columbian Quincentenary of 1992 (see Chapter 3). Other sources of inspiration include the development of tribal casinos and tourism (Bodinger 2007; Cattelino 2008); the rise of the ecology movement (Krech 1999); challenges to the representation of Indians in cosmopolitan museums, sports, and commerce (see Chapter 10); the repatriation movement (Mihesuah 2000; Fine-Dare 2002); and the development of indigenously controlled museums (see Chapter 12). Each of these arenas is marked by vigorous struggles over representation.

Scholarship on representation is interdisciplinary, and it is somewhat artificial to consider anthropological scholarship separately from that of other disciplines. Nevertheless, it may be useful to note certain discipline-specific contributions of anthropology. In addition to the reflexive critiques discussed above, these contributions involve ethnographic methodologies and sensibilities, the development and deployment of practice-based theories of representation, and attentiveness to an increasingly broad array of representational sites and technologies. The remainder of this chapter will briefly consider the promise of each of these contributions of an ethnographically grounded approach to representation.

Although framed as an analysis of verbal play, Keith Basso's 1979 study, *Portraits of "the Whiteman,"* can also be read as a pioneering ethnography of representation. Drawing on years of ethnographic research among Western Apaches, Basso analyzes how "the Whiteman" is represented in spontaneous joking performances as embodying the opposite of appropriate Apache social behavior. Basso's analysis employs a useful theory of typification (adapted from the phenomenologist Alfred Schutz), emphasizing how conventional tropes such as "the Whiteman" are constructed through the selection and exaggeration of distinctive features. This ethnographic deployment of the theory of typification is an important theoretical contribution to the study of representational practices and is used in this book in an analysis of the typification of the Indian as a "captivating Other" in Euro-American captivity narratives (see Chapter 5).

A more recent ethnography of representation, Doug Foley's 1995 *The Heartland Chronicles* concerns Mesquakie portrayals of their White neighbors in the author's hometown (Tama, Iowa) as well as White portrayals of Mesquakies (including those of anthropologists associated with the "action anthropology" of Sol Tax's Fox Project). Making use of auto-ethnography as well as more conventional participant-observation, Foley explores the construction and representation of racial otherness in daily social life. As we will see in subsequent chapters, ethnographic and auto-ethnographic methodologies have also been employed by anthropologists studying the practice of "playing Indian" in children's games and youth organizations (see Chapter 8); the emotional attachment of sports fans to pseudo-Indian mascots (see Chapter 10); and the performance of Indian identity in tourist destinations, courts of law, and tribal casinos. Some of the most extensive ethnographic work on representation has been devoted to the repatriation of tribal artifacts and the development of the tribal museum, analyzed effectively by Patricia Erikson (2002) as a hybrid cultural form. The repatriation of the Zuni *ahayu:da* or "war gods" has generated landmark collaborative research on the politics of representation (Merrill and Ahlborn 1997; Ferguson, Anyon, and Ladd 2000) and demonstrates that the study of representation is of central concern to archaeologists as well as to cultural anthropologists.

Anthropologists in the field of ethnohistory were among the first members of the discipline to focus their attention on representation. Historically inclined anthropologists have studied the development of stereotypical representations of the Plains Indian, the "noble savage," the "squaw," and the "Indian princess" (e.g., Green 1975, 1988b; Albers 1989; Krech 1999; Medicine 2001). Historical and museum anthropologists have also conducted research on such topics as the representation of Indians in world fairs (Chapter 3), popular literature (Chapter 5 and Chapter 6), and folklore and material culture (Green 1988a). Increasingly, as discussed in Chapter 3, anthropologists are focusing on contemporary processes of historical representation and commemoration, at the level of both the community and the nation-state.

The representation of American Indian identity is a highly contested arena, one that has far-reaching political and economic implications. These implications are clear in well-known ethnographies of the Mashpee's unsuccessful bid for tribal recognition (Clifford 1988b; Campisi 1991). A more recent work, Circe Sturm's 2002 ethnography *Blood Politics: Race, Culture, and Identity in the Cherokee Nation of Oklahoma,* is centrally concerned with the symbolism of "blood" and the politics of authenticity (as discussed in Chapter 4).

Theories of commodification and appropriation have come to play a central role in anthropological studies of representational practices. Legal anthropologist Rosemary Coombe (1998) has contributed important work on the economics of representational practice, focusing on the processes of appropriation and commercialization inherent in "Indian" trademarks and logos. Ethnohistorian Shepard Krech (1999) has considered the appropriation of the American Indian as the "original ecologist" by the environmental movement, whereas folklorist John Dorst (2000) and anthropologist Peter Nabokov (2006) have examined contesting claims on the rock formation represented by the Lakota as Bear

Lodge Butte and by others as Devils Tower National Monument. Other studies have examined the commercialization of Native American material culture and cultural performances in tourist destinations and in the art market (Meyer and Royer 2001; Mullin 2001). Finally, anthropologists have joined other scholars in studying the processes of appropriation and commodification involved in representations of Native Americans in photographs and film, as well as the reappropriations achieved in indigenously controlled media (Ginsburg 1991, 1993, 2002; Prins 2002, 2004; Singer 2001; Lewis 2006).

The ethnography of representational practices, like the systematic use of the concept of representation itself, is still emerging. The following chapters aim to show the value of ethnographic and ethnohistorical approaches to the social and cultural processes through which representations are produced, circulated, reproduced, contested, and ultimately transformed.

Bibliographic Note

Overviews of representations of Native Americans include, among others, Honour, *The New Golden Land* (1975); Berkhofer, *The White Man's Indian* (1978); Stedman, *Shadows of the Indian* (1982); Todorov, *The Conquest of America* (1984); Francis, *The Imaginary Indian* (1992); Bird, *Dressing in Feathers* (1996); Bordewich, *Killing the White Man's Indian* (1996); Mihesuah, *American Indians: Stereotypes and Realities* (1996); Cheyfitz, *The Poetics of Imperialism* (1997); P. Deloria, *Playing Indian* (1998); S. L. Smith, *Reimagining Indians* (2000); Bataille, *Native American Representations* (2001); Ellingson, *The Myth of the Noble Savage* (2001); Huhndorf, *Going Native* (2001); Jolivette, *Cultural Representation in Native America* (2006); and P. C. Smith, *Everything You Know about Indians Is Wrong* (2009).

Influential theoretical works on the general topic of representation include Said, *Orientalism* (1978); Fabian, *Time and the Other* (1983); Hobsbawm and Ranger, *The Invention of Tradition* (1983); Clifford and Marcus, *Writing Culture* (1986); Clifford, *The Predicament of Culture* (1988d); Greenblatt, *Marvelous Possessions* (1991a); and S. Hall, *Representation* (1997). Sources on more specific topics are cited in the bibliographic note in each of the following chapters.

PART TWO
REPRESENTING HISTORY AND IDENTITY

The representation of history and identity are closely intertwined, particularly when history is understood as historical memory or tradition. As cultural studies theorist Raymond Williams (1977) wrote, tradition may be understood as "an intentionally selective version of a shaping past and a pre-shaped present, which is then powerfully operative in the process of social and cultural definition and identification" (115). The chapters in Part Two consider how the tropes of *tribe, discovery,* and *Indian blood* are part of an American selective tradition, a "national imaginary," that constructs a national self that excludes indigenous people—positioning them as antecedent to, and outside of, the collective "we" of the nation.

All contemporary treatments of nationalism have been profoundly influenced by Benedict Anderson's (1983) concept of the "imagined community." Annette Hamilton (1990) has built on Anderson's concept in defining "national imaginary" as process through which collective selves and others emerge "not from the realm of concrete everyday experience but in the circulation of collectively held images" (16). Discussing how Aboriginal art and knowledge are used in Australian popular culture to justify settler colonialism, Hamilton draws on Jacques Lacan's treatment of mirroring to describe the "imaginary relations" that Australian settlers construct in media representations of Aboriginal peoples as "ourselves looking at ourselves while we think we are seeing others" (17). In the present context, the concept of national imaginary offers a way to consider how the representational practices of Euro-Americans have constituted an indigenous "other" that reflects back their own categories of civilization and savagery, culture and nature, order and wildness (see also Ginsburg 1993; Conklin and Graham 1995).

Indigenous people are, of course, anything but an inert reflective surface, and settler society is hardly monolithic. The collectively held images that make up the American national imaginary are complex and contested, as the analysis of the tropes of *tribe, discovery,* and *Indian blood* in the following chapters will demonstrate. Chapter 2, "Tribe and Nation," surveys the complex relationship between two forms of political sovereignty in the United States: the sovereignty of the nation-state and the sovereignty of Indian tribes. As we will see in this chapter and throughout the book, contemporary debates over tribal membership, tribal recognition, land claims, hunting and fishing rights, tribal gaming enterprises, and the repatriation of artifacts and human remains all invoke particular understandings of national sovereignty in relationship to tribal sovereignty.

The trope of discovery is considered in Chapter 3, which focuses on struggles over the representation of history and identity during the years surrounding 1992, the five hundredth anniversary of Columbus's momentous transatlantic voyage. This chapter, "Five Hundred Years," explores some of the ways in which the Eurocentric historical paradigm of discovery was challenged during the Columbian Quincentenary by a multicultural discourse of "encounter and exchange" as well as by an indigenous discourse of "conquest, resistance, and survival." To understand *discovery, encounter,* and *conquest* as tropes is to treat them as figures of the historical imagination (White 1973; Fernandez 1986). Discovery, for example, is a trope with recognizable icons (Columbus and his ships), a limited perspective (Euro-American) that presents itself as universal, and a set of metaphorical associations with highly valued activities in American culture (self-discovery, scientific discovery, exploration, ingenuity, originality). The trope of discovery has long been central to the American national imaginary, whereas the tropes of encounter and conquest situate 1492 and subsequent events within very different frameworks, each with distinctive implications.

The problematic trope of "Indian blood" is considered in Chapter 4, which closes Part Two. Departing from a quincentenary installation by the Métis artist Joane Cardinal-Schubert, and taking into account the Kiowa author N. Scott Momaday's notion of "blood memory" as well as Gerald Vizenor's parody of blood reckoning, the chapter considers the implications of locating the essence of indigenous identity not in language, culture, and social relations, but in a physical substance that can be measured in drops and fractions and degrees.

Part Two, in sum, considers some of the representational practices surrounding notions of tribal sovereignty, national and tribal memory, and objectified identity. Among the sites of representation we will consider are court cases and school curricula, expositions and museum displays, and indigenous art and literature. In each case the representational practices are embedded in political struggles, and in each case they have significant social, cultural, and personal consequences. The contested tropes of blood, tribe, sovereignty, and survival are at the heart of indigenous experiences and imaginings of identity, just as the tropes of discovery, progress, and freedom are central to the American national imaginary.

CHAPTER TWO
TRIBE AND NATION

In his comparative analysis of nationalism, Daniel Segal (1988) asks his readers to consider the world map in *The National Geographic Atlas of the World*. Describing that map's presuppositions, Segal notes that the land is divided into "165 independent nations ... distinguish[ed] by colored perimeters.... No contiguous nations are bounded by the same color, and ... there are no interstitial areas outside of national territories, no graded areas where one nation merges into the next, and no areas of multiple nationality" (301–302).

However, if we focus on the United States—or, for that matter, many other settler societies—we will find that these presuppositions are not at all true to political reality. We discover encompassed territories, often labeled "reservations," that are by and large controlled by Native Americans. These areas are, indeed, "areas of multiple nationality"—and, often, of shared sovereignty (Biolsi 2005). The current complex arrangement, in which Native Americans are often citizens of the United States as well as members of 562 officially recognized "Indian entities," is a product of the twentieth century (Biolsi 2004a, 231). Yet its ideological and legal underpinnings date back to the beginnings of settler colonialism (Wolfe 1998) and involve both historical and ongoing processes of dispossession, appropriation, subordination, and resistance.

If modern nationalism is understood as "the forming of boundaried social wholes of supposedly like individuals, and the privileging of such boundaried wholes as the legitimate foundation of sovereign territorial states" (Segal and Handler 1992, 4), then Native Americans pose a distinct challenge to modern nationalism's very foundations. For centuries Native Americans have maintained and created alternatively conceived nations that challenge and constrain the boundaries and sovereignty of the United States. Although of distinct cultural origins, these indigenous nations took their present shape through the same colonial processes that contributed to the rise of the nation-state that encompasses them. And their form and actions strongly affected both the nature and the course of US nationalism.

Indigenous nations have been composed, over time, of a shifting and diverse set of persons conceptualized less often as individuals than as members of social groups. These nations have permeable social boundaries, and their populations are widely dispersed, despite attachment to aboriginal territories, sacred sites, and lands guaranteed by treaty. They are self-governing under federal protection and not under the jurisdiction of the states in which they are encompassed. In having treaties with the United States—by definition an agreement between sovereign nations—these indigenous nations accord collective rights to their members that supplement and sometimes limit the individual rights held by all American citizens. As Jessica Cattelino (2010) has aptly put it, "indigenous nationalism unsettles settler-state sovereignty" (285).

This chapter's treatment of the ambiguous and contested relationship between Native Americans and US nationalism is primarily concerned with the political relationship between what came to be called "tribes" and the United States. (The intriguing symbolic dimension of this relationship—the appropriation of the indigenous as a symbolic resource for the representation of American national identity—is central to subsequent chapters.) With an eye to the shifting significance accorded to indigenous polities in Euro-American discourse and in US Indian policy, this chapter will briefly survey the convoluted course of historical relations between Euro-Americans and the indigenous groups who served as allies and opponents, were eventually subjugated and encompassed, survived policies aimed at fragmentation and incorporation, and even today constrain the continental reach of American nationalism.

Recent manifestations of resistance to American nationalism by Native peoples—attempts to reassert separate nationalisms, sovereignties, histories, and identities in a situation of political encompassment—illustrate the incomplete nature of national hegemony in the United States. Like African Americans, Native Americans fall outside the ideology that "we are a nation of immigrants" (though sometimes indigenous people face attempts to reinterpret archaeological theory in order to assimilate them to the dominant ideology as the most ancient immigrants). In asserting collective rights based on their status as members of indigenous nations, while at the same time demonstrating a patriotism unsurpassed by immigrant Americans, Native Americans challenge modern nationalism's foundational premises of possessive individualism, bounded political sovereignty, and singular national identity (Handler 1988).

Contested Sovereignties: Historical Tensions between Native Americans and American Nationalism

> You know, there are two words which I use when I want to bring fear to the faces of BIA [Bureau of Indian Affairs] officials. One word is *nation*. When I say "Kiowa Nation," they know I am talking about treaties and sovereignty. And the other word is *reservation*. When I refer to the "Kiowa Reservation," they know I am talking about land rights and oil royalties. It makes them scared.
>
> —*Former Kiowa tribal chairman Pressly Ware*
> *(Moore 1992, 107)*

Contemporary political sovereignty in the space now called the United States of America is the result of changing relationships among "colony," "tribe," and "nation" as cultural concepts and as political entities—a history that underscores the historically contingent and ideologically potent definitions of political units in the North American context. The contrast between Native American tribalism and American nationhood that is so central to current American nationalism, and to US Indian policy, emerged only gradually and has repeatedly been subject to revision and challenge.

Nations Facing Nations: The Colonial Period

If today the relationship between American nationalism and indigenous peoples is one of encompassment and subordination, during the whole of the colonial era there was a considerably more balanced relationship of political, economic, and military opposition and alliance. Under an ideology of discovery (Jennings 1975), English legal and political policy conceived of Native Americans as subjects of the Crown, and the Crown and its agents (like those of Spain and France) claimed dominion over wide tracts of land not claimed or occupied by other Christian peoples. However, the earliest English colonies on the North American continent were weak enterprises, numerically small and powerless compared to indigenous groups, upon whom they depended initially for material survival. European settlers quickly established alliances with neighboring indigenous polities—such as Powhatan's empire in the Chesapeake Bay area—that were analogically treated as premodern Old World nations. (As will be discussed in Chapter 5 and Chapter 9, American popular history has mythologized these alliances between nations as personal relationships, such as that between John Smith and Pocahontas.) Although the Crown sought to make British subjects of their indigenous allies, between 1607 and 1775 the Crown and the various colonies entered into at least 185 treaties with indigenous nations (D. Jones 1988, 190–194), treating them as sovereign political entities—if only ultimately to limit their sovereignty.

Indigenous peoples initially welcomed English colonists as trading partners and political and military allies. But the colonial appetite for land quickly resulted in full-scale conflict. In 1622, fifteen years after Jamestown's founding, the Algonquians of tidewater Virginia launched the first of numerous wars of resistance against English expansion. These wars inspired a coalescence of small indigenous groups into larger nations and confederacies, indigenous-European alliances, and conflicting and ambiguous claims of dominion (Dowd 1992). In a complementary fashion, indigenous wars of resistance helped to forge alliances among colonies and an emerging collective identity among English colonials—united in opposition to the Native nations on the western frontier, the French to the north, and ultimately, the British nation across the sea.

For upward of two hundred years, Native Americans—especially the Six Nations of the Iroquois and the "Five Civilized Tribes" of the Southeast—held the balance of power on the American frontier, serving as a barrier to westward expansion by both the English colonists and the early Republic, and as a complementary political and military "other" against whom the colonists defined themselves (Jennings 1988; Richter 1992). This situation changed dramatically, however, with the birth of the American nation-state.

Nation-State and Domestic Dependent Nations: The Early Republic, Land Cessions, and Removal

Native Americans were viewed by the nascent American nation as obstacles to expansion, and often as predators and uncivilized enemies as well. Indigenous alliances with the British and their "savage" mode of warfare entered the list of grievances in the Declaration of Independence. On their side, most Native Americans favored the British over the American colonists, treasuring trade relationships with the former and fearing the expansionist designs of the latter. The powerful Six Nations, although divided among themselves, largely supported the British. Their military defeat by the Continental Army not only led to major land cessions in upstate New York but also signaled the beginning of the end of symmetrical military relations between indigenous nations and the former colonies. Even so, eleven years after the Declaration of Independence, the Commerce Clause of the Constitution treated "Indian Savages" as equivalent to foreign nations and the thirteen states, although they were designated not as "nations" but as "tribes."

The new designation signaled a major shift in policies toward Native peoples. Whereas the British Crown had often respected Native American power, rights, and interests against the interests of the separate colonies, the expansionist republic (and its separate states) demanded land cessions and removal of Native peoples from territory claimed by the states. Indigenous nations, it was held, had lost their "right to the soil" by military conquest at the hands of the colonists. By 1786, the original colonies in the North had ceded their land claims west of their present boundaries to the federal government, which sought to sell these lands, still controlled by Native Americans, to Euro-American settlers in order to ease the federal debt. Hoping to establish and maintain peace in the trans-Appalachian frontier settlements at low cost, the federal government tried to secure lands from Native peoples through compensation and removal rather than warfare—although the United States engaged in 1,642 official military actions against Native Americans (Fixico 2002, 381).

Two major strategies were pursued to achieve the goals of westward expansion, removal, and assimilation. First, indigenous nations were forced into treaties (through military force or its threat) that provided compensation for lands and required them to emigrate north to Canada or west of the Mississippi River, the original western boundary of the United States under the Treaty of Paris (1783). Second, Native peoples were subjected to "civilizing" technologies, including yeoman farming, Christian evangelization, and Western education. Thomas Jefferson went further, predicting that Native Americans would ultimately be subsumed into Euro-American society through intermarriage. Separation and assimilation remained the dominant US Indian policies up to the second and last quarters of the twentieth century (in which the tide turned toward self-determination).

A series of military actions, legislative enactments, treaties, and US Supreme Court cases reflected the new policies. The most important early legislation, the Northwest Ordinance of 1787, provided for the formation of three to five states between the Ohio and the Mississippi Rivers (on land mainly occupied by a variety of Native nations). The ordinance stated in Article III,

> The utmost good faith shall always be observed towards the Indians; their lands and property shall never be taken from them without their consent; and in their property, rights and liberty, they shall never be invaded or disturbed, unless in just and lawful wars authorized by Congress. (Carter 1934, 47)

Despite these principles of exhibiting the "utmost good faith," the lust of Euro-American frontiersmen for "vacant" (i.e., vacated) lands precipitated frequent hostilities against Native nations on the western frontier, only some of which were formalized as "just and lawful wars." The defeat of a coalition of Algonquian-speaking nations in 1794 (in Ohio Territory) led to the first major land cessions in the old Northwest under the Treaty of Grenville. The victory over Tecumseh's coalition in 1811 (in Indiana Territory) and, to the south, Andrew Jackson's victory over the Creeks and Cherokees together signaled the end of large-scale indigenous wars of resistance in the east. This paved the way for further treaties involving land cessions and removal (Satz 2002).

The most infamous of the removals was the forced relocation in the 1830s of the Five Civilized Tribes of the Southeast (the Cherokees, Creeks, Choctaws, Chickasaws, and Seminoles) to what is now Oklahoma. The removal of these nations, considered "civilized" because of their adoption of Anglo-American political, economic, and religious institutions, resulted not only in legislation, treaties, and military campaigns but also in two crucial Supreme Court decisions regarding the status of indigenous nations. It is significant that Native status was codified in cases involving the relatively acculturated and widely admired Cherokees, instead of less acculturated groups widely considered less capable of self-government. In the first case, *Cherokee Nation v. Georgia* (1831), Chief Justice John Marshall characterized the Cherokee Nation as a "state, as a distinct political society, separated from others, capable of managing its own affairs and governing itself" (11). Yet, at the same time, Marshall did not find the Cherokees or other Native groups to be "foreign" states. Instead, he wrote,

> They may, more correctly, perhaps be denominated *domestic dependent nations.* They occupy a territory to which we assert a title independent of their will, which must take effect in point of possession when their right of possession ceases. Meanwhile they are in a state of pupilage. Their relation to the United States resembles that of a ward to his guardian. (12; emphasis added)

In the second case, *Worcester v. Georgia* (1832), the court decided the issue of what right, if any, the Cherokees had to govern themselves. Though Marshall found it difficult to imagine the United States having the right to annul the rights and powers of indigenous nations, he acknowledged that "power, war, conquest, give rights, which, after possession, are conceded by the world; and which can never be controverted by those on whom they descend" (543). Even so, Marshall returned to the opinion expressed in *Cherokee Nation v. Georgia* that Native nations were separate and distinct sovereign states, emphasizing that the Cherokee Nation (and by extension, all indigenous nations that signed treaties) had the status of "a nation claiming and receiving the protection of one more powerful: not that of individuals abandoning their national character, and submitting as subjects to the laws of a master" (*Worcester v. Georgia* 1832, 554). He concluded that a nation may be subjected to a stronger nation and yet still retain its character and much of its independence. In Marshall's words,

> The Cherokee nation, then, is a distinct community, occupying its own territory, with boundaries accurately described, in which the laws of Georgia can have no force, and which the citizens of Georgia have no right to enter, but with the assent of the Cherokees themselves, or in conformity with treaties, and with the acts of congress. (560)

Although President Andrew Jackson famously ignored Marshall's decisions, these two cases contain the germs of the complex and contradictory legal principles that continue to guide US policy toward indigenous nations. To summarize,

- Native nations are *sovereign* political communities, which can make their own laws and govern themselves, without the interference of state and local governments.
- Native polities are also *wards* of the federal government, with their property subject to its trusteeship.
- As *domestic dependent nations,* Native polities have lost their sovereign power to deal with nations other than the United States.
- Native polities are *subject to the plenary power* of the federal government due to conquest.
- Finally, indigenous people are related to the United States not only as individuals, but also as *members of their distinct nations.*

The contradictions inherent in these legal representations are still being played out today, nearly two centuries after the two Cherokee cases were decided. Each of these principles has been challenged—by states, at the federal level, and by indigenous nations—and both tribal sovereignty and federal protection have alternately expanded and contracted over time. Still, the basic framework of limited political sovereignty under federal trusteeship remains intact.

"Savage" Tribes within a "Civilized" Nation: Encompassment, Compression, and Individuation

Land cessions and trans-Mississippi removal remained central elements of US Indian policy until the end of the Mexican War in 1848. At this time, Native nations still controlled more than half the present territory of the forty-eight contiguous states (Gibson 1988, 215). But the growth of American territorial claims culminating in the land cessions following the Mexican War meant that Native groups could no longer easily be removed into non-American or unsettled territory. Removal was now internal and directed to the rapidly filling Indian Territory (now Oklahoma).

A new policy of "reserving" lands within aboriginal territory was formulated—a policy that still included land cessions with compensation. The reservation policy was first used in the Pacific Coast states, where rapid Euro-American settlement had nearly overwhelmed the Native population by the 1860s. But it soon spread throughout the trans-Mississippi region, especially after the Civil War, as the Euro-American population expanded into the West. By 1895, in fact, indigenous holdings were compressed to nearly their present extent (Gibson 1988, 216–217).

Attempts to destroy Native political sovereignty and cultures went hand in hand with the appropriation of land in the expansionist American nationalism of the post–Civil War era. The federal government, often at the behest of local settler interests, carried out widespread and concentrated military, legal, and disciplinary actions designed to subdue and control Native nations and to dismember them into more easily encompassed individuals. This is the now-mythic period of the western "Indian Wars." In reality, however, the remaining independent indigenous nations were not a significant military threat to American expansion, and the federal government used only a small portion of its potential military might to subdue Native American forces. Military actions were most important in enforcing land cessions and restricting indigenous groups to their new reservations.

Bureaucratic activities of the kind Michel Foucault (1979) has called "disciplinary" were as important as military action in constraining Native sovereignty and replacing it with economic and political dependency, and they remained crucial after military campaigns ended (White 1983). The Bureau of Indian Affairs (BIA) sent agents, farmers, and missionaries to impart "civilized" attributes to a dependent population seen increasingly in evolutionary terms as living in an outmoded, "tribal" state of society—a perspective influenced by the work of ethnologists such as John Wesley Powell and Lewis Henry Morgan (Hinsley 1981; Bieder 1986). The enumeration of individuals on tribal rolls, curfews and movement restrictions, the capture and incarceration of recalcitrant leaders in military prisons, the provision (or withholding) of subsistence rations, and increased Protestant evangelization—all these served to control and circumscribe the activities of indigenous individuals and communities.

Perhaps the most important weapon of the government in its cultural and social war against "tribalism" was enforced education at residential schools. Native children were required to attend boarding schools from the age of five through their mid-teens. Often they were forcibly kidnapped and removed from their families and reservations (a practice that continued up to the 1920s in some places). In Indian boarding schools the children lived under military discipline, were required to wear uniforms, were forbidden to use their native languages or to practice their religions, and were expected to prepare themselves for a life of industrial or domestic service (Lomawaima 1993, 2002; Littlefield 2004).

Legally, there was an imposition of federal law on Indian reservations; a formulation of local legal codes; and an establishment of Indian courts, Indian police, and tribal governments. Federal criminal law was extended to previously sovereign nations as a result of public outrage over a case, *Ex parte Crow Dog* (1883), in which the Court found that neither federal nor state governments could try an Indian for the murder of another Indian on a reservation (Harring 1994). In response, the Major Crimes Act of 1885 extended federal criminal jurisdiction to Indian reservations, essentially bringing an end to independent internal governance.

A major threat to collective ownership of reservation lands through the promotion of individuated identities was embodied in the Dawes Allotment Act of 1887, which aimed to turn Native Americans into independent yeoman farmers on 160-acre plots of land. By the time of its passage and implementation (which took more than two decades), most of the arable, fertile, or useful land in the American West had been claimed by White settlers. Native Americans were generally allotted poor parcels that, unlike reservation lands, were often able to be bought and sold. The result of the Dawes Act was a significant loss of tribal land and further compression of the Native population. Additionally, the Dawes Act imposed for the first time a divisive, biologically based definition of indigenous identity, differentiating between "full bloods" and "mixed bloods"—the latter assumed to be more capable of civilization and therefore accorded the dubious right to alienate their lands if they accepted US citizenship (see Chapter 4).

These determined American efforts to eliminate Native sovereignty and federal protection were never, however, totally successful. Some tribes, such as the Crow, actively resisted assimilatory campaigns through political and legal challenges (Hoxie 1984, 1992). By the beginning of the twentieth century, however, Native Americans were viewed within the dominant society as a "vanishing race" doomed to demographic and cultural extinction in their lost Darwinian struggle with the White race (Dippie 1982; J. O'Brien 2010). Even though contemporary scholars attribute the devastating demographic decline of Native Americans during this period to European diseases, warfare, and Anglo-American policies (Thornton 1987), the notion of outmoded savagery has remained a popular ideological justification for conquest.

Tribal Nations within a Nation: Advancing and Retreating from Indigenous Sovereignty

The turn of the twentieth century marked the nadir of concern with Native Americans in the larger American consciousness. The tide began to turn in the 1920s and 1930s, partly as a result of the impressive record of many Native American servicemen during World War I, and partly as a result of the activities of reformers. The Indian Citizenship Act of 1924 finally extended US citizenship to indigenous people. Certain indigenous nations, such as the Hopi, refused to recognize the act, considering it an unlawful extension of American political sovereignty. Elsewhere, full voting and other civil rights were often not achieved until the 1960s and 1970s.

The New Deal brought about a revolutionary change in indigenous-settler relations in the United States. John Collier, the commissioner of Indian affairs under Roosevelt, was a reformer and cultural pluralist who successfully engineered the passage of the Indian Reorganization Act (IRA) in 1934. The IRA acknowledged the sovereign power of Indian nations to govern themselves, albeit on a Western model, and established tribal access to a revolving credit loan fund as well as the ability to form business corporations. Most important, the IRA prohibited future allotments of Native lands and included restrictions against the alienation (sale) of lands. It also included provisions for restoring to tribes some lands that had previously been sold or settled, as well as mechanisms for increasing the land base of reservations. Furthermore, under Collier the Bureau of Indian Affairs followed a policy of preferred employment for Native people, which remains a major employer to this day. The political and economic premises of the Indian Reorganization Act were not accepted by all Native Americans, and there remains on some reservations a deep rift between "traditionalists" and the "progressives" who accept the IRA form of governance.

Opposition to the "Indian New Deal" at the local and federal levels was swift in forming. The Indian Claims Commission, formed in 1946 to settle disputes between tribes and the federal government, became in practice a way to extinguish through monetary compensation any federal obligations to indigenous nations. Seven years later, in 1953, House Concurrent Resolution 108 called for the termination of federal responsibility for Native peoples in six states. Between 1954 and 1962, 109 Native tribes and bands were "terminated," in the starkly realistic government parlance of the time (Wilkinson and Biggs 1977, 152–153).

Individuation policies (consistent with what is today called neoliberalism) were also apparent in the "relocation" programs of the Bureau of Indian Affairs. Throughout the 1950s and 1960s, the BIA encouraged large numbers of unemployed Native Americans from reservations to move to urban areas, where opportunities for wage labor were greater. Although many of those who were relocated returned to their reservation homes, cities such as Chicago, Seattle, Denver, Los Angeles, and Minneapolis–St. Paul developed large Native populations (Fixico 1986). At the same time, government boarding and day schools began to be closed, with Native children shifted to local public schools.

The termination era ended in the late 1960s and early 1970s, when two important trends emerged in the context of the civil rights movement and the increased recognition of minority groups in the United States. First, there was tremendous growth in federal expenditures for Native Americans—for housing, education, health, economic development, land, and so on. In many cases these expenditures were an extension of more general federal antipoverty programs. Second, Indian rights organizations demanded indigenous control over programs affecting Native American communities, resulting in a greater degree of self-determination for indigenous nations. The Indian Self-Determination and Education Assistance Act of 1975 and a series of Supreme Court decisions affirmed and emphasized Indian sovereignty and the ability of tribes to assert economic, political, and cultural authority over their own lands and membership. Notably, in *Santa Clara Pueblo v. Martinez* (1978) the Court upheld the right of a tribe to be governed by its traditional laws and to determine its own membership even if these conflict with civil rights guaranteed under the Constitution.

Native sovereignty, resting as it does on collective rights outside of the Constitution, remains contested even in an atmosphere of increased self-determination. Religious freedom and the ability of tribes to protect sacred sites have not been secured, despite the passage of the American Indian Religious Freedom Act of 1978 (Nabokov 2006). Though some previously unrecognized or terminated tribes have had success in going through the federal recognition process established in the 1970s—thus becoming eligible for federal benefits—others have been caught in the catch-22 of proving that they have maintained their cultural identity to the satisfaction of the very government that systematically sought to destroy that identity (Campisi 1991). Some nations have received satisfactory monetary settlements for lands that were illegally appropriated, but those aiming for the restoration of land have met with little success. Attempts to assert various treaty rights relating to fishing, hunting, and resource use have met fierce, sometimes violent opposition (Nesper 2002). The Indian Gaming Regulatory Act of 1988 has led to dramatic economic development on certain reservations (Cattelino 2008) but has pitted tribal governments against state and local governments, commercial interests, and some tribal members.

In a country based on the individual rights of citizens, there is little understanding among the general population of the collective rights accorded by treaty to indigenous nations. Just as in debates over states' rights and cultural diversity, conflicts over Native American rights devolve easily into debates over the "meaning of America." The continued existence of 562 Native polities within the heart of the United States continues to challenge the premises and constrain the ambitions of American nationalism.

Imagining and Appropriating an Identity: Indigeneity as a Symbolic Resource for American Nationalism

> Shook our hands, Took our lands.
> For the Games, Took our Names.
> What's Next?
> —*Sign at an American Indian Movement demonstration at
> the 1992 Super Bowl, protesting the name and mascot of the
> Washington Redskins (Denlinger 1992)*

Not only as members of sovereign nations preceding and, to some extent, remaining outside of national hegemony, but also as symbolic constructs within American nationalist discourse, Native Americans hold a distinctive relationship to American nationalism—representing, as Roy Harvey Pearce (1965) put it, what Euro-Americans "were not and must not be" (5). As noted in Chapter 1, in the dominant American imaginary the American Indian represents the "wild," "natural," "savage" other that both threatens and tempts the "civilized" Euro-American self. The superiority of the "civilized" as well as their claim to legitimate power rests on dominating the natural, controlling the wild, subjugating the savage. But this national imaginary entails considerable ambivalence—as Pearce suggested in the phrase "must not be." Euro-Americans have both opposed their "civilization" to Indian "savagery" and yearned nostalgically after that savagery; they have both predicated American nationalism on the subjugation of Native Americans and identified with the freedom of their subjugated opponent.

The ideology of savagism was responsible for confining Native Americans within boarding schools, prisons, and reservations. Today, as we will see in the following chapters, the ideology of savagery is replayed in textbooks and literature, in art and movies, and in sports and games. The two main variations upon the theme of savagism involve attitude: Native Americans are viewed as either noble or ignoble opponents, as either obstacles to progress or its victims, as either objects of scorn or objects of pity—but in each case as belonging to the past (Berkhofer 1978). In this way appropriation is justified—appropriation that extends beyond land, labor, and resources to "natural" virtues associated with Indians, such as natural spirituality (Gill 1987; Nabokov 2006) and wilderness prowess (see Chapter 8).

The contest of savagery and civilization is a narrative and a set of attitudes with which all Americans are familiar, if not necessarily comfortable. The narrative was developed in the war and captivity narratives of early American literature (Chapter 5), in the classics of James Fenimore Cooper and nineteenth-century dime novels, in Pocahontas plays and public sculpture, in Western art and films. It is exemplified today in New Age religion and mass-produced "Indian" handicrafts, in the use of pseudo-Indian mascots for sports teams and advertising logos (Chapter 10), and in the names of weapons such as the Tomahawk missile and the Apache helicopter. The narrative has been exported to the rest of the world in such venues as Buffalo Bill's Wild West Shows, world fairs (Chapter 3), and the cinema (Chapter 9).

During the culture wars of the 1990s, the relationship between Native Americans and American nationalism came to the fore, not only on account of the observance of the five hundredth anniversary of Columbus's momentous voyage, but also because of increased political activism on the part of Native Americans and environmentalists, the acrimonious public controversy regarding multiculturalism and political correctness, and increasingly sophisticated scholarship. Critiques of colonial representations of national identity, a subject of intense interest in the academy, entered public space and prime time during the observance of the Columbian Quincentenary, as we will see in Chapter 3. The degree of emotional intensity with which Americans engaged in controversies over Columbus and his ships, sports mascots and parades, museum exhibitions and constitutional history, is indicative of how deeply embedded are customary representations of American Indians in the taken-for-granted assumptions of American culture.

During the observance of the Columbian Quincentenary, it became clear that indigenous people often do not accept or participate in the hegemonic imaginings of American nationalism. At the same time, many Native Americans are deeply patriotic, as is strikingly evident at Indian powwows, those exuberant intertribal celebrations in which elaborately costumed singers and dancers of all ages and both genders perform traditional as well as modern dances, both sacred and secular. Customarily, during the opening ceremony known as the Grand Entry, great respect is shown to indigenous veterans bearing state and national flags.

Just as the existence of Native nations within the boundaries of the United States constitutes a challenge to American nationalism, so too the complex imaginings of national identity found among indigenous people call into question some of the basic presuppositions of modern nationalism. Members of distinct tribal nations as well as the American nation-state, adept at subverting hegemonic nationalist narratives and crossing national borders, familiar with multiple forms of belonging and exclusion, Native Americans represent well the complex form of identity that has come to be known as postmodern. Indeed, the tribal and national identities discussed in this chapter are, in some cases, now being supplemented with transnational identities, either pan-Indian or pan-indigenous. That Native Americans, once expected to vanish, have come to exemplify a postmodern form of identity is an irony eminently worthy of Coyote, that subversive indigenous trickster (see Figure 2).

Figure 2. Harry Fonseca (Maidu), *Shuffle Off to Buffalo #V,* 1983. Fonseca's Coyote paintings imagine the traditional Native American trickster in contemporary contexts. Denver Art Museum: William Sr. and Dorothy Harmsen Collection, by exchange. Photography provided by the Denver Art Museum.

Bibliographic Note

This chapter synthesizes a wide array of scholarly work on Native American political and legal history. Useful overviews include Washburn, *History of Indian-White Relations* (1988); S. O'Brien, *American Indian Tribal Governments* (1990); Castile and Bee, *State and Reservation* (1992); Wilkins and Stark, *American Indian Politics and the American Political System* (2011); and relevant chapters in P. Deloria and Salisbury, *A Companion to American Indian History* (2002) and Biolsi, *A Companion to the Anthropology of American Indians* (2004b).

The works of the Native American scholars Vine Deloria Jr. (1969, 1970, 1971, 1974; Deloria and Lytle 1983, 1984); D'Arcy McNickle (1973); Robert Williams (1990); David Wilkins (1997; Wilkins and Lomawaima 2001); and Taiaiake Alfred (1999a, 1999b, 2002) offer important treatments of Native American tribalism and sovereignty, as do Cattelino's *High Stakes: Florida Seminole Gaming and Sovereignty* (2008) and Wilkinson's *American Indians, Time, and the Law* (1987). Biolsi (2004a) provides an overview of debates concerning the relationship among tribal self-determination, state-recognized sovereignty, and neoliberal governmental policies; Darian-Smith (2010) covers sovereignty and environmental issues. Clifford's "Identity in Mashpee" (1988b) and Campisi's *The Mashpee Indians: Tribe on Trial* (1991) offer revealing accounts of the implications of popular, scholarly, and legal interpretations of the notion of "Indian tribe."

Comparative studies of indigenous peoples and the nation-state are offered in Perry, *From Time Immemorial: Indigenous Peoples and State Systems* (1996); Cook and Lindau, *Aboriginal Rights and Self-Government* (2000); Povinelli, *The Cunning of Recognition: Indigenous Alterities and the Making of Australian Multiculturalism* (2002); Anaya, *Indigenous Peoples in International Law* (2004); and articles by Edmunds (2002) and Harring (2002). Cattelino (2010) discusses the comparative importance of the relatively new concept of settler colonialism.

The References include a section on the federal laws and court cases cited in this and subsequent chapters. Wilkins and Stark's *American Indian Politics and the American Political System* (2011) provides a more comprehensive list of major federal laws affecting Native Americans (265–269) as well as a comprehensive overview of its subject. Prucha (2000) reproduces many relevant statutes and court cases.

CHAPTER THREE
FIVE HUNDRED YEARS

In a *Pogo* cartoon published during the first week of 1992, Churchy Lafemme complained to Pogo and Porkypine: "I don't care if they did make '92 a leap year—they also made it too much else—the 'lympics, the 'lections, the whirl's fair—an' the quincendentaltennial of Columbus discoverin' Ohio! One measle exter day won't cover it! '92 is gonna need to be at least six months longer to shoehorn all that in! Right, you guys? Guys?" By now, however, Churchy has lost his audience. "Must of gone off to write their congersman," he surmises (Sternecky 1992).

Churchy may have been guilty, in Pogo's and Porkypine's minds, of taking public spectacles too seriously, but he had at least one thing right: the year 1992 was filled to overflowing with public events claiming world historical significance. Setting aside the Olympics and the US elections, if not the world's fair in Seville, it remains no mean task to assess the significance of the Columbian Quincentenary (also known as the Quincentennial). While the quincentenary's impact upon American historical consciousness and collective identity may have been less significant than either its proponents or its denigrators expected, it was certainly greater than Pogo and Porkypine's disinterest would suggest.

The quincentenary was notable, above all, for its diffuseness, its heterogeneity, its polyvocality—that is, for its lack of an encompassing vision, an epitomizing symbol, a totalizing discourse. Unlike the four hundredth anniversary of Columbus's first voyage to this hemisphere—remembered as the occasion for the progressivist and imperialist World's Columbian Exposition in Chicago (Rydell 1984)—the five hundredth anniversary cannot be easily located on a central site or characterized in a key phrase. The quincentenary was both highly contested and widely ignored; it aroused emotions ranging from rage to ambivalence to apathy. For those who attended to the quincentenary, it provided an occasion for instruction and revitalization, commodification and entertainment, mobilization and subversion. In the United States it generated transformative scholarship and curricula, memorable Native art exhibits, and debates about the observance of Columbus Day. Elsewhere, it generated a postcolonial world's fair and energized indigenous social movements.

The Columbian Quincentenary, then, was not so much a non-event as a diffuse one that violated preconceptions and defeated glib descriptions. Television coverage on October 12th focused on Denver, Colorado, where a coalition led by the American Indian Movement (AIM) forced the cancellation of the Columbus Day Parade in the very city in which the national tradition began. Before deciding to locate the significance of the quincentenary in Denver, however, we should remember that Columbus Day parades and festivals proceeded according to plan in many American cities in 1992. With this in mind, we might locate the center of the Columbian Quincentenary in Pasadena, California, where Ben Nighthorse Campbell—then a US representative from Colorado—served as co-marshal of the 1992 Tournament of Roses Parade, which was dedicated to the theme "Voyages of Discovery." Campbell, wearing the regalia of his Native nation, the Cheyenne, rode his horse alongside Cristóbal Colón, a lineal descendant of the explorer, in a televised image of postcolonial harmony.

Alternatively, we might focus on Washington, DC, the site of an influential and diverse series of museum exhibitions, ranging from the aesthetic relativism of the National Gallery's *Circa 1492*—where the "age of exploration" was celebrated with art from four continents—to the historical revisionism of the Smithsonian Institution's *Seeds of Change,* where the concept of the Columbian Exchange was illustrated through five metaphorical seeds traded between Europe and the Americas: corn, potatoes, sugar, the horse, and fatal diseases. Also organized by the Smithsonian was *The West as America,* a controversial exhibition that interpreted frontier art as ideological justifications of European conquest and capitalist expansion. Each of these exhibitions brought current scholarly perspectives on 1492 into public discourse, with the impact of *Seeds of Change* magnified through traveling exhibitions, curriculum guides, teacher workshops, and magazine features.

Less obviously, we might choose Gainesville, Albuquerque, and Minneapolis as epitomizing sites—all cities where a traveling exhibition (*First Encounters*) featuring a replica of Columbus's caravel, the Niña, engendered indigenous protests; or the pathbreaking quincentenary art exhibits that featured Native perspectives, such as *The Submuloc Show/Columbus Wohs (… Who's Columbus?),* curated by the Flathead artist and curator Jaune Quick-to-See Smith, and the

Canadian Museum of Civilization's *Indigena: Perspectives of Indigenous Peoples on Five Hundred Years* (see Chapter 4); or other indigenous activities such as the Peace and Dignity Journeys, which brought indigenous and nonindigenous runners from across the hemisphere together in Mexico City.

As the range of these events suggests, it is unwise to search for an epitomizing site or symbol for the Columbian Quincentenary. American observances of the anniversary were far more localized than many of the key planners would have predicted at the outset. It was not an anniversary dominated by the national media—not by the PBS series, "Columbus and the Age of Discovery," nor by the commercial cinematic flops, John Glen's *Columbus: The Discovery* and Ridley Scott's *1492: Conquest of Paradise*. It was not dominated by the various reenactments of Columbus's voyage, which were plagued by mutiny and financial difficulties. Even Expo '92, the Universal Exposition in Seville, Spain, had difficulty in attracting global attention. Still less successful in attracting attention was Columbus, Ohio, the site of AmeriFlora '92, a horticultural exposition that the official US Quincentennial Jubilee Commission considered the "centerpiece" of its productions (hence Churchy LaFemme's characterization of 1992 as "the quincendentaltennial of Columbus discoverin' Ohio!").

Nevertheless, the two quincentenary expositions mounted in Seville and Columbus are worthy of consideration as sharply contrasting attempts to orchestrate elaborate global spectacles in observance of the anniversary. Without overemphasizing their importance—for I believe that the transformative potential of 1992 was more fully realized in local and educational events—this chapter analyzes these expositions as telling moments in the representation of world history. We will also consider two other kinds of representational practices that flourished during the Columbian Quincentenary: museum exhibitions and oppositional indigenous events. We will be particularly concerned with how contrasting historical paradigms of *discovery, encounter,* and *conquest* played out in these sites of representation.

Encounter and Exchange: Domesticating the Past in *Seeds of Change*

The year 1992 was originally billed in the United States as a celebration of discovery, to be presided over by the Christopher Columbus Quincentenary Jubilee Commission. As the year proceeded, however, the quincentenary came to look less like a jubilee than a teach-in, less like a celebration of discovery than, to use a then-fashionable term, an encounter. Indeed, the widespread currency of the term *encounter* seemed—for a time, at least—to signal the shifting of paradigms in public historical discourse (Lunenfeld 1991; Kolodny 1992). In the new paradigm Columbus did not discover a new world but encountered an old one; 1992, then, commemorated the beginning of an ongoing exchange between the two worlds. As museum curator Herman Viola explained in the book *Seeds of Change,* "What Columbus did in 1492 was to link two old worlds, thereby creating one new world" (Viola and Margolis 1991, 12). The quincentenary, in other words, offered scholars, curators, and educators the opportunity to popularize and dramatize the kind of theoretical approach pioneered in geographer William Crosby's important 1972 volume, *The Columbian Exchange: Biological and Cultural Consequences of 1492.* Hence, a spate of quincentenary exhibitions organized around the theme of encounter and exchange: the National Museum of American History's *American Encounters* (H. Morrison 1992); the traveling exhibition *Sacred Encounters* (J. Peterson 1991); the Florida Museum of National History's *First Encounters* (Milanich and Milbrath 1989); and, most broadly and influentially, the Smithsonian Institution's *Seeds of Change: 500 Years of Encounter and Exchange.*

Seeds of Change, on view at the National Museum of Natural History from October 26, 1991, through April 1, 1993, was intended to be itself a seed of change, its impact magnified through the circulation of traveling panel exhibitions, a book of scholarly essays featured in book clubs and sent to all members of the Smithsonian Institution (Viola and Margolis 1991), and prominent features in popular publications such as *Newsweek* ("When Worlds Collide" 1991), *National Geographic* ("1492: America before Columbus" 1991), and *U.S. News and World Report* ("America before Columbus" 1991). Perhaps most significantly, the exhibition generated a wide range of new curricular materials (Crosby 1987; Crosby and Nader 1989; National Council for the Social Studies 1991; Phillips and Weber 1991; Ringle 1991). "Discovery, Encounter, Exchange in History: The Seeds of Change" was the theme of National History Day in 1992. *Seeds of Change* also provided a guiding metaphor for AmeriFlora '92. As a whole, *Seeds of Change* may be taken as representative of the scholarly paradigm of encounter and exchange when it is packaged for mass consumption. This popular version of the Columbian exchange paradigm became a highly influential effort in public historical representation, one well suited to have an impact in education because of its compatibility with multicultural approaches to history and social studies (Gutmann 1994; Rosaldo 1997; Hale 2002).

The *Seeds of Change* exhibition displaced the quincentenary from both the controversial figure of Christopher Columbus and from the year 1492. It was not Columbus's ships that dominated the exhibition but a huge portal of multicolored corncobs inspired by Mesoamerican architecture and South Dakota's Corn Palace. This gateway embodied the first of five metaphorical "seeds" featured in the exhibition—that is, five elements of the biological exchange between hemispheres that was initiated by Columbus's voyages. Two of the seeds, corn and potatoes, were Native cultigens, whereas three were European imports: sugar cane, horses, and deadly diseases new to the Americas. Despite the rather cerebral subject, much of the exhibition was lighthearted, upbeat, and frankly gastronomic. Corn and potatoes were represented nostalgically by memorabilia such as Mr. and Mrs. Potato Head and Jiffy Pop. And Roark Gourley's playful wall sculpture, *Spaghetti Meets Tomato in the Collision of the Continental Plates,* portrayed the culinary encounter of Asia and America as a love story mediated by Europe (see Figure 3).

More traditionally for an ethnographic exhibit, life-size dioramas portrayed an Aztec market, Hopi cultivation of corn, and Andean cultivation of potatoes. The influence of the horse on the indigenous cultures of the Plains was illustrated by an elaborately decorated, life-sized model of a horse. Appropriately, sugarcane and disease received more somber treatments. The section titled "Sugar: The Bittersweet Legacy" counterpoised such fruits of the Columbian exchange as chocolate torte and Caribbean culture against the agonies of the Middle Passage and life under slavery (as narrated by Whoopi Goldberg). "The Invisible Invader: Disease" dramatically demonstrated the devastating demographic effects of European diseases from 1492 through 1992, representing diminishing populations through extinguishing lights.

The aim of the exhibition was for the five highlighted "seeds of change" to become just as familiar to new generations of Americans as Columbus's ships, the Niña, Pinta, and Santa Maria. To portray 1492 as the beginning of an ongoing biological and cultural exchange between two old worlds was exciting for educators eager to move beyond the Eurocentric trope of discovery. Curators and

Figure 3. Roark Gourley, *Spaghetti Meets Tomato in the Collision of the Continental Plates,* 1991 (detail). This work was commissioned for *Seeds of Change: Five Hundred Years of Encounter and Exchange* at the Natural Museum of American History, The Smithsonian Institution. Photography courtesy of the artist.

teachers viewed encounter and exchange as an eminently teachable paradigm—a vivid, constructive, and amicable way to teach an inclusive history and give various constituencies their due.

One of the new paradigm's strengths, given American notions about objectivity, is its appearance of moderation and balance. The concepts of encounter and exchange at once acknowledge the modern world's indebtedness to Native American peoples and the ways in which Europeans affected indigenous cultures. That the exchanges are primarily of material objects plays well in a technological society and allows for the celebration of a rich and complex global civilization. The paradigm gives the appearance of presenting Native American and African perspectives upon what is neutrally called "encounter" and "exchange" while avoiding more critical political and economic concepts such as invasion, conquest, appropriation, exploitation, imperialism, and genocide.

In other words, the encounter and exchange paradigm is notable as much for what it tends to obscure as for what it reveals. The scholarly works upon which *Seeds of Change* built—McNeill's *Plagues and People* (1976), Mintz's *Sweetness and Power* (1986), Crosby's *The Columbian Exchange* (1972), Henry Hobhouse's *Seeds of Change* (1987)—do not avoid critical analysis. Nevertheless, when it entered the realm of public history and pedagogy, the paradigm's critical edge was sheathed. Most striking in the *Seeds of Change* exhibition was its failure to address inequities of power—that is, its tendency to present exchanges as if they all occurred on the proverbial level playing field. The choice of "encounter" rather than more power-laden alternatives—"collision," "clash," "confrontation," "contest"—is revealing. So, too, is the omission of gunpowder as a transformative "seed of change"—an omission that is symptomatic not only of the exhibition's biological emphasis but also of its obfuscation of physical and technological domination. Along similar lines, the omission of tobacco—which, along with quinine, tea, maize, and sugar, was featured in the 1987 volume by Hobhouse that inspired the exhibition—reveals the avoidance of colonial processes of appropriation and commodification.

As a reviewer for the *Washington Post* put it, the exhibit "rises above the accusatory finger-pointing and ethnic posturing so tempting to historic revisionists in our day," demonstrating that "the most seismic changes wrought by the European conquest of the Western hemisphere, whether calamitous or beneficial, were usually unrecognized at the time and almost invariably unplanned" (Ringle 1991). The *Seeds of Change* exhibit, in sum, offered a domesticated version of the Columbian exchange, a respectable and well-bounded interpretation of the past that raised the issue of environmental responsibility in the one world Columbus linked but that did little to challenge the distribution of power and resources that has divided the world anew.

The Age of Discoveries/A Worldwide Encounter: Expo '92

The discourse of "encounter" was prominent at Expo '92, despite its official theme, "The Age of Discoveries." Seville, the site of the Ibero-American Exhibition in 1929, offered to host a Universal Exposition in 1992 because of its abundant historical connections to Columbus and the Americas. Seville is situated on the banks of the Guadalquivir River, Spain's "gateway to the Indies." The relationship of Seville to the Americas is revealed in a number of the city's historical landmarks, including the famous Torre de Oro, the tower in which gold mined in the Americas was stored; the Royal Tobacco factory, where American tobacco was processed; a prominent monument to Columbus's voyages in Seville's central park; and a tomb in the cathedral containing one of several putative sets of the explorer's bones. Plaza de España, dating from the Ibero-American Exhibition, includes scenes in mosaic from each of Spain's major cities and provinces, several of them referring to Columbus. In Barcelona's, for example, Columbus appears before Queen Isabella and King Ferdinand, presenting to them the ten Arawak captives he brought back from the Caribbean on his first voyage.

Similarly, Expo '92 made abundant references to the city's maritime past—geographically, architecturally, and metaphorically. The exposition was located on La Isla de la Cartuja, an alluvial island within the Guadalquivir River. On the island sits a fifteenth-century Carthusian monastery, Santa Maria de las Cuevas, where Columbus stayed prior to his voyage of 1492 and where he was buried for a time. Many architectural features at Expo '92 alluded to sails, and replicas of the Niña, Pinta, and Santa Maria were docked at a reconstructed Port of the Indies. Five "thematic" pavilions were organized around the exposition's theme of discovery. These were strung out along a Route of Discovery and a Canal of Discovery, two of the main pathways through the fair.

Experientially, then, visitors to Expo '92 were encouraged to identify themselves as maritime explorers—traveling along routes of discovery, attending events underneath billowing sails, and visiting caravels and a reconstructed port. More explicitly, promotional material encouraged visitors to become explorers. "Discover Expo," "discover the world," "discover yourself"—these were the tropes around which the experience of the fair was organized and promoted.

Despite the centrality of the trope of discovery, little attention was paid to the figure of Columbus. Apart from the ships docked at the reconstructed Port of the Indies, there were no monuments to Columbus on the fair grounds—no modern counterparts to the historic monuments in Seville and Granada. Spain left it to Italy to commemorate Columbus the explorer in 1992. Indeed, the theme of discovery was generalized to encompass five hundred years of human progress. And even the generalized theme of discovery was muted over the decade that Expo '92 was conceived and constructed, as Spain attempted to respond to internal and international criticism and to head off conflict at the fair. Spain was eager to position itself in 1992 as a modern, prosperous, and democratic nation; as a central player in the European Community; and as a natural bridge between Europe, Africa, and Latin America by virtue of its multicultural history. In line with these goals, and in accordance with the progressive vision characteristic of world's fairs in general, Expo '92 focused more on the future than on the events of 1492—a future envisioned as both technologically sophisticated and harmonious.

Viewed from the city of Seville, the most striking of the exposition's constructions was a series of bridges across the Guadalquivir River. These bridges, which remain as a permanent legacy of Expo '92, were described by King Juan Carlos at the fair's inauguration, on April 20, 1992, as "splendid symbols of the image Spain wishes to transmit of itself: nexus of past and future, of art and technology." Even more central to the exposition's iconography than the bridge was the globe, which served as the fair's logo. The most distinctive construction on the fairgrounds, apart from some of the national pavilions, was the global bioclimatic sphere, a cloud-producing chiller emblematic of the fair's vision of "global solidarity and a balanced relationship with nature," in the words of Emilio Cassinello Aubán, commissioner general of the exposition (*Expo '92 Sevilla* 1992; Strong 1992).

"Global solidarity" was embodied more lightheartedly in the exposition's official mascot, Curro—a friendly white bird with elephant's legs and a rainbow-colored beak and crest. Although Curro was one of the few symbols at Expo '92 not provided with official exegesis, the anomalous creature evidently was meant to allude to interethnic and international harmony. In order to construct an inclusive fair—in fact, the most inclusive in history—Spain subsidized the building of composite pavilions for Latin America, Africa, and the Caribbean. Moreover, in order to diffuse the discordant implications of 1992 as the five hundredth anniversary of the expulsion of Jews from Spain, King Juan Carlos symbolically rescinded Ferdinand and Isabella's edict of expulsion shortly before the opening of the fair. The edict was repealed in conjunction with the dedication of a new monument, *La Tolerancia,* an abstract concrete sculpture located near a decrepit statue of the Dominican "defender of the Indians," Bartolomé de las Casas. Similarly, as an overture to Islamic peoples (for 1492 was also the year of the Reconquest in Spain), a major exhibition of Moorish art, *Al-Andalus,* was displayed at the Alhambra in Granada before traveling to the Metropolitan Museum in New York.

Perhaps the most significant retreat from the theme of discovery at Expo '92 was not by human design. As if colluding in a shift in historical consciousness, an electrical fire destroyed nearly all of the pavilion dedicated to discovery—a high-tech construction billed as genuinely relativistic and highly critical of purely technological advances. Although by opening day the effects of the fire had been somewhat camouflaged by huge cutouts of luck-inducing chimney sweeps and ladders, the hulk of the Discovery Pavilion loomed over the fairgrounds.

Completing the retreat from the trope of discovery were the official inauguration ceremonies, where scant mention was made of either Columbus or the exposition's official theme of discovery. King Juan Carlos described the exposition as a "worldwide encounter," utilizing the alternative discursive framework originally suggested by Latin American critics of the discovery theme. The mayor of Seville, Alejandro Rojas Marcos, spoke even more fully within the alternative discursive framework, speaking not of "the discovery of a new world" but of "the encounter of two old worlds." His inaugural speech invoked Bartolomé de las Casas and his "discovery of human unity"—a striking reinterpretation of the trope of discovery, more typically referencing an ideology of conquest based on essential human differences. Finally, Commissioner General Aubán introduced the thematic pavilions—those dedicated to discovery—as a reminder of common problems and challenges, including environmental degradation and "abysmal disparities of resources." Aubán described all world's fairs as "daring" and "utopian" dreams, but characterized Seville's in particular as revealing "a trust in progress without the obstinate optimism of other periods" (*Expo '92 Sevilla* 1992; Strong 1992). Certainly the inauguration was festive, with bands, balloons, and puffs of colored smoke from the smokestacks of the nineteenth-century Cartuja ceramics factory, but the spectacle was accompanied by both a seriousness of purpose typical of world's fairs and an atypical degree of self-consciousness. This was to be a world's fair that transcended the naive and colonialist discourse of previous world's fairs, offering not so much new technologies for the world to admire and adopt as a new form of discursive practice.

Nevertheless, despite Spain's backtracking from and redefinition of discovery, the "Age of Discoveries" theme set the agenda for many nations' participation in the fair. Some pavilions reduced discovery to a travel slogan: Discover Sri Lanka, Discover Thailand, Explore Canada. New Zealand actually staged a discovery, placing Maori dancers on a rocky coastline before a largely European audience. But some nations, as well as some of the autonomous communities of Spain, took the theme as a serious intellectual challenge, developing their own distinctive visions of discovery. The Basque pavilion emphasized the role of Basques, not Castilians, in the exploration and settlement of America. The Mexican pavilion, alluding architecturally both to pre-Columbian architecture and to the crossing of cultures, invited visitors to discover Mesoamerica *before* 1492. Several other Latin American countries, as well as Australia and Canada, highlighted indigenous art—Canada echoing in Seville the focus on contemporary Native art found in major Canadian museums in 1992 (Rushing 1993). Bolivia, notably, departed radically from both the discourse of discovery and the discourse of encounter, presenting its history in the more politicized terms of *contest* and *synthesis*.

The Trope of Discovery at US Quincentenary Expositions

Unlike its neighbors to the north and south, both of whose pavilions were highly praised, the United States oriented its pavilion around neither the North American landscape (as did Canada) nor its indigenous peoples (as did Mexico). Organized by officials of the United States Information Agency (USIA) and a group of corporate and civic sponsors, the US pavilion devoted itself to promoting American political and economic values. Almost entirely sidestepping the exposition's theme, the US pavilion commemorated not the quincentenary of a discovery, encounter, or invasion but, incredibly, the bicentennial of the Bill of Rights.

Despite highly visible corporate sponsorship, the US pavilion was a low-budget operation, lacking adequate congressional funding. The indoor space of the pavilion consisted of two geodesic domes, veterans of many trade fairs, one of which housed an original ratification copy of the Bill of Rights and a theater in which a multicultural cast imparted a civics lesson on film. A second film premiered in the other geodesic dome, a tearjerker underwritten by General Motors called *World Song*. Also shown at AmeriFlora '92, *World Song* portrays "universal" human experiences from birth to death, including—predictably but incredibly—driving that first car ("About *World Song*" n.d.). In an environment in which audiences expected displays of environmental and cultural distinctiveness—where, for example, Chile displayed an iceberg and Japan offered the largest wooden structure ever built—the United States offered the discourse of political, economic, and emotional universalism, served up in an ambience of commercial American culture. Following the trade show model, displays included futuristic General Motors cars, a "typical American home," and various corporate booths, while young guides hawked Budweiser beer, Coca-Cola, Baskin-Robbins ice cream, and sports paraphernalia. A small section of the pavilion attempted to recreate the ambience of Kansas City, Seville's sister city.

Visually, the only striking element of the US pavilion, and the only one to reference the exposition's theme, was *Discovery,* a pair of allegorical murals by pop artist Peter Max (see Figure 4). The murals, according to the artist, represent two faces of discovery: the "glorious history" of the past five hundred years and the possibilities of the future. Columbus's three ships sail across the center of the mural representing the past, overshadowed by a huge image of Sitting Bull. The mural representing the American past also includes, but much less prominently, a black cowboy. In this panel the sun is setting, and both the warrior and the cowboy seem to be receding before an impending bearded presence. Facing this colonialist representation of the vanishing Indian and the vanishing frontier is Max's imperialist rendering of the future, featuring a White, androgynous, space-age cast.

The murals seemed to hearken back to Chicago's Columbian Exposition of 1893, where historian Frederick Jackson Turner first announced the end of the frontier and the establishment of Euro-American civilization across the continent (Fogelson 1991). This is just the kind of Western art that the National Museum of American Art's controversial exhibition, *The West as America,* analyzed as a justification for dispossessing indigenous people, relegating them to a romanticized past, and appropriating that past as a national origin myth.

Native peoples, however, are not that easily relegated to the past. On opening day, as if to belie both Max's Eurocentric future and the US pavilion's commodified universalism, Austin Two Moons, a Northern Cheyenne elder, was on hand to bless the pavilion's water screen. Although the blessing was highlighted in the United States Information Agency's press release concerning the opening (Associated Press 1992), it came across as an awkward afterthought. The visit of Two Moons and three Native American companions was co-sponsored by the agency and the American Indian Heritage Foundation of Washington, DC. Clearly the foundation and the USIA had conflicting agendas, and these exploded into public view at the opening ceremony. Two Moons brought substance to an otherwise bland event, but the dignity of his blessing was undermined by chaos in the pavilion. Amidst jostling crowds, an occasional war whoop, and an aggressive press corps eager to salvage something of interest from the pavilion's opening, Two Moons became one of a long line of Native Americans exhibited in Europe as exotic curiosities (Feest 1987).

The head of the American Indian Heritage Foundation, who goes by the name of Princess Pale Moon, publicly voiced her anger following the ceremony, claiming that the blessing had been a "farce"; that Two Moons had been exploited

Figure 4. Peter Max, *Discovery,* 1992. One of two panels displayed at the United States Pavilion, Expo '92, Seville, Spain. This panel represents "the past." Photography by Pauline Turner Strong.

and treated as a "token"; that promises had been broken regarding the availability of space at the pavilion for a Native American art exhibition; and that she and her two companions—Miss Indian America and a talented Cherokee hoop dancer—had been excluded from the proceedings (Associated Press 1992). There was considerable irony in Pale Moon's accusations because she herself has been criticized by anti-mascot activists for singing the Star Spangled Banner at games of the Washington Redskins—that is, for engaging in an enterprise in which Native Americans are treated as tokens (see Chapter 10). At any rate, Pale Moon said that she and her companions had come to Seville as ambassadors of peace, and instead found themselves exploited by a governmental agency. Certainly, as Peter Max's murals demonstrate, exploiting a stereotypical Indian was central to the United States' representational practices at Expo '92.

The US pavilion was the subject of some ridicule in Seville, less on account of its retrogressive discourse than its refusal to treat Expo '92 as an event of world historical significance. Unlike nations that had much to gain in international prestige from an impressive self-presentation, the United States seemed to rest on its laurels, offering no architectural statement, no dramatic accomplishment, no evocation of landscape, and little response to the exposition's theme other than colonialist pop art. Nearly as trivial in conception and execution was AmeriFlora '92, billed as the United States' counterpart to Expo '92. So insignificant was AmeriFlora '92 that few people outside of Ohio ever heard of it. It was even ignored, for the most part, by indigenous groups opposing celebratory quincentenary events, although it was billed as "America's celebration of discovery."

Like Expo '92, AmeriFlora was conceived as both a tourist attraction and a means of urban renewal—specifically, a pretext for the expansion of the Franklin Park Conservatory and the development of the riverfront beneath City Hall. A statue of Columbus, a 1955 gift from the City of Genoa, stands in front of City Hall. Like many statues of Columbus elsewhere, in this monument the explorer is shown holding the document in which Ferdinand and Isabella granted him authority over any lands he might discover, as well as a share in any of their resources. The statue illustrates how the paradigm of discovery is, implicitly, a colonial discourse of conquest and domination, but the accompanying plaque presents Columbus primarily as a moral hero worthy of emulation, illustrating how Columbus the Discoverer personifies the virtues of bravery, creativity, resourcefulness, and self-reliance.

A nearby statue, erected in 1992 on the riverfront, represents still another attribute of Columbus: he was the first Italian-American, the first immigrant, in a nation that tells itself, "we are all immigrants"—thereby treating all passages to the continent, voluntary or involuntary, within memory or in the distant and forgotten past, as equivalent. Below this statue floats a full-size replica of Columbus's flagship, the Santa Maria, which was launched in October

1991 as a permanent tourist attraction. Even more than Columbus himself, of whom we have no authoritative portrait, the Niña, Pinta, and Santa Maria serve as icons of discovery—and in Ohio, in contrast to Spain, the floating icon of discovery was part of the dominant discourse of the exposition, rather than in tension with it.

Interestingly, however, just as Seville in 1992 built a monument to tolerance, so did Columbus. Right above the Santa Maria is a new park featuring sculptures of animals that are characters in a Native American tale of discovery, and the plaques from sponsoring groups and individuals advocate raising children in tolerance. It is as though the discourse of discovery and the discourse of tolerance can exist side by side, instantiating American pluralism, neither discourse invalidating the other. Rather than associating tolerance with a figure that questioned colonial discourse and practices, as Spain did in honoring Bartolomé de las Casas, the city of Columbus associated tolerance with the innocence of children, even while offering them an icon of discovery and conquest in the form of the Santa Maria.

On the grounds of AmeriFlora '92 itself, even this degree of historical reflection was generally lacking. A celebrative atmosphere prevailed, with maypoles, clowns, and an "Around the World Carousel" providing the ambience of an innocent, carefree country fair. Like Expo '92, AmeriFlora used the trope of discovery to structure visitors' experience of the fair, but in a banal and unabashedly commercial form, quite without Spain's commitment to expanding and critically examining the discourse. Discovery emerged at AmeriFlora '92 as a flexible and marketable trope, as fairgoers were invited to "discover the world in your backyard," "discover the world on Bridgestone Tires," and "discover yourself" in the military. The Old World became a food court, and children playing with remote-controlled boats could emulate Columbus and subsequent immigrants to America.

Visually, the counterpart at AmeriFlora to Seville's new bridges and bioclimatic sphere was *Navstar '92,* a striking rendering of three sails by Columbus sculptor Stephen Canneto. The intention of this stainless-steel sculpture, according to Canneto (1992), was to use "sleek contemporary forms and materials to reference Columbus's ships and transcend the notion of a colonial past." As a serious work of art, this sculpture certainly transcended the superficial renderings of discovery with which it was surrounded. However, it is not at all evident that *Navstar '92* transcends a colonial past. Canneto's sculpture endures as an aesthetically significant legacy of the quincentenary, but its reference to Columbus's voyage updates rather than replaces the iconography of discovery. In contrast, an indigenous iconography was offered in a much more modest exhibit, the Native American Peoples' Garden, mounted by the Seneca Nation of New York. Inside a modern longhouse, visitors could peruse a small exhibit on Native American cultures, while outside they could view a representation of Turtle Island—as the continent is conceived by the Seneca and many other indigenous peoples.

The paradigm of encounter and exchange was presented at AmeriFlora '92 in a small traveling version of *Seeds of Change*. Like the Seneca display, this exhibition conflicted with the trope of discovery that encompassed it. More generally, AmeriFlora, like Expo '92, was pervaded by two competing discourses: the trope of discovery, in which Columbus discovered a new world, and the new discourse of encounter, in which Columbus brought about an encounter and exchange between two old worlds. At Expo '92, official discourse and key symbols—Curro, the globe, the bridge—emphasized the encounter paradigm, but discovery remained the theme and organizing trope of the fair. At AmeriFlora '92, key symbols—the Santa Maria, the Columbus statue—celebrated discovery, whereas the most fully developed narrative, *Seeds of Change*, offered an implicit critique of that very celebration.

Other notable quincentenary productions in the United States also undermined the trope of discovery at the same time they employed it, including *Columbus and the Age of Discovery*, a seven-part television series broadcast on PBS in 1991 and 1992 (Dor-Ner 1991), and *Circa 1492: Art in the Age of Exploration*, a major exhibition curated by Jay Levenson (1991) that opened at the National Gallery in Washington, DC, on October 12, 1991. Despite their titles, both of these elaborate productions were rather dramatically influenced by critiques and revisions of the discovery paradigm. *Circa 1492*, resolutely apolitical and sparsely contextualized, played "art" to *Seeds'* "artifact": that is, just as *Seeds of Change* employed the text-dependent ethnographic approach featured in natural history museums, *Circa 1492* employed the more decontextualized approach characteristic of traditional art museums (Clifford 1988c; Vogel 1988; Berlo and Phillips 1992). But *Circa 1492* was less traditional in employing a global and pluralistic conception of high culture—one that acknowledged the diversity, creativity, sophistication, and mutual influences of artistic traditions in Europe, the Mediterranean world, Asia, and the Americas. This led to an exhibit as ambitious as the age of exploration it commemorated.

In contrast, PBS's quincentenary series primarily focused on the navigator himself. But the sixth episode, "The Columbian Exchange," explores the same five seeds of change that were developed in the Smithsonian exhibition. By the last episode, when the narrator maintains that "we" should celebrate Columbus's accomplishments, the attentive viewer might well beg to differ, given the series' demonstration of the disastrous consequences of Columbus's voyages for the Taínos of the Caribbean and for Africans imported to work on sugar plantations. Embedding an encounter and exchange episode within a tale of discovery leads to a jarring collision of paradigms, one that potentially destabilizes the dominance of the Euro-American perspective central to the discovery paradigm.

A View from the Shore: Conquest, Resistance, and Survival

Circa 1492 and *Columbus and the Age of Discovery* represent struggles to contain new and volatile representational agendas within old wineskins (Kolodny 1992). In the face of discursive challenges, the wineskin of discovery proved to have powerful advocates. This was brought home forcefully to William Truettner (1991b) and his colleagues at the National Museum of American Art (NMAA), part of the Smithsonian Institution, when in 1991 they mounted their openly revisionist quincentenary exhibition, *The West as America: Reinterpreting Images of the Frontier, 1820–1920.* Drawing on contemporary currents in Western history, *The West as America* situated frontier art within its social context of capitalist expansion, attacking the discovery paradigm head-on as an ideology of dispossession and exploitation. During a public controversy that raged throughout the exhibition's run, the NMAA—like the Smithsonian more generally—was strongly attacked for politicizing art by those who favored the traditional romantic approach to the Western frontier. At the forefront of the attack were two proponents of the discovery and exploration paradigm: Senator Ted Stevens of Alaska, a devoted proponent of the development of his state, the "last frontier," and Daniel Boorstin, Librarian of Congress Emeritus, author of a book on *The Discoverers,* and a contributor to the exhibition catalog of *Circa 1492* (Levenson 1991). The controversy was covered extensively in the media (Truettner 1991a; Wallach 1992). Threats of congressional funding cuts and withdrawal of support by donors ensured that the "new Western history" pioneered by scholars such as Patricia Nelson Limerick (1987, 2000) and Richard White (1993) would not find a congenial home in the Smithsonian. Furthermore, a scheduled tour to the Saint Louis Art Museum and the Denver Art Museum was canceled (Strong 1991).

As the brouhaha over *The West of America* demonstrated, the paradigm of invasion and conquest was perceived as too threatening for American public culture, however influential such books as Jennings's *The Invasion of America* (1975), Todorov's *The Conquest of America* (1984), Limerick's *The Legacy of Conquest* (1987), and Sale's *The Conquest of Paradise* (1990) had become in scholarly quarters. *Invasion* and *conquest* are terms that are largely reserved for "others" in the national imaginary—for Normans, Spanish conquistadors, body snatchers, African killer bees. In oppositional discourse, however, *invasion* and *conquest*— often coupled with *survival* and *resistance*—became central to an influential new paradigm that was promoted throughout 1992 and thereafter by indigenous, environmentalist, religious, and feminist organizations (Barreiro 1990; Bigelow and Peterson 1991, 1998; Jaimes 1992; Sheridan 1992). Tying together past invasions and present injustices, religious organizations such as the National

Council of the Churches of Christ in the U.S.A. (1990), the National Council of Catholic Bishops (1992), and Clergy and Laity Concerned (1991) sounded a call for a quincentenary observed by "repentance and reconciliation." Donald Pelotte (1992), an Abenaki bishop responsible for the Roman Catholic diocese centered in Gallup, New Mexico, assumed a leading role in questioning the Roman Catholic celebration of five hundred years of evangelism, suggesting instead that 1992 be a time for reflection upon the past, reconciliation between Native peoples and other Americans, and a recommitment to social justice. Pelotte had limited success, as suggested by the National Council of Catholic Bishops' (1991a, 1991b) statement on evangelization and a quincentenary poster campaign, "Discover Catholic Schools," that featured one of Columbus's caravels as a logo.

Other Native Americans seized upon 1992 as a "teachable moment," and sometimes their message and style differed radically from that of Pelotte. Russell Means and like-minded activists proclaimed 1992 as a year of "de-celebration": a time of mourning, protesting, disrupting, and countering official quincentenary events, which they denounced as ethnocentric celebrations of conquest and racist justifications of genocide. Means and a local collaborator, Jan Elliott, launched a round of protests in Gainesville, Florida, in November 1989, soon after the opening of the Florida Museum of Natural History's traveling exhibition, *First Encounters: Spanish Exploration in the Caribbean and the United States, 1492–1570* (Milanich and Milbrath 1989). A conventional ethnohistorical exhibition, *First Encounters* presented as its focal point—and as its main icon—a two-thirds' scale replica of Columbus's favorite ship, the Niña. The exhibition's narrative of exploration began in Spain; moved through the Spanish "encounter" with the Taínos; followed the exploration of Juan Ponce de León, Hernando de Soto, and Francisco Coronado; and concluded with "The Native Perspective," declaring this to be elusive, as "we" only have Spanish accounts. The nonnative "we" and native "they" of the exhibition was further expressed in a label observing that "it is disheartening to learn that our society is built on graves." Though the exhibition clearly did not celebrate the destruction of indigenous cultures (Milbrath and Milanich 1991), its theme, despite its title, was exploration, and its collective subject, its "we," was Euro-American. Underscoring this, for critic Jan Elliott (1989/90), was the way in which visiting children identified with Spanish explorers when they boarded the Niña.

As a result of the protests in Florida, curators in Albuquerque and Minneapolis consulted extensively with indigenous community members prior to mounting the traveling version of the exhibition. At the Science Museum of Minnesota the consultation resulted in a full-blown counter-exhibition, *Native Views: From the Heart of Turtle Island*. The counter-exhibition involved some additional items, but it was most effective in directly and succinctly positioning and critiquing the interpretive stance, display techniques, and communicative style of the original exhibition (M. Simpson 2001; Strong 1997; Cooper 2007).

"What is offensive about *First Encounters*?" asked a counter-label beside the replica of the Niña. The answer: "For many Euro-Americans, this replica of the Niña is a source of pride. For indigenous people, the Niña symbolizes death and destruction." Beside a life-size portrayal of the exchange of trade goods, a similar counter-label objected to presenting indigenous people in a case like an exotic, extinct species, thereby calling into question the presuppositions underlying natural history museums in general (Haraway 1989). The exhibition's display of Spanish armor was criticized, like the Niña, for glorifying instruments of conquest, as was the use of "wilderness" and "new world" as labels for what was home to Native Americans for thousands of years. Through embracing controversy, *First Encounters/Native Views* fully realized the exchange and encounter paradigm (Bunch 1992).

Another noteworthy experiment in labeling and juxtaposition was the public artist Scott Parsons's *Quincentenary Project* (see Figure 5), erected on October 12, 1992, in Denver's Civic Center, the site of cowboy and Indian statues as well as a monument to Columbus. In the midst of scores of freshly charred, powerfully haunting tepee frames, Parsons placed a set of signs, most of which imitated National Park Service interpretive signs. These offered, in official guise, an oppositional perspective upon Western history: documenting massacres, presenting apologies of religious leaders to indigenous people, and chastising the Denver Art Museum (located across the street) for displaying sacred Ghost Dance regalia.

The *Quincentenary Project* faced the State Capitol building, where, on October 12, 1992, members of the American Indian Movement faced down Italian-American sponsors of the traditional Columbus Day parade. After the parade sponsors withdrew, the AIM leaders led a victory parade through the installation, after which the burned-out tepee village was extended up to the Capitol itself,

Figure 5. Scott Parsons, *Quincentenary Project*, 1992 (detail). One hundred burnt tepees and twenty-nine historical markers installed at the Denver Civic Center, October 12. Collaboration with Dave Greenlund and the American Indian Movement of Colorado. Photography by Pauline Turner Strong.

where it served as a powerful, if temporary, indictment of Colorado's treatment of its indigenous peoples.

Like *Native Views,* the *Quincentenary Project* appropriated the authoritative medium of institutional labels in order to contest the dominant tropes and the exclusive "we" of the American national imaginary. Another indigenous response to the quincentenary was to ignore Columbus entirely and focus instead on indigenous survival and resilience. For example, the Peace and Dignity Journey had indigenous runners from as far away as Alaska and Argentina converge in Mexico City on October 12, 1992, demonstrating strength, resilience, and unity. More generally, a hemispheric indigenous identity began to coalesce in 1992 (see Part Five). As Diane Nelson (1999) writes, the quincentenary "produced a flurry of hemispheric meetings, Rigoberta Menchú's Nobel Peace Prize, and the United Nations declaring first a Year [1993] and then the Decade [1994–2004] of Indigenous People" (4). In 2007, decades of work culminated in the adoption, by the General Assembly, of the UN Declaration on the Rights of Indigenous Peoples. The only four negative votes were registered by settler states—Australia, Canada, New Zealand, and the United States—and all reversed their opposition by the end of 2010 (Niezen 2003; Richardson 2010; Cultural Survival 2010; Wilkins and Stark 2011, 201). Although the declaration is not binding, it is a significant statement in favor of indigenous cultural survival and self-determination.

Conclusion: Public Historical Representation during the Columbian Quincentenary

Official American quincentenary exhibitions revealed a diversity of approaches to public historical representation, ranging from the regressive US pavilion to the revisionist *West as America.* The encounter and exchange paradigm as popularized in *Seeds of Change* falls midway between these extremes, with its focus on material exchanges and multicultural contributions to a complex world civilization. The fact that *The West as America* was at once the exhibition most fully grounded in the latest historical scholarship and the exhibition most vulnerable to controversy demonstrates the gulf between academic and public history (Wallach 1992). Similarly, the distance between *Seeds of Change* and the US pavilion at Expo '92 demonstrates the gulf between public history and nationalist propaganda.

The encounter and exchange paradigm's ability to mediate between extremes, its widespread promotion among educators, and its transatlantic appeal made it attractive as a pedagogical paradigm. But its assertion of strength through cultural exchange proved to be unacceptable to those who sought to ground US supremacy on universal values and the trope of discovery. On the other side, the encounter paradigm's suppression of conflict made it unsatisfactory for those who sought to understand and emphasize the relationship between the injustices of the past and those of the present. Although the debate continues to be played out in battles over school curricula, both the exchange and the resistance paradigms have grown in strength since 1992. To the extent that the cultural work that occurred during the Columbian Quincentenary contributed to the mobilization and change in public attitudes that enabled the ratification of the UN Declaration on the Rights of Indigenous Peoples, 1992 turned out after all to be an observance of Five Hundred Years of Survival and Resistance.

Bibliographic Note

In this chapter "paradigm" is used as a "lightly held historical metaphor," as George Stocking (1987, xiv) puts it, rather than in Kuhn's (1962) stricter sense. My thinking on the paradigms of discovery, encounter, and conquest was influenced by an international workshop in Seville, Spain, organized by Annette Kolodny (1992). This conference enabled me to attend the opening of Expo '92; quotations of officials are from my field notes (Strong 1992) and from the exposition's press kit (*Expo '92 Sevilla* 1992).

I take the section title "A View from the Shore" from an acrylic stencil of that title by Simon Brascoupé, a Tuscarora/Algonquian artist (Barreiro 1990, cover image). Diane Nelson's *A Finger in the Wound: Body Politics in Quincentennial Guatemala* (1999) is an important analysis of indigenous organizing in Guatemala in the years around 1992, in the wake of a genocidal civil war. For ongoing disputes in Denver, Colorado, concerning the observance of Columbus Day, and an excellent demonstration of why the issue means so much to both sides, see Navajo filmmaker Bennie Klain's documentary, *Columbus Day Legacy* (2010). The film *Journey: Museums and Community Collaboration* (1996) documents the Science Museum of Minnesota's exhibit, *First Encounters/Native Views*; see also Strong (1997).

The study of historical representation is a large and lively field. See, for example, H. White, *Metahistory* (1973); Mitchell, *Colonizing Egypt* (1988); Bodnar, *Remaking America* (1993); Kammen, *Mystic Chords of Memory* (1993); J. Young, *The Texture of Memory* (1994); Trouillot, *Silencing the Past* (1995); Linenthal and Engelhardt, *History Wars* (1996); Handler and Gable, *The New History in an Old Museum* (1997); Klein, *Frontiers of Historical Imagination* (1997); Sider and Smith, *Between History and Histories* (1997); Sturken, *Tangled Memories* (1997); Nash, Crabtree, and Dunn, *History on Trial* (2000); Segal, "'Western

Civ' and the Staging of History in American Higher Education" (2000); Linenthal, *Preserving Memory* (2001) and *The Unfinished Bombing* (2003); Flores, *Remembering the Alamo* (2002); and Nabokov, *A Forest of Time: American Indian Ways of History* (2002). On world fairs, see, for example, Rydell, *All the World's a Fair* (1984); Stocking, *Victorian Anthropology* (1987, chapter 6); Fogelson, "The Red Man in the White City" (1991); and Tenorio-Trillo, *Mexico at the World's Fairs* (1996).

Chapter Four
Indian Blood

In one panel of her provocative installation, *Preservation of a Species: DECON-STRUCTIVISTS (This is the house that Joe built)*, the Canadian artist Joane Cardinal-Schubert arranged, as if on a chalkboard, photographs of herself, her father, and other members of her family. In the midst of the photographs—often displayed in multiple copies—she chalked in the question, "What does *part* Indian Mean? (which Part?)" (see Figure 6). Which part, indeed for, as she wrote, "you don't get 50% or 25% or 16% TREATMENT WHEN YOU EXPERI-ENCE RACISM—IT IS ALWAYS 100%." Stamped across her own photographs were scarlet letters that exemplify this racism, branding her "GOVERNMENT ISSUE/NON STATUS"—a reference to the Canadian classification for persons of mixed ancestry excluded from the recognition and rights accorded to "Treaty" or "Status" Indians (Boldt and Long 1985; Peterson and Brown 1985; McMillan 1988). Another panel featured Cardinal-Schubert's brother Douglas Cardinal, the designer of the Canadian Museum of Civilization. Chalked notations stated, "He is an architect and a non-status Indian," but across his duplicated portraits Cardinal-Schubert stamped not his non-status designation, but the way he de-fined and distinguished himself, as "Architect, Brother, Father, Uncle, Nephew, Son, Son-in-law, Friend, and Colleague" (McMaster and Martin 1992, 134).

Two other panels portrayed historical scenes: screaming children facing colonial authorities, and an altar labeled "FOSTER CHILD" surrounded by objects and texts evoking the history of displacement, residential schooling, and despair. A closed box labeled "CULTURAL IDENTITIES" sat off to the side, and a painting of a lake—unusual for the installation in its use of color—seemed

Figure 6. Joane Cardinal-Schubert (Métis), *Preservation of a Species: DECONSTRUCTIVISTS (This is the house that Joe built)*, 1990 (detail). An installation displayed in the *Indigena* exhibition, Canadian Museum of Civilization. Photography by W. Jackson Rushing. Reproduced with permission of the artist's estate.

to offer the possibility of renewal. In the center of the installation a black fence enclosed five figures, separating them from five similarly clothed forms on the outside. The mournful cry of loons pervaded the room—all in all, a haunted and haunting space, filled with the forces of death and loss, but also with the vital spirit of outrage and resistance.

Various versions of *Preservation of a Species* were displayed in twenty venues in Canada, the United States, and Europe between 1989 and 2000. I saw the installation at the Canadian Museum of Civilization, where it appeared in *Indigena*, a pathbreaking quincentenary exhibition of contemporary Native art (McMaster and Martin 1992; Rushing 1993). In the exhibition catalog Cardinal-Schubert acknowledged the influence of her German and Blackfoot grandmothers and described the work as "an installation that visually discusses RACISM through an examination of labels and imposed stereotypes that I have experienced growing up in a non-Native society"—labels through which "the government declares by number who is Native and who is not" (McMaster and Martin 1992, 132–133). Central to the project were the panels of photographs and chalked-in text, at once evocative of the bureaucratic labeling, the erasing deculturation, the disciplinary subjection, and the graffiti-like resistance of the Indian residential school. The effect of the "chalkboard" gallery was enhanced by the eerie atmosphere created by the entire installation, in which the viewer's experience was fragmented and obstructed by fences, barriers, peepholes, veils, and erasures that materialize the exclusion, disarticulation, and invisibility of Canadians of mixed ancestry.

Cardinal-Schubert allowed that her "construction site" created an "uncomfortable and unsettling experience" for its viewers—whom she identified as the "deconstructivists" of the subtitle—and remarked with satisfaction, "Good! Now you know how I have felt for most of my life." The viewer's task in coming to terms with this site of identity-construction resembled that of the Native "survivors," who "hung on to the fragments of culture they had managed to preserve; began to work together to piece their cultures together and to celebrate their wholeness" (McMaster and Martin 1992, 132–133). In this fractured space, the viewer could not easily escape the poignant cry, "What does *part* Indian Mean? (which Part?)" So concrete, so precise is the official calculation of Native identity—"50% or 25% or 16%"—that Cardinal-Schubert reduced the naturalizing formula to absurdity simply by taking it literally. *"Part Indian?"* *"Which part?"* Making the deconstructive move that Gayatri Spivak (1993) has characterized as "one of Derrida's most scandalous contributions," that is, to begin with the familiar and "to take it with the utmost seriousness, with literal seriousness" (5), Cardinal-Schubert realized in this space the horror of being torn apart, reconstructed, and defined as a fragment.

Preservation of a Species refused to name the essentialized substance underlying the "50% or 25% or 16% treatment." Similarly, when asked his own "percentage of Indian blood," scholar and activist Ward Churchill took the notion of fragmentation with "literal seriousness" but refused to name the expected substance: "I can report that I am precisely 52.5 pounds Indian—about 35 pounds Creek and the remainder Cherokee—88 pounds Teutonic, 43.5 pounds some sort of English, and the rest 'undetermined.' Maybe the last part should just be described as 'human'" (Jaimes 1992, 123). Equally playfully and pointedly, Cherokee artist Jimmie Durham named the substance but denied its amenability to arithmetical calculation: "The question of my 'identity' often comes up. I think I must be a mixed-blood. I claim to be male, although only one of my parents was male" (Jaimes 1992, 123; Gordon and Newfield 1994, 752). Irony aside, Durham, Churchill, Cardinal-Schubert, and their audiences know all too well that Indian identity is fixed, quantified, and delimited through an elaborate calculus operating upon "blood": pure, full, or mixed blood; Indian, White, or Black blood; Blackfoot, Creek, or Cherokee blood; blood in fractions, blood in degrees, or blood in drops.

Langston Hughes (1953) once had his fictional character, Simple, remark, "It's powerful ... that one drop of Negro blood—because just *one* drop of black blood makes a man colored. *One* drop—you are a Negro!" (85; ellipsis in original). Vis-à-vis "White blood," the power of a drop of "Negro blood" is to contaminate (Wright 1994; Davis 1995; Zack 1995). In contrast, the power of a drop of "Indian blood"—if no more than a drop—is to enhance, ennoble, naturalize, and legitimate. As the nineteenth-century Southern novelist William Gilmore Simms put it, "Properly diluted, there is no better blood than that of the Cherokee and Natchez. It would have been a good infusion into the paler fountain of Quaker and Puritan" (quoted in Fogelson 1985, 16). Given this desire to enhance the pale, it is perhaps appropriate that a 1967 history of Quakers in the Alleghenies bears (without irony) the title *Indian Blood* (Olsen 1967), deriving from local statements such as "I show my Indian blood in the way I walk," or "My love of beads and bangles comes from my Indian blood" (9).

The enhancing power of "Indian blood" is invoked more critically in Jamaica Kincaid's novel, *Lucy* (1990), when the title character, a West Indian au pair, is told by Mariah, her North American employer,

> I was looking forward to telling you that I have Indian blood, that the reason I'm so good at catching fish and hunting birds and roasting corn and doing all sorts of things is that I have Indian blood. But now, I don't know why, I feel I shouldn't tell you that. I feel you will take it the wrong way. (39–41)

Lucy, the astute au pair, reflects,

> This really surprised me. What way should I take this? Wrong way? Right way? What could she mean? To look at her, there was nothing remotely like an Indian about her. Why claim a thing like that? I myself had Indian blood in me. My grandmother is a Carib Indian. That makes me one-quarter Carib Indian. But I don't go around saying that I have some Indian blood in me. The Carib Indians were good sailors, but I don't like to be on the sea; I only like to look at it. To me my grandmother is my grandmother, not an Indian. My grandmother is alive; the Indians she came from are all dead. If someone could get away with it, I am sure they would put my grandmother in a museum, as an example of something now extinct in nature, one of a handful still alive. In fact, one of the museums to which Mariah had taken me devoted a whole section to people, all dead, who were more or less related to my grandmother.
>
> Mariah says, "I have Indian blood in me," and underneath everything I could swear she says it as if she were announcing her possession of a trophy. How do you get to be the sort of victor who can claim to be the vanquished also? (39–41)

Kincaid's question is pivotal: *"How do you get to be the sort of victor who can claim to be the vanquished also?"* What is this peculiar form of appropriation that lays claim not only to land, labor, and knowledge but even, when "properly diluted," to "blood," the presumed (though colonially imposed) substantive basis of the colonized's identity? This is what Jack Forbes (1987), speaking of Virginians who claim descent from Pocahontas, called "fooling Genocide, managing somehow to hold on to Indian-ness" (120). In claiming drops of "Indian blood"—and especially in tracing it to Pocahontas or another "Indian princess"—the victors naturalize themselves and legitimize their occupation of the land. Meanwhile (and this is the flip side of "managing somehow to hold onto Indian-ness"), the vanquished are required to naturalize and legitimize themselves in terms of "blood quantum"—an imposition of the victor's essentialized reckoning of identity that becomes an integral, often taken-for-granted aspect of Native subjectivity. The need to objectify identity in the idiom of blood courses through Native American life.

The shared experience of objectification has generated a wry corpus of Indian humor, as in a delightful, if haunting, passage from "Cheeky Moon" (Baker 1990), by the Canadian poet Annharte: "I'm left to defend / one lonely drop of blood. / I might terminate / if I get nosebleed" (38). Like Cardinal-Schubert, Annharte destabilizes the concept of "Indian blood" simply by taking it literally. *"I might terminate if I get nosebleed"*: To get the joke, we must understand both the blood-reckoning that defines Native identity and the history of governmental efforts to "terminate" the official status of Indian tribes (Fixico 1986; McMillan 1988). In the image of a life-threatening nosebleed, Annharte deftly captures the precariousness of both tribal sovereignty and individual identity.

In "Cheeky Moon" the subjective experience of being defined through blood-reckoning is expressed from inside the reservation boundary, if just barely, while in Cardinal-Schubert's installation it was expressed from outside looking in. Annharte and Cardinal-Schubert share, however, the experience of possessing a naturalized, individualized, and fractured identity. Such identities are also potentially conflicted, as the Chickasaw poet Linda Hogan (1987) reveals, again using the idiom of blood, in "Old Men at War, Old Women," a poem about her dark and blond grandfathers. "Be silent / old men who live inside me," she begins,

> dark grandfather that was silent
> though I was his blood
> and wore his black eyes.
> He's living in my breath
> when it's quiet,
> all his people are walking
> through my veins without speech.
> And blonde grandfather
> fishing the river for Chubs,
>
> ...
>
> I'm wearing your love and hate
> like silver
> and blue stone.
> this face
> this body
> this hair
> is not mine.
> This war inside me
> is not mine. (235–236)

Similarly, with "literal seriousness," the Laguna poet Paula Gunn Allen invokes blood conflict in her poem, "Dear World" (1988):

Mother has lupus.
She says it's a disease
of self-attack.
It's like a mugger broke into your home
and you called the police
and when they came they beat up on you
instead of your attackers,
she says.
I say that makes sense.
It's in the blood,
in the dynamic.
A halfbreed woman
can hardly do anything else
but attack herself,
her blood attacks itself.
There are historical reasons
for this … (121)

Historical reasons, yes, and cultural ones as well. *Her blood attacks itself*: the reckoning of Indian identity that gives rise to this image is grounded in the same discourse about "blood relationship" that David Schneider analyzed in a more benign form in *American Kinship* (1980). As Schneider explained Euro-American common sense, "Because blood is a 'thing' and because it is subdivided with each reproductive step away from a given ancestor, the precise degree to which two persons share common heredity can be calculated, and 'distance' can thus be stated in specific quantitative terms" (25). Among Native Americans, such precise, quantified distance has immense political and personal ramifications, dividing "full-bloods" from their "mixed-blood" or "half-blood" descendants; half-bloods or, more derogatorily, "half-breeds," from their quarter-blood relatives; eighth- and sixteenth-, thirty-second-, and sixty-fourth-bloods from each other; on down the line to those who, like Annharte, struggle to defend "one lonely drop of blood."

"What difference a blood quantum can make," muses Terry P. Wilson (1992, 109). But "blood quantum," as important as it may be, is never the sole marker of Indian identity. Biolsi (1995) has shown how genealogy, private property, and "competence in civilization" articulated with blood quanta in the construction of reservation identities and subjectivities; Lomawaima (1994) gives evidence of the social and cultural inflection of the categories "full-blood" and "mixed-blood"; Blu (1980) has described the Lumbees' refusal to designate tribal identity in terms of blood; and Clifford (1988b) and Campisi (1991) have shown Mashpee identity to be grounded in shared history, social ties, and attachment to place more than in objectified ancestry. But among federally recognized tribes in the United States, blood quantum (often 25 percent) is the most common criterion of membership. Used in specific cases since the Sauk and Fox Treaty of 1830 (Stiffarm and Lane 1992), "blood quantum" was given a more generalized application in the administration of Indian boarding schools and land allotments and in census reports (Kelly 1983; Wilson 1992; Lomawaima 1994). Subsequently, "blood quanta" were codified in various forms in many of the tribal constitutions and bylaws written as a result of the Indian Reorganization Act of 1934, which defined tribal members and non-enrolled Indians through a mixture of descent, residence, and "blood" (Baca 1988; Resnick 1989). Directly or indirectly (through its role in defining tribal membership), blood-reckoning is also significant in the administration of federal laws relating to jurisdiction over crime, American Indian religious freedom, the adoption of Indian children (Chapter 6), the marketing of Indian art, the repatriation of artifacts and human remains (Chapter 11), economic enterprises on reservation lands, and the like.

Like tribal governments and federal Indian policy themselves, "blood quantum" is highly contested—as a general concept, in its various and variable applications, and as an individual "possession." Nevertheless, "Indian blood"—and especially its more differentiated, tribally specific varieties—is a dominant discourse within and against which indigenous identity is defined. The Cherokees of Oklahoma, for example, have been engaged in conflicts over tribal membership that Circe Sturm (2002) describes explicitly as "blood politics."

The works of Cardinal-Schubert, Annharte, Hogan, and Allen expose the tragic absurdity of the essentialized discourse of "Indian blood" and the pain of those the discourse divides, excludes, and marginalizes. Other indigenous people, however, have chosen to reinforce and refigure, rather than deconstruct and displace, the symbol of Indian blood. The work of Kiowa author N. Scott Momaday is notable in this regard, and because Momaday's image of "memory in the blood" has been criticized as "absurdly racist" in an influential volume of literary criticism, Arnold Krupat's *The Voice in the Margin* (1989, 14), it calls for careful consideration.

In *The Way to Rainy Mountain* (1969), Momaday writes,

> Although my grandmother lived out her long life in the shadow of Rainy Moun-tain, the immense landscape of the continental interior lay like memory in her blood. She could tell of the Crows, whom she had never seen, and of the Black Hills, where she had never been. (7)

Here "memory in the blood" is simply a simile, a literary device that seeks to convey the power of narration to transcend the limitations of individual experi-ence. In subsequent works, however, "memory in the blood" comes to take on a more naturalized quality. In the essay "I Am Alive" (1974), Momaday describes and comments upon the giveaway ceremony in which his Kiowa grandfather, Mammedaty, who died before he was born, received a fine black horse:

> I remember it, as it were, in the way that we human beings seem at times to remember Genesis—across evolutionary distances. It is a memory that persists in the blood, and there only....
>
> This blood recollection, which is an intricate image indeed, composed of innumerable details, is especially vivid and immediate to me, a whole and irrevocable act of the imagination. I have the sense always that the event, the dramatic action, is just now, in a moment, taking place in the real world. I have held on to this vision for many years, keeping it within my reach, bringing it into focus in moments of peace and quiet. I have walked about in this vision, taken it into account from many different angles, across many distances, in many different lights. And I have thought about it; I have tried to understand it in its own terms; I have tried to perceive myself in it.
>
> In this experience which I have related concerning Mammedaty and the horse, which experience is of a very particular kind, there is a synthesis of other, more general experiences, I believe. In such things there is an evocation of the tribal intelligence, an exposition of racial memory. (11–14)

In these passages, "memory in the blood," "blood recollection," and "racial memory" are all introduced in a struggle to describe the author's experience of a timeless, unmediated, and especially vivid act of vision or imagination. This is the kind of extraordinary experience that others might attribute to divine possession, artistic inspiration, genius, madness, or physiological alterations, but Momaday's "very particular" experience has the quality of a memory from the distant past, a distinctive inheritance from his ancestors. Thus he locates it in blood, a substance he construes as persisting over time and connecting him to his remote ancestors. In doing so, as in his reference to Genesis and to "evolutionary distances," Momaday is speaking from a hybrid consciousness, one that shares aspects of a mythopoetic worldview with his ancestors and a more materialist one with his audience.

Momaday's experience of "memory in the blood" is probed further in *Ancestral Voice*, a series of conversations between Momaday and interviewer Charles Woodard (1989). Discussing his book *The Way to Rainy Mountain*, Momaday remarks, "The imagination that informs those stories is really not mine, though it exists, I think, in my blood. It's an ancestral imagination. It's important to understand that dimension." Likewise, referring to a "racial memory" of crossing the Bering land bridge, Momaday says, "There are times, Chuck, when I think about people walking on ice with dogs pulling travois, and I don't know whether it's something that I'm imagining or something that I remember. But it comes down to the same thing" (22). Pressed on this, Momaday more decisively naturalizes his vivid experience of the past:

> I think that each of us bears in his genes or in his blood or wherever a recollection of the past. Even the very distant past. I just think that's the way it is.... In the case of the Kiowa, it's a remembering of the migration. A remembering of coming out of the log. A remembering of crossing the Bering land bridge. (21)

Later in the same conversations Momaday equates Kiowa "blood memory" with "the racial memory of life in the mountains" (53) and says of the Big Horn Mountains in particular,

> That landscape represents to me, in the best sense, the cultural memory of the migration of the Kiowas. I look at it and I wonder who before me in my own line of descent has looked upon it. And what did it mean to that person. That is a very exciting thing to think about. And thinking about it in such a way is an appropriation, too. You know, I take possession of the landscape when I look at it in that way. I feel that I'm gathering it into my experience and I'm becoming richer because of it. (211)

"Memory in the blood" is a persistent trope indeed in Momaday's writing, though at times it is located more imprecisely "in the genes or the blood or wherever," and is characterized as "imagination" rather than "recollection," or as "cultural" rather than "racial." The imprecision is revealing: it is as though none of these formulations adequately captures Momaday's vivid apprehension of ancestral experience on the landscape. What is most consistent about Momaday's "recollection of the past[,] even the most distant past" is not its embodiment in blood, but its connection to Kiowa movements across the landscape. To locate memory in the blood as Momaday does may be as essentializing as to locate identity in "blood quanta," but Momaday's use of blood imagery aims not to differentiate but to relate; not to administer but to imagine; not to impose quantified identities upon others but to make sense of the intersubjective quality of his own experience; not to appropriate the land of others but to appropriate the experiences of his own ancestors. When read in the context of the Native American experience with blood-reckoning, Momaday's "memory in the blood" becomes a refiguring of "Indian blood" that makes it a vehicle of connection and integration—literally, what Paula Gunn Allen calls a "re-membering" (Owens 1992)—rather than one of calculation and differentiation.

These contextual and pragmatic dimensions of "memory in the blood" are elided in Krupat's claim that Momaday's notion is "absurdly racist." Approaching Momaday's work in terms of what James Clifford (1988b) has called a "literalist epistemology" (340), Krupat (1989) states categorically that "there is no gene for perception, no such thing as memory in the blood." He charges that such "mystifications" place "unnecessary obstacles in the way of a fuller understanding and appreciation of Native American literature," and goes on to criticize Momaday more generally for writing in a mystical, monological, and authoritative voice (13–14, 177–187). I wish to argue against the charge that Momaday's "memory in the blood" is a racist mystification, but it would seem that by confining his critique to the realm of literature Krupat has understated the issues involved. It is not its challenge to literary appreciation that is most troubling about "memory in the blood," but its chilling resonance with racist ideologies used to justify genocide.

However, even in this stronger form—or perhaps especially in this stronger form—the charge of racism can be answered by taking into account the contextual and pragmatic dimensions of Momaday's "memory in the blood." For Momaday to refigure "Indian blood" so that it is a signifier of "tribal intelligence" and "ancestral imagination" is essentialist, to be sure, but hardly racist: nowhere does Momaday express the superiority of those possessing what he figures as "blood memories," nor does he advocate political, economic, or social distinctions on the basis of the possession of such memories. To the contrary, through his writing Momaday is extending those memories beyond the sphere of his own ancestry. Furthermore, if it is "absurdly racist" to speak poetically of "memories in the blood," is it not equally so to speak transparently, as Krupat does, of the "mixed blood father" of the early Pequot author William Apes, or of anthropologist Jack Forbes as "a mixed blood of Powhatan-Lenape-Saponi background" (143, 204)? Blood is, by now, thoroughly embedded, one way or another, in the construction of Native American identity, and any act of speaking or writing within, through, or against this idiom must be assessed in terms of the particular "cultural work" (Tompkins 1986) that it does.

Nevertheless, nonessentializing strategies promise, in the end, to be more effective in subverting the hegemonic power of "Indian blood." "Like the mockingbird, I have more than one song" (80), writes Osage poet Carter Revard (1987) in a remarkable autobiographical essay. The power of voice-shifting to mock and subvert fixed, essentialized identities is also celebrated in the writings of that mischievous self-described "crossblood," Gerald Vizenor (1987), who writes as one "bound with mixedblood memories, urban and reservation disharmonies" (1987, 102). In *Crossbloods* (1990), as well as in several other loosely autobiographical works, this heir to the Anishinaabe trickster Naanabozho identifies himself and other crossbloods with the "mournful," "whimsical," and "wild" trickster (1981, 1987). "Mixedbloods," writes Vizenor in a particularly memorable passage, "loosen the seams in the shrouds of identities" (1987, 101). His writings are filled with outrageous, revitalizing loosenings of both bureaucratic and anthropological "shrouds," at times expressed through one of his characters, at times in his own voice.

One of Vizenor's characters in *Earthdivers* (1981), for example, wryly proposes "an organization of mixedblood skins which demands one-fourth degree of tribal blood or *less*, to be enrolled as a member" (16; emphasis added). Another petitions

> to be recognized as a mixedblood tribal person, claiming that his great grand-mother was a pure Indian princess, or something, and she was so powerful she even had slaves ... well, she fooled around with one of those slaves, and here stands me, a mixedblood tribal black with a smooth tongue, brother. (14)

A third character, Capt. Shammer, who holds "The Chair of Tears" in a Department of American Indian Studies and is the founder of the Halfbreed Hall of Fame, lectures,

> Geometric blood volume was introduced by colonial racists, and from time to time, measure to measure, depending upon the demands of federal programs and subsidies, tribal blood volume increases or decreases. You could say that tribal blood volume follows the economic principles of supply and demand. Accordingly, Capt. Shammer proposes a scheme in which "tribal faculties and students would be paid a basic wage according to their volume of tribal blood," based upon a color wheel offering a "scientific approach to blood volume, degrees, and quantities of tribalness." (16)

No one, of whatever type or degree of blood, is immune to Vizenor's biting wit, but he is not to be typecast. Even "crossblood assurance" comes in for reflexive critique as "a descent from pure racial simulations" in the "literature of dominance" (Vizenor 1994, 59). In a more visionary vein, Vizenor (1987) suggests that "The mixedblood is a new metaphor ... a transitive contradancer between communal tribal cultures and those material and urban pretensions that counter conservative traditions" (101). Evoking the earthdiver of many tribal traditions—the creature who successfully retrieves, from the bottom of the primordial sea, the earth out of which the world was fashioned—Vizenor (1981) imagines mixed-bloods plunging "into unknown urban places now, into the racial darkness in the cities, to create a new consciousness of coexistence." Further drawing on tribal traditions in imagining the world created by the earthdiver as resting on a turtle's back, Vizenor summons "white settlers" to

> dive with mixedblood survivors into the unknown, into the legal morass of treaties and bureaucratic in search of a few honest words upon which to build a new urban turtle island. (x–xi)

Like Carter Revard, like the mockingbird, Vizenor speaks in many voices, and at first glance there appears to be no sharper contrast to Momaday's "ancestral voice," his "memory in the blood," than the crossblood trickster. Still, like Momaday, Vizenor is preoccupied with redefining the meaning of "Indian blood," finding an opportunity as well as a burden in the particularly objectified form in which Euro-Americans have construed and institutionalized their racism vis-à-vis the indigenous inhabitants of the landscape. And herein lies a challenge for scholarship on race and racism, particularly in anthropology. At one time anthropologists' overriding task was the Boasian program of de-objectifying race, disengaging it from language, culture, and nationality. That remains important. If, however, we simply transfer the strategy of de-essentializing race to our analyses of the discourse of those who have been construed as racial others, we end up, like Krupat, treating all essentialisms alike and calling them racist. Some even end up, like ethnohistorian James Clifton (1989, 1990), opposing Indian rights on the basis of the fictional nature of Indian blood. If the hegemonic calculus of Indian identity is perverse, it is doubly perverse to use deconstruction to delegitimate those who have been forced to frame their identity and their claims in terms of that calculus.

Spivak's (1993) warning is well-taken: "Deconstruction, whatever it may be, is not most valuably an exposure of error, certainly not other people's error, other people's essentialism" (4) (especially, one might add, subordinated people's essentialism). She continues, "The most serious critique in deconstruction is the critique of things that are extremely useful, things without which we cannot live on, take chances; like our running self-identikit" (4). "Indian blood," essentialist as it may be, is at present a tragically necessary condition for the continued survival and vitality of many individuals and communities—if only until Vizenor's crossblood earthdivers succeed in their efforts to dredge up those "few honest words" upon which to create a new "turtle island."

Bibliographic Note

Other treatments of essentialized Native identity include Sturm's *Blood Politics: Race, Culture, and Identity in the Cherokee Nation of Oklahoma* (2002) and Garoutte's *Real Indians: Identity and the Survival of Native America* (2003). Comparative treatments are offered in Kauanui's *Hawaiian Blood: Colonialism and the Politics of Sovereignty and Indigeneity* (2008) and in *Blood Narrative: Indigenous Identity in American Indian and Maori Literary and Activist Texts*, which discusses what author Chadwick Allen (2002) calls a "blood/land/memory complex" common to the Maoris and Native Americans. Several contributors to

Franklin and McKinnon's (2001) *Relative Values: Reconfiguring Kinship Studies* (Carsten 2001; Tapper 2001; Weston 2001) consider metaphorical renderings of kinship in terms of blood. Naturalized, constructed, and hybrid identities are discussed by the contributors to *Resisting Identities* (Segal 1996), a theme issue of *Cultural Anthropology* (see especially Briggs 1996), and "Theorizing the Hybrid," a theme issue of *Journal of American Folklore* (Kapchan and Strong 1999).

Among the many treatments of indigenous kinship practices are E. Deloria's (1988) *Waterlily*, a fictionalized portrayal of Lakota kinship practices; Foster's (1992) ethnohistory, *Being Comanche: The Social History of an American Indian Community*; J. Brown's (1996) ethnohistory, *Strangers in Blood: Fur Trade Company Families in Indian Country*; Witherspoon's (1996) ethnography, *Navajo Kinship and Marriage*; Kan's (2001) anthology, *Strangers to Relatives: The Adoption and Naming of Anthropologists in Native North America*; and J. Miller's overview, "Kinship, Family Kindreds, and Community" (2002). An earlier, coauthored version of this chapter (Strong and Van Winkle 1996) contrasts traditional Washoe kinship practices with the objectified identity of Indian blood (555–559).

PART THREE
CAPTIVITY, ADOPTION,
AND THE AMERICAN IMAGINARY

One of the few Native Americans known to the proverbial American schoolchild is Squanto, who brought seeds of maize to the starving Pilgrims and taught them how to cultivate it. The hospitality of Squanto and indigenous people more generally is acknowledged each year at the Thanksgiving table, at once a representation of salvation, peaceful communion, and legitimized occupation of a plentiful land. A complementary role in Euro-American "foundational fictions" (Sommer 1991) is played by Pocahontas, the "Indian princess" who represents salvation, communion, and colonial legitimacy in a distinctly female way (see Chapter 9). As John Smith's savior, as a cultural mediator and convert to Christianity, and as the wife of tobacco planter John Rolfe and the mother of his child, Pocahontas is at once an icon of the commingling of Indian and English "blood," the conversion of the American "heathen," and colonial appropriation of American abundance (see Figure 7).

Squanto and Pocahontas are all the more appropriate as legendary figures in the national imaginary because they are tragic heroes, early personifications of the noble, but vanishing, Indian (O'Brien 2010). Neither Squanto nor Pocahontas lived long after ensuring the survival of the fledgling English colonies—Squanto dying in a lonely exile in his own land, Pocahontas, in England aboard a ship bound for Virginia. Less well known is another tragic dimension of Squanto and Pocahontas's lives: both were captives among the English before they became valued allies.

Figure 7. Antonio Capellano, *Preservation of Captain Smith by Pocahontas,* 1825. Carving above the west door of the US Capitol Rotunda. Courtesy of the Architect of the Capitol.

That Squanto and Pocahontas were prisoners as well as saviors and converts of the English is suppressed in Euro-American mythology not only because it is inconsistent with their personification of peaceful communion. More, their captivity conflicts with a third dominant representation of the relations between Euro-Americans and Native Americans: the captivity of "White" among "Red." Like Squanto and Pocahontas, the White captive represents a kind of communion between Natives and settlers, but one that is achieved through violence and generally repudiated. John Smith is probably the most famous of the White captives, but as an adult male captive saved from execution by a young Indian woman (as the story goes), he is unusual. No single figure personifies the complex selective tradition of captivity that has, for more than three centuries, served as a potent and resilient vehicle for the imagining of national identity.

Captivity across the indigenous/settler frontier and its representation has a history as long as the European presence in North America. Chapter 5, "Captivity in White and Red," considers the practice and representation of captivity across cultural boundaries in the seventeenth and early eighteenth centuries, years that included the first and most devastating indigenous war of resistance against the English (King Philip's War of 1675–1676) as well as the first two intercolonial wars between Britain and France (or "French and Indian Wars"). The most significant vehicle for representing captivity during these years and into the nineteenth century were narratives written or dictated by captives upon their return to colonial society. The narratives are considerably more complex and variable than the typifications of captivity they engendered, so we are able to trace the development of a selective tradition of captivity out of a complex set of historical encounters and a multiplicity of representations.

Since the colonial era, the narratives of colonial and frontier settlers have appeared in a variety of genres, from print and painting to sculpture and film. Considerably less well known—in fact, excluded from what, following Raymond Williams (1977), I call the selective tradition of captivity—are the experiences of Native American captives, whether held by other indigenous groups or by Europeans or Euro-Americans. Scholars are beginning to examine more carefully the tales of various kinds of indigenous captives, whether they were kidnapped, enslaved, incarcerated, or forced to attend residential schools. A more multidimensional picture of captivity on the indigenous/settler frontier is emerging in current scholarship and, to some extent, in popular culture as well. An example of this more complex representation of captivity is the 1996 novel *Indian Killer* by the Spokane-Coeur d'Alene author Sherman Alexie. Chapter 6, "The Contemporary Captivity Narrative," interprets this novel as a powerful transformation of the selective tradition of captivity. This chapter discusses the experience of Native American children forcibly removed from their homes and placed in adoptive or foster families, as well as the remedy offered in the Indian Child Welfare Act of 1978.

Part Three concludes with "On Captivity as Digital Spectacle" (Chapter 7), a brief consideration of certain iconic representations from the twenty-first-century "war on terror" in the context of the captivity tradition. While it is not possible to trace the whole of the Euro-American captivity tradition in this book, Chapter 6 and Chapter 7 point to the continuing significance of representations of captivity in the American national imaginary.

Another reminder of the continuing salience of captivity imagery occurred as this book was being completed. On May 1, 2011, the US Navy special operations force (the SEALs) reported to President Barack Obama the successful completion of their action against Osama bin Laden's compound in Pakistan with the code "Geronimo EKIA" (enemy killed in action). Whether "Geronimo" referred to bin Laden himself, as early reports indicated, or the mission to kill or capture him, as the White House insisted, the military was employing a long-standing practice in appropriating an indigenous name from the Indian Wars to refer to a contemporary military action (actually two names, since the Blackhawk helicopter used by the SEAL commandos was named after the nineteenth-century Sauk leader, Black Hawk).

The historical Geronimo, a famous Apache warrior, eluded US and Mexican forces for years, surrendering in 1886. He was still a prisoner of the United States—a captive—when he died thirteen years later (Sayre 2000). Paratroopers in the Second World War used his name as a battle cry, a practice that diffused to others taking daring leaps, including workers on oil rigs and children at swimming holes ("Geronimo," *Oxford English Dictionary*). The conflation of Geronimo with the terrorist Osama bin Laden was deeply offensive to many Apaches and other indigenous citizens, who protested in various forums, including Facebook ("Osama is not Geronimo"), YouTube ("Geronimo E-KIA, a poem by the 1491s"), and a congressional hearing on racist stereotypes of indigenous people (US Senate Committee on Indian Affairs 2011). Although this episode involved assassination rather than captivity, it reveals, once again, the continuing significance of the captivity tradition in the American national imaginary.

CHAPTER FIVE
CAPTIVITY IN WHITE AND RED

Books Written in Blood

On a public fast day in 1698 commemorating the close of King William's War, an eight-year struggle against the French and their indigenous allies, the prominent Boston minister Cotton Mather (1978 [1699]) delivered a sermon, "Observable Things," in which he interpreted the grueling events of the war as "a sort of Book put into our Hands; a Book indeed all written in Blood; a Book yet full of Divine Lessons for us" (201–202). Reading that bloody book was properly the work of the clergy, he insisted, for only clergymen could discern the hand of Providence behind the events of the war.

Prominent in Mather's providential interpretation of the war (Bercovitch 1978) was the captivity of English women and children, portrayed in one vivid passage as the defenseless prey of carnivorous beasts. "How many *Women* have been made a *prey* to those *Brutish men,* that are *Skilful* to *Destroy?*" Mather (1978 [1699]) asked.

How many a *Fearful Thing* has been suffered by the *Fearful Sex,* from those *men,* that one would *Fear* as *Devils* rather than men? Let the *Daughters* of our *Zion* think with themselves, what it would be, for fierce *Indians* to break into their Houses, and brain their *Husbands* and their *Children* before their Eyes, and Lead them away a Long Journey into the *Woods*; and if they begin to *fail* and *faint* in the Journey, then for a Tawny Salvage to come with Hell fire in his Eyes, and cut 'em down with his Hatchet; or, if they could miraculously *hold out,* then for some *Filthy* and ugly *Squaws* to become their *insolent Mistresses,* and insolently to abuse 'em at their pleasure a thousand inexpressible ways; and, if they had any of their *Sucking Infants* with them, then to see those Tender Infants handled at such a rate, that they should beg of the *Tygres,* to dispatch 'em out of hand. Such things as these, I tell you, have often happened in this Lamentable *War.* (220–221)

Even more distressing to Mather than the fate of Puritan goodwives was the fate of their children:

Our Little *Boys* and *Girls,* even these Little *Chickens,* have been Seized by the *Indian* Vultures. Our Little *Birds* have been Spirited away by the Indian Devourers, and brought up, in a vile Slavery, till some of them have quite forgot their *English Tongue,* and their *Christian Name,* and their whole *Relation.* (222)

In "Observable Things" this master of Puritan rhetoric developed a compelling and influential representation of English vulnerability in a threatening New World. Declaring a clerical monopoly over interpretation and utilizing systematic oppositions in ethnicity, gender, and Christian civility, Mather portrayed the English colonists as weak and innocent victims of brutish, demonic Indian captors. Today, the representation of brutish enemies destroying domestic tranquility and seizing and abusing the most vulnerable representatives of Christian civilization remains remarkably familiar and powerful. Over the course of three centuries, the capture of a defenseless settler by Indians has been featured in Anglo-American folklore and popular media—expanding from sermons and historical narratives to sculpture, textbooks, fiction, children's games, the cinema—becoming in the twentieth century a conceptual model for representing American relations with currently more threatening Others.

Though Cotton Mather's representation of captivity is complex and requires extensive analysis, we may begin by noting that it relies on three kinds of symbolic oppositions between Indian predators and their English prey. Of the three, it is mainly the opposition between a vulnerable female captive and her brutish male captor that came to dominate subsequent typifications of captivity. Certainly, the other two symbolic oppositions had considerable rhetorical power. The opposition between a fearful female captive and her insolent and abusive "mistress" portrays captivity as a violation (in both gender and ethnicity) of colonial patterns of domination. And the opposition between "little chickens" and the "Indian vultures" who consume them encapsulates the colonial fear of Christian civility being consumed by the dark and demonic forces of the Wild. Nevertheless, as a dominant representation of Anglo-American captivity developed, it was the opposition between a vulnerable White female and her Red male captor that came to the fore. Again and again in representations of captivity—and visual iconography makes this particularly clear—the relationship between captive and captor maintains (and symbolically employs) male dominance over women while reversing the ethnic power relations that were established through conquest (see Figure 8). Red males threaten and prevail over their vulnerable White female victims. This is not to say that Red ultimately prevails over White, for the captive is generally rescued by Providence or His representative, a White male redeemer. The redeemer, through a violence that is both heroic and redemptive, reestablishes the dominance of White over Red (Slotkin 1973).

So familiar and so removed from historical context is the dominant representation of captivity that even contemporary scholarship often fails to acknowledge the extent to which it is a highly selective rendering of a long and complex course of intercultural encounters. As we will see, the consistency in the representations of Red male captor and White female captive, together with the frequent appearance of a White male redeemer, has considerably less to do with captivity as a historical practice than with the ideological potency of parallel and simultaneous oppositions in ethnicity, gender, Christian civility, and power—the very oppositions used so successfully by Mather.

The use of three analytical concepts thus far—*dominant representation, typification,* and *opposition*—reveals several somewhat disparate sources of theoretical inspiration for this chapter. Perhaps most significantly, my approach to the representation of captivity is influenced by the Gramscian concept of cultural hegemony (Gramsci 1972). Control over the production of meaning is a significant part of a ruling class's hegemony, as Cotton Mather and his fellow clergymen understood so well (hence Mather's insistence that only the clergy

Figure 8. John Vanderlyn, *The Murder of Jane McCrea*, 1804. This representation of a Revolutionary War event is typical of captivity imagery in contrasting a vulnerable female victim to powerful male captors. Wadsworth Atheneum Museum of Art, Hartford, CT. Purchased by subscription.

could properly read the divine lessons contained in the bloody text of warfare). The dominant representation of captivity may be considered an "element of a hegemony" (R. Williams 1977) insofar as it is part of the process through which a dominant social group legitimates its power through grounding it in a set of authoritative understandings that are taken for granted and, thus, permeate and structure lived experience. More specifically, the hegemonic representation is a *selective tradition* in Williams's sense.

The phenomenologist Alfred Schutz (1964–1973) called such taken-for-granted understandings *typifications.* The usefulness of Schutz's concept for ana-lyzing typifications of "Others" is indicated by Basso's (1979) study of Western Apache typifications of "the Whiteman," which analyzes how Western Apache jokes typify or "epitomize" the Whiteman through highlighting the structural oppositions between Anglo-American and Apache behavior. In embedding the concepts of structural opposition and typification within an analysis of cultural hegemony, I aim to reveal the social process and cultural forms through which the typifications of White female captive, Red male captor, and White male redeemer achieved and maintained ideological dominance; the relationships among these typifications; the relationship between the captivity tradition and captivity as an intercultural practice; and, finally, the relationship between the hegemonic representation of captivity and alternative or oppositional representations, such as that featuring Pocahontas, the redeemer who is neither White nor male and a captive (John Smith) who is male and only temporarily vulnerable.

As we shall see, the rhetorical power of the hegemonic representation relies in large part upon decontextualizing captivity from European colonial expan-sion and aggression—thus portraying colonial captives as innocent prey of marauding and aggressive beasts. The decontextualization of captivity is found in scholarship as well. Until fairly recently, scholars have neglected the extent to which the warfare, captivity, and diplomatic practices of Native American people were transformed by their engagement with European colonial pow-ers—and specifically the extent to which indigenous captivity practices were affected in significant ways by the European colonial enterprise. We can now see that those captivity practices coded as "Red" in the hegemonic representa-tion are instead a "convergence" (Vaughan and Richter 1980, 77) of multiple Native and European practices. The nature of this convergence is illuminated by considering captivity across the British colonial frontier as a "structure of the conjuncture" in Sahlins's (1981, 1985) sense of the term. Like the Ha-waiian capture and sacrificial incorporation of Captain Cook that to some ex-tent they resemble, Native American captivity practices involved a conjuncture of distinct cultural categories deployed by socially situated (thus differentially interested and empowered) actors. Whereas Sahlins is particularly concerned with the transformative effect of the conjuncture upon relations among native

Hawaiians—nobles and commoners, men and women—I will outline how the conjuncture of captivity practices in eastern North America entailed transformations in both settler and indigenous societies, at the same time that it structured relations among them.

This chapter, then, views captivity as both a *structure of the conjuncture* and as a *hegemonic representation*. Combining a structural approach to history with a cultural approach to hegemony provides a way to conceptualize the dialectical relationship between captivity as historical practice and captivity as symbolic representation, and, further, the way in which both practice and representation are embedded in structures of domination. This approach allows me to bring together the strengths of two largely separate traditions in the study of captivity among Native Americans: cultural or literary history, which focuses on relationships among texts, and ethnohistory or social history, which offers detailed historical and sociocultural contextualization. Like several other scholars (including Vaughan and Clark 1981; Salisbury 1997), I try to attend both to textual analysis and to social and cultural context. In addition, like Colley (2002) and Voigt (2008), among others, I am concerned with bringing the subject of captivity and its representation into the comparative framework offered by contemporary analyses of colonial discourse, colonial structures of domination, and the construction of national imaginaries.

This chapter proceeds from the general and speculative to the more determinate. Dominant representations to the contrary, by far the largest number of captives on the British colonial frontier were Native Americans, an important point to emphasize if we are to understand what the representation of captivity suppresses. To this end we begin with a consideration of the earliest Native captives of the British, exemplified by Squanto. This is followed by a general review of indigenous captivity practices and a brief discussion of their transformation in the colonial situation. Given this historical and cultural context, we turn to the earliest accounts of English captives among Native peoples, concentrating (after a glance at Jamestown) on the New England colonies because it was there that captivity first took on ideological significance. The major texts we consider include the four earliest and most influential narratives of captivity published in the English colonies—those of Mary Rowlandson (1682), John Williams (1707), Hannah Swarton (1697), and Hannah Dustan (1697), the latter two narratives as interpreted and published by Cotton Mather. All four narratives derive from the period of heightened warfare in New England that extended intermittently from 1675 through 1713. My conclusions regarding the development of a captivity tradition also take into account the remainder of the dozen narratives of captivity published in the English colonies during the half century between 1682 and 1736, the publication date of the last account by a captive taken during the first two intercolonial wars.

European Devourers and Their Prey

In an intriguing legend of the Wampanoags, the Algonquian-speaking inhabitants of southeastern Massachusetts, Europeans were first encountered riding a gigantic bird up the Taunton River. The newcomers seized several Wampanoags, holding them captive on the giant bird. The Wampanoags attacked the bird when it stopped at a spring for water, managing to rescue its human prey despite the barrage of thunder and lightning with which the bird defended itself (W. Simmons 1986, 70).

Our only source for this revealing Native construction of a first encounter with Europeans is a skeletal fragment of local history collected in the early nineteenth century. Without the reference to captivity, this legend would resemble a number of other northeastern woodland legends that assimilate European ships to the powerful Thunderbird of indigenous cosmologies (Hammell 1987). However, considering this legend in the context of other northeastern Algonquian folklore reveals that it assimilates early encounters with Europeans to the most fearsome cultural model available of a kidnapper and human devourer. A huge cannibal bird, called *gulluoa* by the Abenakis of Maine, figures prominently in Algonquian mythology across the Northeast (Gyles 1977 [1736], 115–116; K. Morrison 1979). The monster is described by a nineteenth-century folklorist who grew up among Wampanoags, James Athearn Jones, as "a great bird whose wings were the flight of an arrow wide, whose body was the length of ten Indian strides, and whose head when he stretched up his neck peered over the tall oak-woods" (W. Simmons 1986, 189). In Wampanoag lore, the cannibal bird would carry away children in its talons to its nest on Nantucket or Martha's Vineyard, where it feasted upon them, dropping their bones in heaps on the ground below.

That Wampanoags would represent the earliest European invaders as kidnappers and potential devourers of their people is striking as a reciprocal construction to Cotton Mather's representation of Indians as vultures who preyed upon European children. It is also consistent with the accounts we have by English explorers, traders, and fishermen of their earliest forays along the eastern coast of North America. Following European precedents reaching as far back as Columbus's kidnapping of ten Arawaks on his first voyage, English expeditions habitually abducted a few, and occasionally scores, of the Native people they encountered, often luring them aboard ship with trade goods. Unlike the Wampanoags rescued from the giant cannibal bird, most Native captives were forever lost to view (Strong 1999, 19–42).

Judging from accounts concerning those few captives who survived the journey to England, the abductions had various motivations. Captives taken in large groups—such as about two dozen Wampanoags, including Squanto, who were kidnapped in 1614—were generally destined for slavery. Individual captives, in contrast, were often displayed as exotic curiosities and captured in drawings in order to substantiate their captors' claims of discovery and to arouse interest in further expeditions. Among the earliest were several Baffinland Inuits kidnapped by explorer Martin Frobisher in 1576 and 1577, whom the expedition's chronicler, George Best, described as "new prey" and "tokens from thence" (Sturtevant and Quinn 1999 [1987], 69–70). In more contemporary parlance, these captives might be considered "tokens of Otherness" (Mullaney 1983), but they were seldom, if ever, treated as irreconcilably "Other." Rather, captives from the New World were pressured for information regarding their homeland; exposed to English life and power in an effort to win their allegiance; and groomed to serve as guides, interpreters, and emissaries. There was little interest in converting the captives to Christianity, a further indication of the instrumental nature of the abductions.

A rare exception to the anonymity of most indigenous captives and one of the few whose allegiance was won through the dubious strategy of abduction is Squanto, whose Algonquian name, Tisquantum, likely refers to the spiritual power he gained in a vision quest (W. Simmons 1986, 39–43). Despite his widespread fame, it is not generally known that Tisquantum's ability to communicate with the Pilgrims derived not only from his unusual resourcefulness but from five years of involuntary exile in Spain, England, and Newfoundland. Tisquantum was among twenty-seven natives of the Wampanoag towns of Patuxet and Nauset who were kidnapped in 1614 by John Hunt in the absence of his commander, Captain John Smith. These captives were taken to Malaga, Spain, where some were sold into slavery and others were claimed by the Church.

After a period of slavery or apprenticeship in the Church, Tisquantum made his way to London by 1617, where he lodged with the treasurer of the Newfoundland Company. In Newfoundland, he encountered Thomas Dermer, who had served John Smith on the expedition that kidnapped him. Dermer, now working for the commander of Plymouth Harbor, Ferdinando Gorges, introduced Tisquantum to his employer. Gorges had attempted to use indigenous captives to promote various colonization schemes since 1605, when explorer George Waymouth turned over to him five Abenaki captives.

The abductions that Gorges encouraged created lasting enmity against the English among coastal Algonquians. Most disastrous was Edward Harlow's kidnapping in 1611 of six natives, including Epenow, a sachem (headman) on Martha's Vineyard. Gorges pinned his colonial ambitions on Epenow, who learned English well, impressed would-be financiers with his noble bearing, and told intriguing tales of gold in New England. However, Epenow proved disappointing upon his return to Martha's Vineyard in 1614, when he escaped from the gold-seeking expedition he was expected to guide. Henceforth Epenow was the foremost leader of Wampanoag opposition to the English.

Tisquantum proved to be more enduringly useful to the English than Epenow, probably because by the time he managed to return to Patuxet with Dermer in 1619, his village had been completely deserted. During Tisquantum's absence, the people of Patuxet had almost all died from a European disease to which the Algonquians had no immunity. The epidemic—which claimed 75 to 90 percent of the coastal Algonquians living from southern Maine to Cape Cod—opened prime agricultural land to European settlement. Characteristically, the Pilgrims attributed the devastation of Tisquantum's people to Providence, seeing the hand of a God who "would destroy them, and give their country to another people" (Crosby 1978).

Tisquantum facilitated contacts between Dermer's party and the leadership of several Wampanoag towns, an ability that has suggested to historian Neal Salisbury (1981) that he had been trained as a *pniese* or shaman, an office with political and military as well as religious significance among the Wampanoags. But Tisquantum's efforts to forge an alliance between the English and the semi-autonomous Wampanoag settlements were not able to prevail over the hostility created by earlier English visitors. Tisquantum was captured once again, this time by Gorges's former protégé, Epenow.

Tisquantum soon found himself in the hands of Massasoit, the paramount sachem of Pokanoket. Once the most powerful Wampanoag village, Pokanoket had been weakened by the epidemic and Massasoit forced into a tributary relationship to his inland enemies, the Narragansetts. When the Pilgrims arrived in 1620, establishing Plymouth on the abandoned site of Patuxet, Massasoit decided that an alliance with the English would be superior to his present subordination to the Narragansett. As emissaries to Plymouth he sent an Abenaki sachem named Samoset (himself perhaps a former captive of the English) and his captive, Tisquantum. The latter won his freedom from the Pokanoket through successfully negotiating a treaty with the Pilgrims. Living on the site of his ancestral home as an interpreter and intermediary for Massasoit, Tisquantum helped Plymouth extend its influence over several Wampanoag towns, ensuring a reliable supply of corn and pelts. He also taught the English how to gather native foods and cultivate corn, planting it in hills fertilized with whole fish. Ironically (but consistent with the complexity of colonial-indigenous cultural exchanges), the use of fish as fertilizer may not have been an indigenous Algonquian practice but, instead, a product of Tisquantum's exile in Newfoundland (Ceci 1975, 1990).

Then, as now, a prominent symbol of alliance between natives and colonists, Tisquantum suffered one more period of captivity among Wampanoag opponents of an alliance. This time his captor was Corbitant, the leading sachem of the Pocassets. Tisquantum was rescued by Plymouth's Captain Miles Standish from this, his third captivity, and spent the next year of his life, the last, attempting to establish himself as an independent political leader. Thus arousing the enmity of Massasoit, Tisquantum was forced to live under the protection of the English, who continued to consider him a special instrument of God (Sanders 1978; Humins 1987). Soon after Massasoit called for his execution, Tisquantum died. Bereft of kin and branded a traitor by Massasoit, Tisquantum requested conversion to Christianity upon his deathbed.

Few cases of captivity among the English are as well documented as Tisquantum's, so the extent and outcome of English abductions of Native Americans is difficult to assess, especially prior to colonization. To generalize, the English abducted the indigenous inhabitants of North America more often than the French, though probably less frequently than the Spanish and Portuguese, who preceded the English in slave raids as well as in kidnappings along the North American coastline. English enslavement of Native Americans became especially significant during the colonial period, particularly in two regions: Carolina, Georgia, and northern Florida, where a flourishing trade supplied thousands of slaves for the West Indies; and New England, where indigenous slaves or indentured servants were imported from the West Indies and, in greater numbers, captured from local tribes during periods of hostility.

In contrast to both the English and the Iberians, the French more often obtained consent before transporting Native Americans across the ocean, hoping to win over persons of influence to the cause of the Crown and the Church. The most notorious exception is revealing in its conspicuous breach of indigenous expectations regarding hostages. Upon meeting a party of fishermen from the Iroquoian village of Stadacona (at the site of Quebec) in 1534, Jacques Cartier abducted two teenage sons or nephews of Donnacona, the headman. Cartier returned to Stadacona two years later with the boys, Domagaya and Taignoagny, both now highly suspicious of the French.

Iroquoians would have understood Cartier's motivations for training interpreters, but would have expected him to leave French boys in their place, following a traditional pattern of creating kinship ties between trading partners through temporary child-exchange. Indeed, Donnacona entrusted Cartier with several Iroquoian children as a token of alliance on his second visit. Although Europeans of the sixteenth century had their own conventions of hostage exchange, Cartier did not reciprocate; rather, wishing to impress his king with the Stadaconans' knowledge of precious metals (probably native copper), Cartier abducted Donnacona, two additional headmen, and (once again) the two interpreters. Neither these captives nor the children were seen again in Stadacona. By 1541, when Cartier established a short-lived settlement west of Stadacona, only one of the captives remained alive. She was not allowed to return to her people, lest she reveal the sad fate of her compatriots.

Indigenous Captives: Hostages, Kin, Sacrificial Victims

As the tales of Tisquantum and Donnacona suggest, both the captivity of enemies and hostage-exchange among allies were practiced among the Algonquian and Iroquoian peoples of the eastern woodlands. Indeed, at least among Iroquoians, the taking of captives was a primary goal of indigenous warfare. In what have been aptly characterized as "mourning wars" (M. Smith 1951; Richter 1983), an Iroquois woman whose grief remained unassuaged after a series of condolence rituals (involving, most centrally, gifts of wampum) might influence the sons of her matrilineally related male kindred to "set up the war kettle," that is, send out a war party. The warriors would attempt to obtain a captive from among traditional enemies, who would be treated in a highly ritualized fashion in order to revitalize the lineage and "dry its tears." First, the mourners would generally vent their rage against captives as they "ran the gauntlet," that is, ran into the town through two lines of villagers who administered physical and verbal abuse. At the behest of the bereaved women of the lineage, the gauntlet might be followed by further torture. Then a captive might be incorporated into the lineage through adoption. If a woman or child, the captive would most often be welcomed as a valuable addition to the lineage, her cultural identity transformed through a variety of institutionalized inducements and punishments. A male captive, however, was considered less malleable and compliant, and he would sometimes be further tortured, executed, and ritually ingested.

The adoption of a captive filled the vacant social position left by the deceased and, additionally, was thought to replenish the spiritual power of the lineage. Spiritual power might also be replenished symbolically through ritual cannibalism—perhaps especially when the captive had exhibited particular bravery during torture—or, in the absence of a captive, through performing an adoption ceremony over a dead enemy's scalp lock, considered the seat of the soul. Torture and scalping were also offered as sacrifices to Agreskwe, the spirit responsible for success in war. Alternatively, in eloquent rites of condolence, the bereaved lineage would be presented with gifts of wampum, furs, or other valuables in place of a captive or enemy scalp. These rites came to form the basis of colonial diplomacy (Jennings 1984; Jennings et al. 1995).

Our major source on Iroquoian warfare and treatment of captives, the *Relations* of the French Jesuits, documents events in the mid-seventeenth century when warfare and captivity had reached an unprecedented intensity in response to the European presence. In contrast to seventeenth-century warfare, indigenous warfare had been limited in scale, in large part due to the goal of taking captives without sustaining casualties (because any additional casualties among the raiding party would require the mounting of still another raid). War, therefore, consisted mainly of isolated ambushes, conducted with a restraint and caution that was as ludicrous to Europeans as the European practice of total war was horrifying to Iroquoians. Following sustained contact with Europeans in the 1620s, however, Iroquoian peoples suffered a demographic crisis of unparalleled proportions—a crisis that dramatically intensified their search for captives or scalps to restore the numerical and spiritual power of the population.

The serious decrease in population that Iroquoian villages suffered in the early seventeenth century had a number of related causes: devastating European epidemics, depletion of fur-bearing animals because of the European trade, an intensification of warfare from the 1640s through the 1670s due to the introduction of firearms and the struggle to control the colonial fur trade, and the emigration of large numbers of converted Iroquois to mission villages in Canada. Increasingly, Iroquoians adopted non-Iroquoian captives, formerly spurned because of the difficulty of integrating them into the society. So many war prisoners and refugees were adopted that by the 1660s, according to French missionary estimates, they outnumbered natives in many Iroquois villages. Even so, massive adoptions could not offset Iroquois losses to disease, the missions, and warfare—losses augmented by serious conflicts with the French after 1674. In the early eighteenth century, the Five Nations of Iroquois (including Mohawks, Oneidas, Onondagas, Cayugas, Senecas) turned increasingly to peacefully assimilating entire Native groups, most notably the Tuscarora (after which the confederation became known as the Six Nations).

In the seventeenth century, then, Iroquoian captivity practices were affected in significant ways by the European presence. The taking of captives and scalps increased greatly in scale, and the potential pool of adoptive kin was broadened from Iroquoians to non-Iroquoians. A significant proportion of the adoptees were Algonquians, which led to a commingling of populations that likely contributed to a convergence of Iroquoian and Algonquian captivity practices. Algonquians adopted elements of the Iroquoian condolence complex that were previously foreign to them. In turn, the Iroquoians may have learned a more instrumental approach to captivity from the Algonquians—one that proved to be compatible with the warfare practices Europeans imported to America.

The nature of the convergence between Iroquoian and Algonquian captivity practices remains a matter of conjecture because indigenous Algonquian practices are much more poorly documented than those of their Iroquoian neighbors; additionally, there are significant debates about Iroquoian practices themselves, with some scholars viewing Iroquoian practices more in terms of subordinating outsiders as slaves than incorporating them as kin (Starna and Watkins 1991; Strong 2002). It appears that captivity lacked the central role in Algonquian religious and social life that it had among the Iroquois, with the possible exception of those groups heavily influenced by the latter such as the Montagnais, Mahican, and Lenape. Algonquians apparently lacked a sacrificial motivation for torture, reserving it for revenge against those enemies who practiced it, both Iroquoian and European. Individual captives were not a major objective of Algonquian warfare, which focused instead on the heads or scalps of enemies, which were utilized as sacrificial offerings (at least among the more southerly coastal peoples). Algonquians augmented their populations not through adopting individual captives but through subjugating their enemies by military means and adopting the refugees collectively.

In indigenous Algonquian societies, then, captives were taken less for spiritual reasons than for instrumental ones—for example, to neutralize a political enemy such as Tisquantum, or to extort wampum or other ransom settlements. As Sayre (1997) puts it, they were more a part of an "economy of exchange" than an "economy of vengeance" (277). The Algonquian practice of using wampum to ransom captives was first revealed to Europeans in 1622 when a Dutch trader kidnapped a Pequot sachem for ransom. The Pequots responded with more than 140 fathoms of wampum—a striking revelation to the Dutch of the value of these strings of purple and white shells (Salisbury 1982, 148–149). These instrumental practices were readily incorporated into colonial modes of warfare: seventeenth-century Algonquian and Iroquoian war parties took captives, heads, and scalps in order to fulfill conditions of alliance imposed by colonial officials and to obtain ransom or bounty payments from them. At the same time, the Iroquois allies of the English or the French insisted on using captives, refugees, or scalps in purely indigenous ways, adopting captives or refugees to replenish their numbers and spiritual power, and offering captives and scalps as sacrifices.

What has been called the mourning war or condolence complex in the eastern woodlands was clearly extended and transformed in important ways by the colonial encounter. In their intercultural scope; expanded scale; and responsiveness to demographic, political, and economic changes, the Native American captivity practices of the colonial period were a complex "structure of the conjuncture." However, the European contribution to indigenous captivity practices is denied in the English representations of captivity that developed in the seventeenth and early eighteenth centuries.

Mary Rowlandson and the Representation of Captivity during King Philip's War

For the most part, the captivity of English settlers among Native Americans as well as its representation in colonial accounts dates to the last quarter of the seventeenth century. An exception is John Smith's account of his imprisonment by Powhatan in 1607 and his timely rescue from execution by that chief's daughter, Pocahontas. There is reason to question Smith's veracity, however, partly because he was silent on the matter until after Pocahontas had married John Rolfe, had become famous in England as a convert to Christian civility, and died. A further reason to refrain from taking Smith's account at face value is that rescue from captivity by a native maiden is a conventional motif in travel narratives, a motif utilized previously by Smith himself and featured prominently in one of the two previously published accounts of Europeans taken captive in North America. Juan Ortiz, a sixteenth-century explorer captured and adopted by Timucuans of Florida, reported that he had twice been saved from sacrifice through the intercession of his captor's daughter (Voigt 2008).

Whatever the historical status of Smith's account, Pocahontas came to play a prominent role in Anglo-American captivity imagery by the early nineteenth century (Tilton 1994). By this time, hopes for a peaceful alliance between settlers and indigenous peoples had largely been consigned to the realm of myth, and captivity had been established as a representation not of alliance and acculturation but of the struggle of Christian civility against savagery in the American wilderness. That is, a tradition of captivity had developed in New England in the late seventeenth and eighteenth centuries in which Divine Providence, not Indian mercy, served as the agent of salvation.

The dominant Anglo-American representation of captivity took its form during the extended series of wars beginning in 1675 during which northeastern Algonquians and English colonists—soon joined by Iroquoians and the French— struggled for control over northeastern America. Only one earlier captivity of colonists was recorded in New England, involving three young women who were seized in 1637 when Pequots attacked the new settlement of Wethersfield, Connecticut, to protest English expansion and treaty violations. Two of the three English girls were returned safely after showing themselves unable to make gunpowder. Following this incident, hostilities between the Pequots and Connecticut intensified, culminating in the destruction of the Pequots' major village on the Mystic River. Some three to seven hundred inhabitants of the village were burned alive or shot while attempting to escape. The refugees were hunted down by colonial forces and their Mohegan allies, who were offered a bounty for severed Pequot heads. Over the next several months, most Pequot refugees were captured and either executed or enslaved. Four to fifteen hundred Pequot refugees were assigned to colonists or their Mohegan and Narragansett allies, while a small group, including fifteen boys and two women, were shipped to the West Indies. Those distributed among Algonquian groups were generally adopted and supplied with houses and fields according to indigenous custom. The English, however, counted the refugees as slaves, and required the Mohegans and Narragansetts to pay an annual tribute payment for each Pequot.

Not until the next major Puritan-Algonquian conflict over land and political sovereignty, some four decades later, were other colonists taken captive. "King

Philip's War" of 1675–1676 pitted the United Colonies (Massachusetts Bay, Connecticut, Plymouth, and New Haven) and their Christian Indian allies against Wampanoag and (later) Narragansett forces led by Metacomet (or Philip) of Pokanoket, the son of Plymouth's ally Massasoit (Lepore 1999). In this war, unprecedented in scale in the English colonies, the English put an end to Algonquian resistance to colonial expansion in southern New England. The cost of victory, however, was high: some twenty frontier towns were destroyed, the colonial male population was literally decimated, and at least forty-two colonists were abducted from frontier settlements. Like the girls from Wethersfield, these colonists seem to have been captured primarily for utilitarian reasons, namely, the ransom payments and political concessions they might bring. The captives shared the hardships of their captors, who were short of food and in constant movement to escape colonial forces. Slightly more than half of the captives were eventually ransomed; most of the remainder were killed in captivity or died from wounds or illness. One case of torture was reported, involving an uncooperative pregnant woman and her child.

The English, for their part, captured, enslaved, scalped, and tortured their indigenous enemies during King Philip's War and its aftermath—all practices that would come to be coded as typically Indian in the representations of captivity developed subsequently by the clerical elite. Much as Connecticut had done during the war against the Pequots in 1637, that colony and Massachusetts Bay offered a bounty for enemy heads or scalps to their Narragansett allies. Despite the bounty, most Narragansetts attempted to maintain neutrality in the conflict, and soon the two colonies extended the bounty payments to colonial soldiers, who received thirty shillings for every enemy head. Narragansett neutrality soon foundered on the issue of Wampanoag refugees: the Narragansetts refused to turn them over to the English, instead preferring to assimilate the Wampanoags as they had the Pequots. The English response was a massive attack on the major Narragansett village, during which some three to six hundred Narragansetts and Wampanoags were killed. Massachusetts alienated other Native allies—the Christian inhabitants of missionary "praying towns"—by incarcerating some five hundred of their number on Deer Island in Boston Harbor, where they suffered from starvation, disease, and exposure.

After achieving victory, the colonists quickly consolidated their gains, appropriating Wampanoag and Narragansett lands and dispersing or destroying the former inhabitants. Philip and other Algonquian leaders were executed for treason, Philip being tortured as well: drawn, quartered, and decapitated as were domestic traitors. Cotton Mather, a youth at the time, personally disengaged Philip's jaw from the rest of his skull (Silverman 1984, 20). Philip's head was displayed on a pole in Plymouth for twenty years thereafter, while the head of his sister-in-law and ally, the "squaw sachem" Wetamo, was likewise displayed at

Taunton, Rhode Island. At least one additional Algonquian captive was tortured by the English during the war, a woman whom the Hatfield court ordered to be torn to pieces by dogs. Philip's wife and nine-year-old son, together with at least one thousand captives or refugees, were sold into foreign slavery, while hundreds of others were sold to colonists as slaves or indentured servants. The remainder were forced to live on small reservations for "praying Indians" (Axtell 1985; J. O'Brien 2003) or to take refuge in New York or Canada.

The English, true to their providential hermeneutics, discerned God's hand in both the indigenous challenge to New England's expansion and in their antagonists' defeat. Providential interpretations of the war were developed in fast-day sermons; histories; and, most compellingly, in a personal narrative published six years after the war titled *The Sovereignty and Goodness of God, Together, with the Faithfulness of His Promises Displayed: Being a Narrative of the Captivity and Restoration of Mrs. Mary Rowlandson* (1682). One of only four works by women published in seventeenth-century New England, Rowlandson's narrative was among the most widely read colonial works of her century and the next. A clergyman's wife, Mrs. Rowlandson adapted the Puritan genre of spiritual autobiography to the New World experience of captivity, interpreting as a personal spiritual trial and opportunity for redemption her hardships during three months as a captive of the female sachem Wetamo of Pocasset and her Narragansett husband.

Beginning with a vivid description of a seemingly unprovoked attack upon the frontier settlement of Lancaster, Massachusetts, Rowlandson's narrative continually situates her captivity in the context of spiritual, not political, conflict. Structurally the narrative consists of twenty "Removes ... up and down the Wilderness" (Salisbury 1997 [1682], 70), a formulation that, as Hambrick-Stowe (1982) has pointed out, is reminiscent of the stages of Christian's pilgrimage "through the wilderness of this world" in the contemporary *Pilgrim's Progress* (1678). Rowlandson's description of these removes farther and farther from home—these separations from previous experience—is coupled throughout with observations on her parallel spiritual journey. The Indian attack came at a time of personal prosperity, complacency, carelessness, and vanity, Rowlandson declared, when she was almost wishing for God to submit her to trial in order to test and strengthen her faith. "Affliction I wanted and affliction I had, full measure" (Salisbury 1997 [1682], 112), she reflected, seeing her captivity as a trial analogous to the captivities of God's chosen in the Old Testament. In captivity, Rowlandson finds herself stripped of the comforts of domestic life; isolated from her family and the supports of Christian existence; reduced to a near-bestial state exemplified by her "wolfish" appetite; and forced to abandon herself and her children into the custody of masters and, worse, a mistress who themselves served the Devil. Returned to her essential human condition of isolation and vulnerability—figured as nakedness—Rowlandson at last abandons all vanity and complacency, acknowledging her utter dependence upon God's power. When she is returned to her husband through a ransom agreement facilitated by "praying Indians," she feels herself to be spiritually as well as physically redeemed.

Reading her experiences as evidence of the workings of Providence, Rowlandson portrays her captors as instruments of God whose actions, whether abusive or merciful, were ultimately oriented to her own spiritual condition rather than to any indigenous values, grievances, or interests. When "wild, ravenous beasts," the Indians were serving as scourges of God; when kind, they were restrained in their furious lust and rage by the hand of God. The narrative abounds in vituperative epithets characterizing her captors as bestial and diabolical: they are "bloody" and "merciless heathen," "barbarous creatures," "hell hounds," "black creatures in the night." However, Rowlandson's descriptions of individuals are considerably more varied. She knows the names of many of her captors; indeed, among those most despised by Rowlandson are former inhabitants of the nearby praying town of Marlboro. Rowlandson describes as her primary antagonist the female sachem Wetamo, who apparently took delight in taunting her captive and depriving her of food, fire, and shelter.

The "squaw sachem" Wetamo, indeed, appears to be a model for Cotton Mather's "filthy and ugly squaws," the "insolent mistresses" who abuse captives "at their pleasure a thousand inexpressible ways." Yet Rowlandson's portrait of Wetamo is more complex than this, for foremost among the traits in Wetamo that she criticizes are her pride and vanity—two of the very same traits Rowlandson criticizes in herself. Wetamo, it seems, served her captive not only as a scourge but as a spiritual object lesson—possible only because of the qualities she *shares* with her captive.

In contrast to her antipathy toward Wetamo, Rowlandson thanks God for the kindness of Wetamo's husband, Quanopin, who "seemed to me the best friend that I had of an Indian both in cold and hunger" (51). Quanopin often protected Rowlandson from the abuses of his wife and reassured her that he would return her to her husband for a ransom payment. Rowlandson also remarked upon the kindness of Philip himself and marveled at the numerous "common mercies" shown to her by Indians who were total strangers.

Rowlandson's well-nuanced descriptions of her captors is one aspect of her general attentiveness to the details of her experience, all of which were significant in the context of a spiritual autobiography. Also characteristic of the genre of spiritual autobiography is Mary Rowlandson's prose—simple, direct, vivid—and her highly personal viewpoint. Apart from certain passages near the close of the narrative that, like a jeremiad, censure her society's shortcomings, Rowlandson's descriptions of her experiences are mainly concerned with the condition of her own soul under adversity. Her interpretations are closely intertwined with the course of events she relates, and her references to Scripture are in the context of her need for comfort or instruction at particular times. In sum, although Scripture was essential in sustaining her, in true nonconformist fashion the narrative presents experience as the sine qua non of knowledge.

The creative blend of experience and interpretation found in Mary Rowlandson's narrative makes it an exceptional captivity narrative, just as Mary Rowlandson, a minister's wife, was an exceptional captive. The other captivity narratives published in New England for half a century after Rowlandson's were written or edited by clergymen, including Cotton Mather, his father Increase Mather, and John Williams, a minister related by marriage to the Mathers who was himself taken captive in 1704. These narratives by the Puritan clergy tend to subordinate immediate experience to dogmatic interpretation, presenting captivity less as a personal spiritual trial than as a divine lesson to an unregenerate society. In clerical hands, captivity narratives depart from the form of spiritual autobiography and become jeremiads, taking a hegemonic form that explicitly reinforced clerical authority.

Even Rowlandson's narrative—internally free of overt clerical "improvements"—is framed by clerical interpretations. Preceded by an anonymous preface, the narrative is followed in early editions by an outline of the last sermon Mary Rowlandson's husband preached before his death. The preface, written in the literary style of the clergy and contrasting strongly with Rowlandson's truly "plain style," was probably written by the foremost minister of the time, Increase Mather, whose church provided a house for the Rowlandson family after Mary's return from captivity.

The preface, even while establishing Mary Rowlandson's authority as a writer, undermines that authority in two ways. First, the narrative is commended less as a record of inner spiritual trial and redemption than for "particularizing" instances of Divine Providence in outward events. The preface summarizes the particular knowledge Rowlandson's narrative imparts:

> as none knows what it is to fight and pursue such an enemy as this, but they that have fought and pursued them: so none can imagine, what it is to be captivated, and enslaved to such atheistical, proud, wild, cruel, barbarous, brutish, (in one word) diabolicall creatures as these, the worst of the heathen; nor what difficulties, hardships, hazards, sorrows, anxieties, and perplexities do unavoidably wait upon such a condition, but those that have tryed it. (Salisbury 1997 [1682], 67)

Ironically, Rowlandson's narrative becomes reduced here to a general account of sufferings amid a diabolical enemy. The "particular" nature of Rowlandson's portrayal of her sufferings—the imaginative correlation of inner and her outward "removes"—as well as Rowlandson's "particular knowledge" of her various captors are elided.

A second manner in which Mary Rowlandson's authority is undermined is that the narrative is introduced and its publication justified by reference to "that Reverend servant of God, Mr. Joseph Rowlandson." In contrast to the narrative, the attack appears in the preface through the eyes of Joseph Rowlandson, who returned home after seeking aid for the defense of Lancaster only to find his own house in flames and "his precious yokefellow, and dear Children, wounded and captivated ... by these cruel and barbarous Salvages." Other inhabitants of Lancaster were captured or killed, but the preface presents the catastrophe that befell the Rowlandson family as "the most solemn and remarkable part of this Trajedy" because it occurred to "Gods precious ones" (64). Mary Rowlandson was herself a "saint," but her afflictions and deliverance were all the more of public concern "by how much nearer this Gentlewoman stood related to that faithfull Servant of God," her husband (66).

The preface, in sum, defines Mary Rowlandson primarily by her relationship to her husband and justifies the publication of her narrative by virtue of her marriage to a legitimate spokesman of Puritan society. *The Sovereignty and Goodness of God* was only the second work by a woman to be published in seventeenth-century New England (following Anne Bradstreet's poetry), and Mrs. Rowlandson's affinity to the clergy provided the requisite justification for allowing her words to enter the public realm of elite males. Still, her character needed protection, and the preface dwells on her modesty and her status as a saint, assuring the reader, as does the title page, that the narrative was written for the author's "private Use," and was only "made public at the earnest Desire of some Friends" (62).

Given the emphasis on Joseph Rowlandson's perspective in the preface, it is unfortunate that no reference to his wife's captivity or to any captivity appears in the outline of the appended sermon (for a fast day in 1678). Still, the sermon, entitled "The Possibility of God's Forsaking a People that have been near and dear to him" (149–164), is congruent with the captivity narrative in an intriguing way. Warning God's chosen people that they must stop forsaking God lest they be forsaken, Joseph Rowlandson made use of a common Puritan trope: the proper relationship of a wife to her husband exemplifies the Saint's relationship to God (Ulrich 1982). Like the faithful wife, who retains good and respectful thoughts toward her husband, even in his absence, the Saint remains faithful to God even when seemingly being forsaken. The sinner who forsakes God in this situation is like an adulteress; the sinner who, in response, is utterly forsaken by God is like a widow. Although we cannot know how Joseph Rowlandson developed his sermon, when it is juxtaposed with the captivity narrative, Mary

Rowlandson emerges as doubly faithful in her captivity: to her husband in his absence, and to God, who seemingly had forsaken her.

These correspondences between the faithful wife, the faithful saint, and the faithful captive are what Cotton Mather would play upon more explicitly in developing the female captive as the typification of colonial vulnerability. Unlike Mary Rowlandson, who was able to maintain her faith, although with difficulty, when removed from the influence of her husband and the clergy, weaker captives were liable to forsake family, community, and God. Like the adulteress, they would fall prey to the seduction of Satan and his worldly servants; like the widow, they risked being utterly forsaken.

Indeed, when Rowlandson's narrative was published in 1682, the clergy were particularly concerned over what they perceived as faithlessness, spiritual vulnerability, and foundering identity. The death of the first generation of Puritan emigrants had left their descendants without the direct connection to England they had embodied. Millennial expectations had been dashed with the restoration of the monarchy in England, church membership in New England was declining, and the vacated lands won in King Philip's War were enticing settlers away from the authoritarian confines of the older towns. Meeting in 1679 under the leadership of Increase Mather to consider spiritual degeneracy, a clerical synod deplored the colonists' "insatiable desire after Land, and worldly Accomodations, yea as to forsake Churches and Ordinances, and to live like Heathen, only so that they might have Elbow-room enough in the world" (Hambrick-Stowe 1982, 256–265).

The clergy feared that frontier settlers were succumbing to what missionary John Eliot called "wilderness temptations" (Nash 1982, 102), willingly abandoning the lawful and godly order of Puritan settlements and embracing the individualistic anarchy presumably characteristic of Indian life. One significant manifestation of this anarchy was the lack of hierarchical relations taken to be natural and ordained by God: the subordination of women to their husbands, children to their parents, servants to their masters, and laity to the clergy. Such a subordination of the weak, wild, and spiritually vulnerable to their natural masters, who were stronger, more reasonable, and more godly, was central to Puritan notions of domestic and civic order (Morgan 1980; Koehler 1980). Just such notions of the natural subordination of wife to husband were at the base of Joseph Rowlandson's sermon when he used the proper husband-wife relationship as a model for that between God and the Saint. And just such notions of the natural vulnerability of women and children were called into play in the representation of captivity developed by Cotton Mather. In either case, a woman and her children were easy prey to physical assaults and spiritual seduction in the absence of the master of the house.

Cotton Mather, John Williams, and the Representation of Captivity during the Intercolonial Wars

The synod's fears of the disastrous consequences of the search for "elbow room" seemed to materialize around the turn of the century. The new English settlements on the northern and western frontiers were vulnerable to intermittent attacks by Algonquians and Iroquoians from across the Canadian border, many of whom French Jesuits had converted to Catholicism. Hostilities intensified from 1689 through 1697 (King William's War) and again from 1702 through 1713 (Queen Anne's War), when England and France were engaged in European power struggles that in the colonies took the form of contests for control over northeastern North America. During these two early intercolonial (or "French and Indian") wars, parties of Native warriors from Canada commanded by French officers attacked frontier settlements, taking some six hundred captives for adoption, occasional use as victims in torture rituals, and for sale to the French for bounty payments. The French, like the English, also offered a bounty for enemy scalps, European as well as indigenous, but they paid more for captives, owing to their desire for an increased population. A large number of ransomed captives remained in Canada, converting to Catholicism, although many others were eventually returned to English officials for ransom or exchange.

In the context of its concerns over the colonies' spiritual vulnerability, the clergy interpreted the intercolonial wars primarily as spiritual battles against the heathenism of Rome and America alike, expanding the captivity metaphor to encompass a redemptive experience not only for captives but for the community as a whole. Captivities—taken as signs of God's displeasure with the Puritans for their collective unfaithfulness—were seen as God's way of evoking a renewed acknowledgment of His power while confirming the Puritans' identity as His chosen people. Three prominent clergymen—Increase Mather, his son Cotton Mather, and his niece's husband John Williams, himself a captive in the second intercolonial war—developed this interpretation between 1684 and 1707, presenting captivity as a divine punishment for internal degeneration.

Such an interpretation of captivity largely excluded a reexamination of colonial relations with Native peoples or the French because captivity was seen as a punishment for internal degeneration rather than a consequence of political relations. Puritan identity had become so dissipated on the frontier, went the logic, that Puritans were doubly vulnerable: to physical attack and to the spiritual onslaughts of Catholic Indians and Jesuits. As we have seen, Cotton Mather's jeremiad of 1698, at the close of King William's War, underscored the vulnerability of New England through his typification of young and female captives. These captives, although a minority of those taken during the intercolonial wars, were the most likely to be assimilated into indigenous or French society. Mather's concern with assimilation is perhaps most forcefully expressed in the image of Indian vultures devouring Puritan chicks, but it was more fully developed in the most extensive captivity narrative he published, that of Hannah Swarton, which appeared first as an appendix to a sermon, "Humiliations Follow'd with Deliverances" (Mather 1977 [1697]) and again in his major work of providential history, *Magnalia Christi Americana* (Mather 1702).

Swarton's narrative, written in the first person although undoubtedly heavily edited by Mather, presents her five-and-a-half years of captivity among Catholic Abenakis and then the French as a personal trial and opportunity for spiritual rebirth. Her perceived failings, however, differ greatly from the vanity and complacency of Rowlandson, the pastor's wife: Swarton's involved abandoning an established Puritan settlement in pursuit of worldly goods in the frontier community of Falmouth, Maine. Swarton, then, is the personification of those Puritans so deplored by the synod of 1679 who "lived like heathen" on the frontier. In this context, her captivity in 1690 and the loss of several family members become exaggerated versions of the independence that she herself had sought on the frontier; the spiritual temptations of French Canada, likewise, exaggerations of the temptations she had courted at home. Like Rowlandson, Swarton presented captivity as a profound isolation from all that had sustained her, here figured not as nakedness but as bereavement. She emerged from captivity with a renewed appreciation for God's power and with a revelation concerning her identity. Indeed, her repentance over her past inattention to her spiritual needs and those of her children assume the quality of a conversion experience.

Despite its message of spiritual redemption, Swarton's narrative lacks some of the experiential immediacy that makes Rowlandson's so effective. Passages from Scripture are less well integrated with experience, and Indians are portrayed as generically satanic, notable mainly for the conjunction of brutality and Catholic piety. This characterization serves Mather well in both his denigration of Catholicism and in his censure of growing Puritan worldliness. Ironically, the Abenakis, though "idolaters," are more faithful than Swarton; it is they who first offer a providential interpretation of the captivity, reminding the despairing captive that her fate is in the hands of God. As in the case of Wetamo, Mary Rowlandson's Algonquian mistress, who shares the vanity Rowlandson comes to repudiate, Swarton's captors serve as object lessons, exemplifying the piety Swarton has lacked—albeit Catholic piety.

Mather's version of Swarton's narrative, in sum, moves toward a more abstract presentation of captivity, one that emphasizes the Catholic assault upon what Swarton calls her "inward man" over the sufferings of her "outward man" among the Abenakis—themselves characterized abstractly. The narrative of another

Hannah, the most famous of Mather's exemplary captives, moves toward abstraction from experience and typification of Indians in a different way, through telling the story in the third person. Hardly an example of feminine vulnerability, Hannah Dustan, of Haverhill, New Hampshire, murdered and scalped her captors in their sleep, turning in the scalps of two men, two women, and six children to the colonial government for a ransom payment. Hannah Dustan would thus seem to lie completely outside the representation of captivity that Mather developed elsewhere but, as we shall see, Mather managed to contain her within that representation, for his own generation at least.

Mather first told Dustan's story in his jeremiad, "Humiliations Follow'd with Deliverances," which he preached shortly after she returned from six weeks as a captive of a small Abenaki band. Pointing to Dustan, sitting in the congregation, as a woman who had been humiliated but subsequently delivered through God's providence, Mather told her story in his own metaphorical style. When the Dustan house was attacked, Mr. Dustan escaped with seven of their children, leaving Mrs. Dustan, her week-old infant, and their nurse behind. After seeing "the raging dragons rifle all that they could carry away and set the house on fire," the three captives were led away by the Abenakis, "but ere they had gone many steps they dashed out the brains of the infant against a tree." In vengeance for the infant's death and fearful of being "stripped and scourged" when they arrived at the "rendezvous of savages which they call a town," Hannah Dustan resolved "to imitate the action of Jael upon Sisera." One night, she awakened her nurse and an English youth held captive with them, convincing the latter to help her kill all but two of the twelve members of her captor's family, making use of the Abenakis' own tomahawks. The Abenakis "bowed, they fell, they lay down" in Mather's telling, echoing the Book of Judges (5:27): "at their feet they bowed, they fell where they bowed; there they fell down dead" (Mather 1981 [1697], 162–164).

Mather's account justifies the axings both through biblical references and, implicitly, through formulaic typifications of the Abenakis as "raging dragons," "formidable savages," "furious tawnies," and (evoking Proverbs 12:10) "those whose tender mercies are cruelties." Even so, acknowledged Mather, Dustan's captors, like Swarton's, put many an English family to shame in their regular observance of prayer. Indeed, Dustan's master, like Swarton's, gave his captive a lesson in spiritual resignation, asking "'What need you trouble yourself? If your God will have you delivered, you shall be so.' And," Mather added, "it seems our God would have it so to be." Still, Mather seems to suggest in his "improvement" (interpretation) of the narrative, Hannah Dustan's deliverance may have been too easy. He admonished Dustan and her companions to guard against undue pride, against the temptation of believing that their deliverance was testimony to their righteousness. They must "make a right use of the deliverance," he insisted, repenting and humbling themselves before God. Warned Mather, "You are not now the slaves of Indians, as you were a few Days ago; but if you continue unhumbled, in your sins, you will be the slaves of Devils; and, let me tell you, a slavery to Devils, to be in Their hands, is worse than to be in the hands of Indians!" (Mather 1978 [1699], 47–50). Perhaps it was as an example of the desired humility that Mather appended to the sermon upon its publication the narrative of the more humble and vulnerable Hannah Swarton.

Mather published and interpreted the narratives of a number of other captives in his sermons and histories, all third-person accounts. None of these accounts is as significant or as divergent as those of the two Hannahs, and all of these accounts serve the same interpretive end. Captivity was a work of Divine Providence designed to humiliate and chastise God's people, to call attention to their collective lack of piety and subservience to the clergy. Within this interpretation, Indians were God's instruments, even in their pious "idolatry." The interpretation is supported through an abstraction from individual experience and a typification of Indians, in marked contrast to the sharp and concrete detail of Rowlandson's spiritual autobiography. One might attribute this abstractness to Mather's lack of direct experience as a captive, if it were not for the fact that this quality is also found in the widely read captivity narrative of his relative and colleague, the Rev. John Williams.

The pastor of the frontier town of Deerfield, Massachusetts, Williams was captured in 1704 along with his family and over one hundred members of his congregation. Although he suffered severe personal losses and hardships during his captivity, including the death of his wife, Williams's *Redeemed Captive Returning to Zion* (1976 [1707]) is preoccupied with his efforts to counter the spiritual "seduction" of the French Jesuits, who successfully converted some of his flock, including his own son. Williams eventually convinced his son to return to the fold, but to his dismay completely lost his daughter Eunice, who was seven years old at the time of her capture. Eunice eventually married a Catholic Mohawk and remained in the community of Caughnawaga. She forever refused to return to New England, except for brief visits with her Mohawk husband and children, when she is said to have camped in her brother's apple orchard wearing buckskin and moccasins. For much of the first half of the eighteenth century Eunice Williams symbolized the fragility of English identity in the New World, personifying Mather's "little chickens ... seized by Indian vultures, ... little birds ... spirited away by the Indian devourers."

John Williams was the only Puritan captive to publish a full-length account of captivity between the Rowlandson narrative of 1682 and a narrative by captive John Gyles in 1736. Thus, he might be seen as the male counterpart of Mary Rowlandson. Williams's work, however, is not a spiritual autobiography but, rather, a polemic against the French Jesuits. If Mary Rowlandson appears in her narrative as the isolated individual struggling to maintain her faith in the absence of her husband and community, John Williams appears as God's representative in the fight against indigenous and French idolatry and as the mainstay of his congregation's faith. Indeed, *The Redeemed Captive,* despite its title, presents Williams less as a captive redeemed after undergoing spiritual trial than as himself a spiritual redeemer. That he was unsuccessful in Eunice's case underscored the vulnerability of the English colonists before the joint French and indigenous threat.

To summarize the representational trajectory, four captivity narratives published in the quarter century between 1682 and 1707—Mary Rowlandson's spiritual autobiography of 1682, Hannah Swarton's and Hannah Dustan's accounts as recounted in Cotton Mather's jeremiad of 1697, and John Williams's narrative of 1707—exhibit an increasing abstraction of the captivity experience and increasing typification of the Algonquian captors. Rowlandson's narrative, the first extended interpretation of captivity to appear in the English colonies, is notable for its immediacy, its correlation of spiritual and physical experience, and its somewhat multifaceted portrayal of individual Algonquians. However, despite its attention to concrete experience, Rowlandson's narrative abstracts the captivity experience from its nexus of political conflict and typifies Indians both through dehumanizing epithets and through the use of providential hermeneutics. In other words, the narrative is highly univocal, to use Bakhtin's (1984) phrase: Indians serve as instruments of God to chastise, instruct, and deliver the captive and are denied motivations, a perspective, and a voice of their own.

Although the narrative denies Algonquians a voice, hardly unusual in colonial New England, it is notable for articulating the experience of captivity through the voice of a female captive, with minimal clerical "improvements." This is no doubt due to Rowlandson's status as one of the elect and a clergyman's wife, but may also be because her own voice was extraordinarily effective in describing and interpreting the captivity experience. Still, the narrative is framed by clerical interpretations, and these provide strong indications of the dominant direction that the interpretation of captivity would take once the clergy claimed interpretive hegemony (as Cotton Mather did when claiming in his 1698 fast-day sermon that it was properly the work of the clergy to read these texts "written in blood").

First, the experience as a whole would be read as a deliverance by Divine Providence from slavery to diabolical and idolatrous forces. Neither the concrete details of the captivity (as in Rowlandson's diary of her removes) nor concrete variations among Native individuals (as in her contrasting portraits of Wetamo and her husband) were essential to establishing this interpretation. No such narrative structure as Rowlandson's parallel spiritual and physical "removes" are found in subsequent narratives. As regards the indigenous captors, general typifications substitute for description, and laudable characteristics are reduced to one: their misguided faithfulness in observing an idolatrous religion. In other words, Captors become typified as demonic, pagan Others defined almost completely in opposition to the Puritan Self. While such oppositional typification is not absent in Mary Rowlandson, it is complicated by her observation of differences among her captors and similarities between herself and her captors. The narratives published by Cotton Mather and John Williams contain no such memorable figure as Wetamo, the proud and vain female sachem who seems to serve as Rowlandson's alter ego, to represent her own sins taken to the extreme.

Secondly, as the representation of captivity became more abstract, it was joined more explicitly to orthodox representations of feminine vulnerability and subservience. Whereas Rowlandson's gender added poignancy to her captivity, one can imagine a male captive writing a similar spiritual autobiography, as John Bunyan had in another setting. Not so in the case of Hannah Swarton, Hannah Dustan, and Eunice Williams: the interpretations of their captivities are all highly dependent on their vulnerability as females to seduction and violation when removed from the paternal supervision of their husbands or fathers and the clergy. Dustan's apparently anomalous case is especially revealing. Her decision to tomahawk her captors is attributed to fear of having to run naked through the gauntlet, she is compared to a female character from Scripture (Jael), and she is counseled to eschew any inappropriate pride in her act.

Appropriately, given the typification of the exemplary captive as female and the general oppositional logic, the gender of the Indian captor becomes coded primarily as male, though abstractly male. While the captor may be accompanied by "filthy," "ugly," "insolent squaws," they are secondary and dispensable to the overall interpretation: captivity is an improper subservience to men who are themselves subservient to the Devil rather than to God.

In short, during the decade between 1697 and 1707, Cotton Mather and John Williams began to develop a representation of captivity that is highly condensed in the passage from Mather's "Observable Things" that opens this chapter. In this interpretation, the figure of the female captive represents the vulnerability of the English colonists in the New World, where they are the prey of brutish and diabolical forces that destroy domestic and civil order, threatening to seduce or devour them. The opposition between a vulnerable female captive and a male captor unrestrained in his savagery is fundamental to this interpretation. Furthermore, a White male redeemer seems to be prefigured in the person of John Williams—a less successful redeemer, to be sure, than the more famous Daniel Boone and Leatherstocking of subsequent decades. To complete the clerical configuration, the Red female captor—so prominent in Mary Rowlandson's narrative—is subordinated to her male counterpart.

Alternative Voices: Quaker and Other Eighteenth-Century Captivity Narratives

This clerical typification of captivity gained its influence from both social and cultural sources: it bore the authority of those who articulated it, the clerical elite, as well as the hegemonic system of assumptions regarding gender, savagery, and civility that it deployed. However, during the half century following the publication of Mary Rowlandson's narrative, there were significant challenges to the clerical representation. To begin with, Mary Rowlandson's spiritual autobiography continued to appear in new editions. And it was supplemented by three other full-length captivity narratives: two of them by male captives, two of them spiritual autobiographies written by Quakers.

The first of the Quaker narratives ranked in popularity with the Rowlandson and Williams narratives in the English colonies. It was published abroad as well, in Dutch and German as well as English editions. First appearing in 1699, the narrative bore the following vivid title: *God's Protecting Providence Man's Surest Help and Defence in the Times of the Greatest Difficulty and Most Imminent Danger: Evidenced in the Remarkable Deliverance of Divers Persons, from the Devouring Waves of the Sea, and Also from the More Cruelly Devouring Jawes of the Inhumane Canibals of Florida amongst Whom They Suffered Shipwreck* (Dickinson 1977 [1699]). This detailed journal records the experiences of Jonathan Dickinson, a prosperous merchant who was shipwrecked in Florida, together with his family and a famous Quaker missionary, Robert Barrow. The desolate party was captured by a group of coastal Natives known as Ais or Tequesta.

Dickinson's narrative is similar to Rowlandson's in its immediacy and its interpretation of captivity as a lesson in resignation to God's will, a lesson both articulated and exemplified by the missionary. The account contrasts with Rowlandson's narrative, however, in its highly stereotypical portrayal of the captors, dominated by fear of the "cruelly devouring jaws" of these reputed cannibals. Indeed, it seems that the Dickinson narrative fleshes out the possibilities inherent in Mather's image of Indian vultures and devourers, using cannibalism to represent loss of self through a literal incorporation by the Other. This interpretation is supported by the nature of Dickinson's second overriding concern: that his infant son would survive himself and his wife and be raised by his captors. This remained a horrifying prospect despite the tenderness of the indigenous women, who repeatedly nourished the starving infant at their own breasts. One wonders if Dickinson and his wife experienced this act of mercy as itself a threatening transformation of the infant's substance.

The second Quaker account related the experiences of Elizabeth Hanson, a pacifist abducted by Algonquian allies of the French during one of the skirmishes that intermittently plagued the frontier between 1713 and the beginning of the third intercolonial war in 1744. Upon her return from captivity, Hanson narrated her experiences to an English minister, who edited and published the narration anonymously as a testament to God's power and a reminder of the importance of spiritual resignation. *God's Mercy Surmounting Man's Cruelty* (1728), as Hanson's narrative is titled, retains a providential interpretation of captivity but lacks the oppositional typification of Indians found in Dickinson's and the Puritan narratives. Hunger is the focal condition in Hanson's account, plaguing captive and captors alike, and motivating both the cruelties of her master and the compassion of the Algonquian women, who showed Hanson how to supplement her failing breast milk with a gruel of walnuts and corn. Notably, Hanson's willingness to acknowledge her captors' perspective includes religion. For example, she is willing to acknowledge a spiritual dimension to the scalp dance she witnessed upon the war party's return home.

This move toward what, from a contemporary perspective, appears as ethnographic curiosity and rudimentary cultural relativism is furthered in the final narrative published before the intercolonial wars resumed. "Memoirs of Odd Adventures, Strange Deliverances, &c. in the Captivity of John Gyles," published in 1736, concerns Gyles's abduction in 1689, when he was ten years old. Gyles, who spent six years among the Eastern Abenaki and three as a prisoner of the French, explicitly imparts material on ethnography and natural history, adding separate sections on these subjects to the chronologically ordered narration of his experiences. For example, Gyles's section on "Indian fables" is one of our earliest sources on the Algonquian cannibal bird, "called gulloua," he writes, "who buildeth her nest on a high rock or mountain." As Gyles tells the story,

> A boy was hunting with his bow and arrow at the foot of a rocky mountain when the gulloua came diving through the air, grasped the boy in her talons, and though he was eight or ten years of age, she soared aloft and laid him in her nest, a prey of her young, where the boy lay constantly on his face but would look sometimes under his arms and saw two young ones with much fish and flesh in the nest and the old bird constantly bringing more, so that the young ones not touching him, the old one clawed him up and set him where she found him, who returned and related the odd event to his friends. (Gyles 1977 [1736], 15–16)

It is tempting to imagine that Gyles identified with the Abenaki boy who was taken captive but ultimately returned home to tell his tale. Although he does not do so explicitly in the narrative, he does devote considerable attention to the myth, locating the bird's nest at the top of a specific mountain, identifying the bird as a larger version of a speckled eagle, and comparing it to Virgil's "hungry harpies."

Gyles's reference to Harpies is only one of many classical references in the narrative, which departs from Puritan and Quaker precedents in identifying the captive with a classical hero, Odysseus, rather than with Hebrew prototypes. Like Odysseus, Gyles returned home transformed, and he put the extensive linguistic, cultural, and environmental knowledge he had gained to good use, serving as an interpreter and diplomat for the colonies after his release from captivity. Gyles's willingness to adopt certain Abenaki traits marks a strong departure from the Puritan preoccupation with maintaining an unsullied identity in the New World. Also a departure from earlier narratives is Gyles's emphasis on physical survival rather than spiritual redemption—survival that he attributes as much to his own human wit as to Divine Providence. Gyles survives the hardships of captivity and emerges to tell his tale, it seems, because his flexible identity incorporates knowledge of Abenaki culture while still remaining oriented primarily to colonial values. Although this narrative is among the least well known, the power of a partially acculturated identity, as Slotkin (1973) has shown, was to become a central theme in Anglo-American representations of captivity after the Revolution—embodied in male captives such as Daniel Boone and in fictional characters such as Cooper's Leatherstocking.

Given the existence of, first, a more multivocal interpretation of the captivity experience in the Hanson and Gyles narratives (again invoking Bakhtin) and, secondly, narratives of two male captives, Gyles and Dickinson, who present themselves as vulnerable, at least to the dangers of torture, it is important not to overstate the extent to which the Puritan clergy dominated the interpretation of captivity in the English colonies during the period we are considering. This half century after Mary Rowlandson first explored the meaning of the captivity experience was a time in which a number of interpretations of captivity coexisted. However, the interpretation fashioned in the works of Increase Mather, Cotton Mather, and John Williams has left the most enduring legacy. Their interpretation of captivity—which justifies colonial domination and aggression as a response to savage threats to vulnerable civility—was developed in the voluminous captivity literature that began to appear during the third and fourth intercolonial wars (especially the latter, the Seven Years War of 1755–1763). The hegemonic interpretation was further developed in narratives deriving from the Revolutionary War and the various frontier wars in which the nation engaged in the late eighteenth century and throughout the nineteenth century. Especially important in the development and dissemination of a hegemonic representation were illustrations of the captivity experience, which only began to appear in colonial editions in the 1770s; anthologies of captivity narratives and "Indian atrocities," which date to the 1790s; narratives included in children readers and Sunday School literature, dating to the early nineteenth century; and fictional accounts, dating to the 1790s and appearing with greater frequency in the nineteenth and twentieth centuries (including in films such as *The Searchers* and *Dances with Wolves*).

As the selective tradition of captivity developed, the processes of abstraction and typification noted in Mather's and Williams's interpretations of captivity continued to be significant. The historical and cultural contexts of captivity became even more thoroughly suppressed. Especially in visual and fictional versions of the captivity experience, the captive became more completely typified as a vulnerable while female, the captor as a threatening Indian male. Meanwhile, the White male redeemer became an ever more prominent figure. Just as the clerical version carried the authority of the Puritan elite, later typifications of captivity would carry the authority of local and national historians, school and church publication boards, the mass media, and representative government—as in Horatio Greenough's 1853 sculpture, *The Rescue*, which for a hundred years stood at the eastern entrance to the US Capitol, reinforcing the hegemonic trio of Captive, Captor, and Redeemer (see Figure 9).

Alternative representations would continue to exist, however, such as the 1824 narrative of Mary Jemison, a captive adopted by the Seneca (Seaver 1995 [1824]), and the many literary and dramatic treatments of Pocahontas and King Philip that began to appear about the same time. These alternatives can be recognized precisely by the manner in which they transgress the oppositional logic on which the hegemonic representation is built: Jemison is a "white squaw"; Pocahontas a Red, female redeemer; and Philip a Red male captor become captive. Rarely,

Figure 9. Horatio Greenough, *The Rescue* (1853). The sculpture was displayed at the east entrance to the US Capitol for over a century (1853–1958). Courtesy of the Architect of the Capitol.

however, do these alternatives function truly as counter-hegemonic representations, for they tend to appear as romantic possibilities for contemplation rather than as visions for action.

Especially in Native American discourse, however, the oppositional power of alternative representations of captivity sometimes emerges. Indigenous authors in the nineteenth, twentieth, and twenty-first centuries have countered the hegemonic tradition of captivity with accounts of being captured as prisoners of war, impounded on reservations, forcibly enrolled in boarding school, and forcibly removed from their families. It is to these narratives that we turn in the next chapter.

Bibliographic Note

Captivity narratives (particularly Mary Rowlandson's) are part of the canon of American literature, and the scholarly literature is voluminous. Some of the more important works are Slotkin, *Regeneration Through Violence* (1973); Drinnon, *Facing West* (1980); Vaughan and Clark, *Puritans among the Indians* (1981); Ulrich, *Good Wives* (1982); Kolodny, *The Land before Her* (1984); Namias, *White Captives* (1993); Demos, *The Unredeemed Captive* (1994); Tilton, *Pocahontas: The Evolution of an American Narrative* (1994); Ebersole, *Captured by Texts* (1995); Castiglia, *Bound and Determined* (1996); Burnham, *Captivity and Sentiment* (1997); Scheckel, *The Insistence of the Indian* (1998); Strong, *Captive Selves, Captivating Others* (1999); and Sayre, *American Captivity Narratives* (2000). For a comparative perspective on captivity, see Brooks, *Captives and Cousins* (2002); Colley, *Captives* (2002); Voigt, *Writing Captivity in the Early Modern Atlantic* (2008); and Snyder, *Slavery in Indian Country* (2010). Bibliographies are found in Vaughan (1983), Derounian-Stodola and Levernier (1993), Salisbury (1997), Strong (1999, 2002), and Sayre (2000).

Ethnohistorical literature on the indigenous peoples of the eastern woodlands is extensive. Useful overviews include Trigger, *Northeast* (1978); Washburn, *History of Indian-White Relations* (1988); Perdue and Green, *Columbia Guide to American Indians of the Southeast* (2001); Bragdon, *Columbia Guide to American Indians of the Northeast* (2001); Richter, *Facing East from Indian Country* (2003); Fogelson, *Southeast* (2004); and the collected essays of James Axtell (1981, 1985, 1988, 1992, 2001).

The most readily available source for most of the narratives discussed in this chapter is Vaughan and Clark, *Puritans among the Indians* (1981); see also Calloway, *North Country Captives* (1992). Annotated editions of the Rowlandson narrative (Salisbury 1997 [1682]), the Williams narrative (1976 [1707]), and Cotton Mather's *Humiliations* (Orians 1970), are also available, edited by

Salisbury, Clark, and Orians, respectively. Washburn (1977–1980) has edited a useful set of facsimiles.

For an expanded analysis and more extensive documentation, see Strong, *Captive Selves, Captivating Others* (1999). Regarding indigenous captivity practices across the continent, see Strong, "Transforming Outsiders" (2002).

CHAPTER SIX

THE CONTEMPORARY CAPTIVITY NARRATIVE

The year 2008 marked the thirtieth anniversary of the Indian Child Welfare Act (ICWA), which was enacted in 1978 after more than a decade of intensive work by the Association on American Indian Affairs, Inc. (AAIA) and other Indian rights organizations. Prior to the passage of the act, generations of Native American children had been removed from their relatives and communities by governmental officials, missionaries, and social workers convinced that assimilation into the dominant society through adoption, foster care, or education in off-reservation boarding schools was in the Indian child's best interests (Adams 1995). The use of boarding schools had decreased by the mid-1970s, but not the widespread practice of placing indigenous children in nonindigenous foster and adoptive families. According to an AAIA study (Unger 1977), 25 to 35 percent of all Native American children were separated from their families, the adoption rate for Native American children was twenty times the national rate, and adoptive and foster families for Indian children were largely non-Indian. Following Senate and Congressional hearings reporting these statistics and demonstrating the deceptive, coercive, and discriminatory practices through which Native American children were often separated from their families, as well as the extent to which indigenous patterns of kinship and child-rearing were disregarded in judgments regarding neglect, abuse, and abandonment, the ICWA was enacted to restore tribal jurisdiction over the adoption of Indian children and prevent the decimation of Indian communities.

The ICWA takes the sovereign status of Indian tribes as its point of departure and strengthening sovereignty as one of its main goals. As we have seen in Chapter 2, the continued existence of Native American tribes within the borders of the United States poses distinct challenges to dominant conceptions of American nationalism and possessive individualism. In this chapter I consider how Native American tribalism as codified in the ICWA specifically challenges (and is challenged by) dominant conceptions of kinship grounded in Euro-American ideologies of possessive individualism and the nuclear family (Macpherson 1962; Schneider 1984; Carriere 1994).

In keeping with the centrality of tribal sovereignty in the formulation, interpretation, and implementation of the ICWA, I use the term "extra-tribal adoption" to refer to the placement of an Indian child with adoptive parents who are not members of a tribe to which the child belongs (or is entitled to belong). This term serves to distinguish the issues involved in the adoption of Native American children from those involved in the equally contested field of transracial adoption (Simon et al. 1994). The legal status of Indian tribes as "domestic dependent nations" brings the issues involved in extra-tribal adoption closer to those encountered in transnational adoption (Volkman 2005) than those found in transracial adoption. Though cultural identity and cultural survival are at stake in both extra-tribal and transracial adoption, extra-tribal and transnational adoption share the additional considerations of sovereignty and citizenship.

This chapter focuses on the treatment of extra-tribal adoption in two important novels published in the 1990s: Sherman Alexie's *Indian Killer* (1996) and Barbara Kingsolver's *Pigs in Heaven* (1993). Together these novels crystallize and illuminate the often polarized positions found in public and legal discourses. First, however, we will look briefly at several historical cases of captivity, adoption, and transculturation in order to underscore the context in which extra-tribal adoptions developed. We begin with a discussion of *The Unredeemed Captive: A Family Story from Early America,* a prizewinning work by social historian John Demos (1994). This innovative "family story" offers a multivocal rendering of the captivity and adoption of John Williams's daughter Eunice, with multiple beginnings (in England, Spain, Massachusetts, and Iroquoia), a multicultural cast (English, French, Mohawk), multiple endings (Catholic, Puritan, Mohawk), and a speculative epilogue that echoes a forward-looking eighteenth-century Puritan sermon in envisioning reconciliation through the blending of English and Mohawk "blood." In his polyphonic retelling of Eunice Williams's captivity and adoption, Demos suggests how the violence of abduction and the intimacy of adoption are implicated in the uneasy relations that often obtain between indigenous peoples and settlers in North America.

Captivity and Adoption in Iroquoia

As was noted in Chapter 5, Eunice Williams was seven years of age when she was abducted, in 1704, from Deerfield, Massachusetts, by Catholic Mohawks—whose clans were accustomed to "requicken" the name of a deceased relative through adopting a captive enemy to take the relative's place (Richter 1983; Haefeli and Sweeney 2003; A. Simpson 2009). She remained a resident of the Canadian mission town of Kahnawake for the remaining eighty years of her life. As the daughter of Puritan minister John Williams, who recounted his own captivity in 1707 in a widely read spiritual autobiography, *The Redeemed Captive Returning to Zion* (J. Williams 1976 [1707]), Eunice is among the most well-known of the colonial children who were adopted into indigenous families and assimilated into their societies. On the basis of Jesuit and Puritan accounts Demos has reconstructed the complicated course of Eunice's life. Shortly after her captivity, Eunice was adopted into a Mohawk matriclan as A'ongote (meaning "she has been planted as a person"). Living with her adoptive mother's extended family, A'ongote would have experienced the dispersed mothering of a Mohawk matriclan as well as child-rearing practices the English considered overindulgent. Within two years, she had forgotten English and refused to return to her English family. Upon her baptism as a Catholic, she was given a new Christian name, Marguerite. At sixteen she married a Catholic Mohawk man named Arosen, and they had several children, including a daughter who married a prominent chief, Onnasategen. At some point she acquired a new Mohawk name, Gannenstenhawi ("she brings in corn"), probably marking her status as a mature woman or clan matron. As a clan matron and as the mother-in-law of a chief, Gannenstenhawi exercised a degree of authority unknown to women in New England. Although Gannenstenhawi, clad in buckskin and moccasins, paid a visit with her husband to her New England family (reportedly camping in her brother's apple orchard), she could not be persuaded to remain. Unable to "redeem" his daughter in either the material or the spiritual sense, John Williams died with a profound sense of loss and failure.

It was captives such as Eunice that her cousin Cotton Mather had, in a 1698 sermon, likened to "little chickens ... seized by the Indian vultures, ... little birds ... spirited away by the Indian devourers" (Mather 1978 [1699], 222). Half a century later, Titus King would echo Mather in his own unpublished captivity narrative, describing captivity as

> an awful school for children when we see how quick they will fall in with the Indians' ways. Nothing seems to be more taking. In six months time they forsake father and mother, forget their own land, refuse to speak their own tongue and seemingly be wholly swallowed up with the Indians. (Axtell 1985, 322)

For John Williams, Cotton Mather, and Titus King, the captivity of children among Indians constituted a profound threat because they were so readily "devoured" or "swallowed up" into a life of savagery and slavery to the Devil. Children, already so close to a wild state, easily "fell in with the Indians' ways," forgetting their language, their family, their country, their religion, and even their English name. Vulnerable fledglings who were "seized" and "spirited away" by "Indian vultures," adopted captives were seen as altogether lost to their natal family and society.

So it appeared to many colonists. But Gannenstenhawi's visit to Deerfield indicates that she and her Kahnawake Mohawk relatives viewed her adoption differently. Gannenstenhawi wished to maintain ties with her English family, viewing adoption as a way of gaining new relatives without severing her ties to the old. Likewise her Mohawk descendants: in 1837, nearly fifty years after Gannenstenhawi's death, two dozen of her descendants visited her home town of Deerfield for about a week. Deerfield's minister was so affected by the visit that he welcomed the Mohawk visitors with a sermon that asserted "a common origin for all the differing tribes and races of men" and praised "the workings of that mysterious Providence which has mingled your blood with ours" (Demos 1994, 247, 252). One and one-half centuries previously, the inhabitants of Deerfield had recognized Providence's work in the destruction of the Native villages that preceded the establishment of Deerfield in the Pocumtuck valley. Now their descendants were asked to recognize their membership in a "common family" with Mohawks, their sharing of the "same life-blood," and their living under "one hospitable roof" as "brethren of a single, united, harmonious household" (249, 251). In the minister's sermon the Christian rhetoric of universal kinship was strongly inflected by Deerfield's kinship relations with their former enemies. The Mohawk pattern of "extending the rafters" through alliances based on kinship (Foster, Campisi, and Mithun 1984) had shown to have transcultural appeal.

Captivity and Loss in Boarding School Narratives

Read against the grain, Cotton Mather's words evoke not only the little English chicks who were "seized," "spirited away," and "brought up" by their indigenous captors but also the generations of Native American children, sometimes called Lost Birds (Melanson 1999), who were removed from their families and "devoured," as it were, by the dominant society. As we have seen, the captivity of Native Americans among Europeans dates to Columbus's first voyage, and indigenous captives were sold into both domestic and foreign slavery during Cotton Mather's time. Closer to our own day, the Hopi priest Don Talayesva articulated a sense of violence and loss similar to that of Cotton Mather. *Sun Chief,* Talayesva's autobiography, tells of US troops coming to the town of Oraibi at the turn of the century "to take the children by force and carry them off in wagons" to the boarding school at the Keams Canyon Agency. Talayesva remarked that "the people said that it was a terrible sight to see Negro soldiers come and tear children from their parents" (L. Simmons 1942, 89). Later his sister went to the day school at New Oraibi, where "the teacher cut her hair, burned all her clothes, and gave her a new outfit and a new name, Nellie." The unhappy girl managed to stay away for about a year by hiding, but when she went to the spring to fetch water for a religious ceremony she was "captured by the school principal, who permitted her to take the water up to the village, but compelled her to return to school after the ceremony was over. The teachers had then forgotten her old name, Nellie, and called her Gladys" (89).

Unlike his sister and a brother, Talayesva chose to enter day school on his own terms. He arrived unaccompanied, thus avoiding the humiliation of being ushered to school by the police, and he wore only a Navajo blanket so that his shirt would not be ripped from his back and burned. Later he attended two separate boarding schools, where like most students he suffered from homesickness, illness, and physical punishment. At boarding school he was required to engage in such seasonal labor as picking sugar beets in Colorado, pitching hay on a California ranch, and picking cantaloupes in the Imperial Valley. School taught him, he reported sardonically, "that a person thinks with his head instead of his heart" (99). After a near-death experience and a spiritual vision, Talayesva finally returned home, "to become a real Hopi again, to sing the good old Katcina songs, and to feel free to make love without fear of sin or a rawhide" (134).

Talayesva's tale is repeated, in essence, in many other autobiographical accounts. Indeed, indigenous abduction, captivity, and resistance narratives can be read as a counter-hegemonic version of the Anglo-American selective tradition of captivity considered in Chapter 5. Zitkala Ša (Gertrude Bonnin), who chose to leave the Yankton Sioux reservation in 1884 at the age of eight to attend a Quaker boarding school, wrote in the *Atlantic Monthly* of crying herself to sleep; having her braids cut off while she was tied to a chair, struggling all the while; and, finally, losing her health and her spirit. When she was grown, she taught at the Carlisle Indian School, which sent her on a recruiting mission, searching, as she put it, for "overconfident parents who would entrust their children to strangers" (Zitkala Ša 2003 [1900], 106). Looking back on her own schooling, Zitkala Ša likened herself to an uprooted tree:

> For the white man's papers I had given up my faith in the Great Spirit. For these same papers I had forgotten the healing in trees and brooks. On account of my mother's simple view of life, and my lack of any, I gave her up, also. I made no

friends among the race of people I loathed. Like a slender tree, I had been uprooted from my mother, nature, and God. (112)

Talayesva and Zitkala Ša were to take opposite paths—he returning to his village "to become a real Hopi again," she taking a prominent role in the nascent Indian rights movement—but boarding school was, for both, profoundly alienating and disorienting. Talayesva's sense of being unreal; Zitkala Ša's sense of being uprooted; and their relatives' sense of powerlessness, sorrow, and loss as their children were captured, whether by force or promises—these are all recurrent emotions in the narratives of Native Americans removed from their families and placed in institutions, foster families, or adoptive families. Though some narratives recount the kindness of adoptive and foster families and the camaraderie and broadened horizons of boarding school, many tell of violent separation from their families, harsh discipline, forced labor, and prohibitions against any manifestations of Native language, religion, or culture. That Euro-Americans fail to appreciate the strength of these historical memories, even while repeatedly reproducing the somewhat analogous experiences of colonial captives such as John Smith, Mary Rowlandson, and Eunice Williams, is one measure of their estrangement from the experiences and perspectives of indigenous people.

Captivity, Adoption, and Loss in Alexie's *Indian Killer*

> We are what
> We have lost.
>
> —*Alex Kuo*

Spokane/Coeur d'Alene author Sherman Alexie begins his complex and hard-hitting novel *Indian Killer* with this poignant couplet from his mentor, the Chinese American poet Alex Kuo. Treated by many critics as an angry revelation of racial hatred, *Indian Killer* is more precisely a novel about the loss of self generated by extra-tribal adoption—and by the more general losses and dislocations that extra-tribal adoption represents. An inversion of Euro-American captivity or "Indian hater" narratives (Slotkin 1973), *Indian Killer* tells of an adopted Indian's search to become "a real person" (Alexie 1996, 19). Alexie's novel develops skillfully, if elliptically, many of the themes commonly found in the narratives of displaced and adopted Indians, including the theme of captivity. In order to highlight these themes I have selected, subtitled, and occasionally rearranged a number of crucial scenes in the life of the protagonist, not coincidentally named "John Smith" by his adoptive father—and ultimately, of course, by his creator Sherman Alexie, whose characters, including a Professor Mather, bear names revealing the affinity of *Indian Killer* to the Euro-American captivity genre.

Let us begin, as does Alexie, with John Smith's "mythology":

The Birth Story

The sheets are dirty. An Indian Health Service hospital in the mid-sixties. On this reservation or that reservation. Any reservation, a particular reservation....

The Indian woman on the table in the delivery room is very young, just a child herself. She is beautiful, even in the pain of labor, the contractions, the sudden tearing. When John imagines his birth, his mother is sometimes Navajo. Other times she is Lakota. Often, she is from the same tribe as the last Indian woman he has seen on television....

... The doctor cuts the umbilical cord quickly. There is no time to waste.... His mother is crying.

I want my baby. Give me my baby. I want to see my baby. Let me hold my baby.

The doctor tries to comfort John's mother. The nurse swaddles John in blankets and ... carries John outside.... Inside the hospital, John's mother has fainted. The doctor holds her hand, as if he were the loving husband and father. (3–6)

The Captivity

With John in her arms, the nurse stands in the parking lot. She is white or Indian. She watches the horizon. Blue sky, white clouds, bright sun. The slight whine of a helicopter in the distance. Then the violent whomp-whomp of its blades as it passes overhead, hovers, and lands a hundred feet away....

A man in a white jumpsuit steps from the helicopter.... The nurse meets him halfway and hands him the baby John.... The sky is very blue. Specific birds hurl away from the flying machine. These birds are indigenous to this reservation. They do not live anywhere else. They have purple-tipped wings and tremendous eyes, or red bellies and small eyes....

Suddenly this is a war. The jumpsuit man holds John close to his chest as the helicopter rises. The helicopter gunman locks and loads, strafes the reservation with explosive shells.... Back at the clinic his mother has been sedated.... Gunfire in the distance. Nobody, not even the white doctor, is surprised by this.

... The pilot searches for the landing area. Five acres of green, green grass. A large house. Swimming pool. A man and woman waving energetically. Home....

John cries as the jumpsuit man hands him to the white woman, Olivia Smith. She unbuttons the top of her dress, opens her bra, and offers John her large, pale breasts with pink nipples. John's birth mother had small, brown breasts and brown nipples, though he never suckled at them. Still, he knows there is a difference, and as John takes the white woman's right nipple into his mouth and pulls at her breast, he discovers it is empty. (6–8)

The Best Thing

"Indian?" asked Daniel. "As in American Indian?"

"Yes," said the agent.... "Now, ideally, we'd place this baby with Indian parents, right? But that just isn't going to happen. The best place for this baby is with a white family. This child will be saved a lot of pain by growing up in a white family. It's the best thing, really." (10)

Sealed Records

... The adoption agency refused to divulge John's tribal affiliation and sealed all of his birth records, revealing only that John's birth mother was fourteen years old. Olivia spent hours looking through books, searching the photographs for any face like her son's face. (12)

The Difference

John was five years old when he first realized his parents were white and he was brown, and understood that the difference in skin color was important....

... He did not look like his parents, especially when they were naked.... He wanted to look like his parents. He rubbed at his face, wanting to wipe the brown away. (305–306)

The Movies

"Smith," Michael said, because white boys always called each other by their last names. "I was just wondering. I mean, you're adopted, right? I mean, she's not even your real mother. Not really."

... "She's a gorgeous white woman and you're an Indian, right? Don't you watch the movies? Don't Indians always want to fuck white women?" (77)

Generic Indians

"What's your name?"

"John."

"What tribe you are?"

He could not, would not, tell her he had been adopted as a newborn by a white couple who could not have children of their own....

His adopted parents had never told him what kind of Indian he was. They did not know.... John only knew that he was Indian in the most generic sense.... When asked by white people, he said he was Sioux, because that was what they wanted him to be. When asked by Indian people, he said he was Navajo, because that was what he wanted to be.

"I'm Navajo," he said to Marie. (31–32)

Real Indians

"So," the foreman had said. "Why do you want to work construction?"

"I read about it," John had said. "In a magazine. Indians like to work construction. Mohawks. In New York City." (132)

To Kill a White Man

"Hey, chief, what you doing? Trying to land a plane?" . . .

John knew if he were a real Indian, he could have called the wind. He could have called a crosscutting wind that would've sliced through the fortieth floor, pulled the foreman out of the elevator, and sent him over the edge of the building. . . .

John needed to kill a white man. (24–25)

His Real Name

. . . He was not afraid of falling. John stepped off the last skyscraper in Seattle.

John fell. . . . Falling. Because he finally and completely understood the voices in his head. . . .

. . . He stood above his body embedded in the pavement. . . . John looked at himself and saw he was naked. Brown skin. . . . John stood, stepped over that body, and strode into the desert. . . . An Indian father was out there beyond the horizon. And maybe an Indian mother with a scar on her belly from a Cesarean birth. She could know John's real name. (411–413)

Coercion, displacement, secrecy, anonymity, rootlessness, emptiness, alienation, inauthenticity, fantasy, rage, despair—John Smith's experience of adoption mirrors that described in Judith S. Modell's ethnography of the experience of adoptive kinship in the United States (Modell 1994, 115–168). The particular intensity with which these experiences are expressed in *Indian Killer* is not only a result of Alexie's fictional treatment. Rather, each aspect of the adopted child's experience is intensified by John Smith's identity as a generic Indian. John Smith envisions his displacement as an extension of the Indian wars and the Indian removals—that is, as a physical and psychological assault upon his ability to survive. Sealed records hide not only his name but also his tribal affiliation, without which he has no hope of being a "real Indian." Even among other Indians he does not belong; he truly belongs only to that singular reservation where birds have "purple-tipped wings and tremendous eyes, or red bellies and small eyes." Like the birds, John Smith is "indigenous to this reservation," and he can live nowhere else. His experience of emptiness and his sense of estrangement are heightened by the physical difference between himself and his adoptive parents. His sense of inauthenticity is intensified by the simulations of authentic

Indianness with which he is surrounded (Vizenor 1994). In search of the "real" he mimics these simulations, only to become increasingly more "generic." In the end, John Smith identifies with the stereotypical savage. Then, like seven of every ten thousand Indians placed in non-Indian homes, he commits suicide (Johnson 1991, vi, 153). In death he hopes to fulfill his search for his Indian parents and his real name. An inversion of the stereotypical Indian-hater, John Smith imagines himself as not only born in violence but "regenerated through violence" (Slotkin 1973).

Both the historical John Smith and Alexie's character are captive to families seeking to transform them into relatives. But unlike the historical character, Alexie's John Smith has no past and no future—only a brown skin that marks his difference. "It's the best thing, really," said the "agent" who arranged the adoption, just as Indian agents for generations thought it best to send children to boarding school and foster families, employing violence when necessary. "Nobody, not even the white doctor, is surprised by this," for in the mid-1960s, when John was born, the "best interests" of an Indian child were routinely thought to be placement off the reservation, with a White family. Such a placement signified escape, opportunity, advancement. As the agent put it, "This child will be saved a lot of pain."

The Best Interests of the Indian Child

The guiding principle of legal adoption in the United States is "the best interests of the child" (Goldstein, Freud, and Solnit 1973; Rodham 1973; Carriere 1994). Adoption is viewed as moving a child from "unfit" parents to "fit" ones, and from an "unstable" to a "stable" home (Modell 1994, 28–29, 41–42). High levels of intervention in indigenous families, as in Native Hawaiian families (Modell 1998), reflect the imposition of ethnocentric principles of fitness and stability upon families organized according to different principles. As Steven Unger of the Association of Indian Affairs argued in advocating passage of the Indian Child Welfare Act,

> The continuing bias of government policy is to coerce Indian families to conform to non-Indian child-rearing standards. Indian tribes are asking state and federal governments to stop "saving" Indian families in this way and, instead, recognize and respect the rights and traditional strengths of Indian children, families and tribes. (Unger 1977, iii)

Interpreting extra-tribal adoption as a threat to tribal sovereignty and survival, Unger called governmental interference with family life "perhaps the most flagrant infringement of the rights of Indian tribes to govern themselves in our time and the most tragic aspect of contemporary Indian life" (iii).

During legislative hearings, advocates of the ICWA pointed out not only the disproportionate percentage of Indian children separated from their natal families, but also that many of these separations were effected without regard to the rights of either birth parents or tribes. Often the birth parents did not understand the documents or proceedings, were threatened with the loss of welfare benefits, or were neither represented by counsel nor advised of their rights. Tribal authorities and community agencies were frequently not consulted. Nor were "Indian children's rights to live with their families" taken into account (Unger 1977, 59). Children were removed for conditions that were not demonstrably harmful to the child, or were removed before supportive services were extended to families experiencing problems. Few children were removed from their families because of physical abuse: most often they were removed for "neglect," "abandonment," or "social deprivation," which might consist of simply living on a poverty-stricken reservation; being under the care of grandparents, siblings, or other members of an extended family; or being raised under less restrictive conditions than were tolerated in the dominant society (Unger 1977, iii, 4). Likening the "epidemic" of extra-tribal adoptions to a "modern Trail of Tears" (a reference to the removal of the "Five Civilized Tribes" from the Southeast in the 1830s), psychiatrist Joseph Westermeyer noted "a social imperative operating against Indian families in our institutions. The result is a de facto ethnocide of values, attitudes, and customs" (Unger 1977, 54–55).

Evelyn Blanchard, a Laguna-Yaqui social worker known as the "mother of the Indian Child Welfare Act" (Johnson 1991, 149), criticized "culture of poverty" theories for ignoring the US government's role in destroying Indian family life:

> Indian families are continually subjected to theories of child abuse and neglect that have been developed in the non-Indian community. The basis for those positions is that people who abuse and neglect their children are people who themselves have been abused and neglected. We do not deny that there are many Indian parents who lived in neglectful situations. However, we do contest the interpretation and the application of that theory ... [because] we can clearly demonstrate that the circumstances in our lives that have contributed to the presence of abuse and neglect in our communities have been directly caused by activities, policies, and regulations of the federal government. It has consistently sought to destroy the Indian family. (Myers 1981, 87)

Acknowledging abusive situations on reservations, Blanchard argued for providing Indian tribes the power and resources to address the abuses, rather than continuing with destructive policies destined to compound them. She and other proponents of the ICWA also offered a cogent and far-reaching critique of a universalizing and ethnocentric interpretation of the principle of best interests. As Navajo legal specialist Leonard B. Jimson put it,

> A judge who thinks in terms of the comfort and stability of a middle-class Anglo home may unconsciously think about this when he looks at a Navajo hogan where people do not have these same comforts. He may not see the importance of rais-ing children to speak Navajo or to know their own culture and religion, because he assumes that all Navajos want to speak and think like Anglos, and this is best for them. In short, the way that the caseworker and judge look at family life may be so different that Navajo people cannot ever satisfy them, even though they also want to do what is in "the best interests" of the children. (Unger 1977, 69)

Senator James Abourezk of South Dakota (who chaired the Subcommittee on Indian Affairs and ran the Senate hearings on the ICWA) made a similar point, noting that "public and private welfare agencies seem to have operated on the premise that most Indian children would really be better off growing up non-Indian" (Unger 1977, 12). Indeed, they did: off-reservation placements were one of the main ways of implementing governmental policies of "termi-nating" Indian tribes and assimilating Native children to the Euro-American value of possessive individualism (as discussed in Chapter 2). The most dramatic example of this is the American Indian Adoption Project, initiated in 1958 as a joint program of the Bureau of Indian Affairs and the Child Welfare League of America. During the ten years in which this experiment in "transracial adoption" was in effect, 395 Native children were placed in non-Indian families, generally in the East and Midwest. On the basis of interviews with the adoptive parents, the project was declared a success, in large part because Native children were relatively easy to place because of Euro-Americans' idealization of the country's original inhabitants. Researchers did not interview the children's natal families, nor follow the development of the children beyond the first five years (Fanshel 1972; Johnson 1991, 22).

Blanchard went beyond the notion of culturally determined best interests in asserting that "the question of best interest is much broader in Indian country than it is elsewhere. Termination hearings sever not only rights of parents but rights of children and rights of tribes" (Unger 1977, 60). She referred here, like Jimson, to the right of parents to follow culturally specific child-rearing practices, but also to the right of children to be affiliated with their tribes and the right of tribes to ensure their cultural and demographic survival. In all these ways the proponents of the ICWA sought to broaden the principle of best interests beyond its individualistic basis and to establish that the balancing act any determination of best interests entails should be the responsibility of Indian tribes.

Blanchard, Jimson, Abourezk, and others argued that the best interests of the Indian child could only be ascertained in tribal terms, not in the individualistic terms of the dominant society. While arguments for the passage of the ICWA were grounded in empirical observations about the destructive consequences of extensive extra-tribal adoptions upon children, the devastating impact of these adoptions upon families and tribes was also emphasized. Building upon well-established principles of tribal sovereignty, the act offered a radical challenge to the principle of best interests by recognizing the interest of tribes in their children and of children in their tribes. In order to underscore the political significance of the reconceptualization of best interests embodied in the ICWA, it is useful to employ models formulated by feminist anthropologists for analyzing the politics of kinship (Strathern 1992; Ginsburg and Rapp 1995; Franklin and Ragoné 1998). In these terms the ICWA establishes

- the right of Native American children to have their best interests understood *relationally, or in terms of culturally constructed personhood*;
- the right of Native American parents and families to have the *dispersed nature of their modes of social and cultural reproduction* taken into account; and
- the right of Indian tribes as quasi-sovereign nations to *control their social and cultural reproduction*.

When stated in these ways, the counter-hegemonic nature of the Indian Child Welfare Act is evident. Like the concept of tribal sovereignty itself, the ICWA establishes collective rights that are in considerable tension with hegemonic constructions of possessive individualism and the liberal state. In the twenty years since its passage, however, the act has successfully withstood several constitutional challenges based on claims that it legislated "disparate treatment of parties in state courts based on the parties' race" (B. J. Jones 1995, 8). The failure of these challenges is largely because courts have found that the classification "Indian child" is "not based upon race but upon the unique legal status of Indians and the political relationship between the quasi-sovereign tribes and the federal government" (Myers 1981, 53; Hager and Law 1997, I–7). In other words, for the purposes of the act, an "Indian child" is any child who is potentially a member of any federally recognized Indian tribe—a designation that varies from tribe to tribe but has a legal and political rather than a purely biological basis.

The ICWA is far from being fully implemented, especially in urban areas (largely because of inadequate resources and expertise), and it continues to be challenged in state and federal courts, the federal legislature, and the court of public opinion. A handbook published by the American Bar Association notes that "the custodial fight between biological parents as opposed to psychological parents is a common thread woven through many of the ICWA cases involving adoption and foster placement" (B. J. Jones 1995, viii). Such disputes occur in a small minority of cases, generally in voluntary adoptions that are completed without involvement of the tribe in question (either due to negligence, misrepresentation, or because the child had not been identified as a tribal member or potential member). But these rare cases, which pit a tribe's interest in a child against the emotional bond between the child and its adoptive parents, are most prominent in public discourse and in the developing case law (Metteer 1996; Monsivais 1997; Philips 1997; Myers, Thorington, and Myers 1998).

Contested Kinship in Kingsolver's *Pigs in Heaven* and in the Courts

In *Pigs in Heaven* Barbara Kingsolver imagines a fictional dispute of this kind, one based on extensive research into the intent, interpretation, and implementation of the Indian Child Welfare Act. Kingsolver has described *Pigs in Heaven* as an exploration of the "tension between individualism and community" through a reexamination of the relationship between Taylor and her adopted daughter Turtle, the two central characters of a previous novel, *The Bean Trees* (1988). Realizing she "hadn't even touched on the political ramifications of taking a Cherokee baby away from her tribe," Kingsolver "felt an obligation to pick up those characters and address that part of the story" (Fleischner 1994, 14–15). As we have seen in the case of *Indian Killer*, extra-tribal adoption offers a productive context for the exploration of the construction, contestation, and negotiation of individual and social identities as well as individual and collective rights. Indeed, Kingsolver's original neglect of the impact of Turtle's loss to her Cherokee family and tribe is itself indicative of the individualistic assumptions underlying extra-tribal adoption. Also indicative of underlying hegemonic assumptions is Kingsolver's characterization of Turtle in *The Bean Trees* as an abused orphan left in Taylor's car by her maternal aunt. This plus the abrasive nature of the Cherokee lawyer Annawake Fourkiller, who characterizes herself as a "hawk" and seeks to restore Turtle to tribal control, reproduces the hegemonic "structure of feeling" (Williams 1977) in which the bond between adoptive parent and child is far more emotionally compelling than any tribal interest in the child.

The deck is completely stacked against a tribally based interpretation of the best interests of the Indian child until the reader becomes familiar with Annawake Fourkiller's own loss of a twin brother to adoption and, eventually, with the many tragedies suffered by Turtle's Cherokee grandfather, Cash. Kingsolver has said she conceived of Cash after an attorney whose practice is devoted to

ICWA cases pointed out "that no child would simply vanish from a tribe without leaving a hole. There would be someone there who needed her back" (Fleischner 1994, 15). Kingsolver has Fourkiller use similar words in trying to convince her Cherokee boss, Franklin, that she should pursue the case. "Don't you think there's a hole in somebody's heart because that child is gone? Did you ever hear about a Cherokee child that nobody cared about?" Franklin replies, "But somebody cares about her now, too. That mother who found her." He adds, "No matter what her story is, a lot of hearts are involved" (Kingsolver 1993, 66–67).

As the story proceeds, Annawake Fourkiller learns to appreciate the strength of Taylor and Turtle's attachment to each other, while Taylor comes to understand the importance of Turtle and her grandfather to each other. In exploring Taylor's and Fourkiller's learning curve, Kingsolver educates her readers in the experiences and perspectives underlying the ICWA, as well as its amenability to flexible and humane application in tribal courts. In the kind of magical ending possible in fiction, Turtle's two families are blended through the marriage of Cash to Taylor's mother.

Sherman Alexie has criticized Kingsolver, a non-Indian, for writing on Indian themes (Egan 1998), and his dark treatment of extra-tribal adoption might be read as a response to hers. But I would argue that the issue of extra-tribal adoption is not solely an Indian theme but a transcultural one that, like the captivity of Eunice Williams, benefits from multiple tellings. *Indian Killer* is a tale of the kind of estrangement that ICWA was enacted to prevent, just as *Pigs in Heaven* imagines the kind of reconciliation that the sensitive implementation of the act can effect. Several centuries of extra-tribal adoption and two decades under the Indian Child Welfare Act have generated a host of stories that are only beginning to be told. Alexie's and Kingsolver's novels are valuable not only as works of fiction but also as indications of the rich narratives of captivity, loss, regeneration, and reconciliation that further historical and ethnographic studies of extra-tribal adoption are likely to reveal.

Bibliographic Note

The text of the Indian Child Welfare Act is posted on the National Indian Child Welfare Association's Web site (www.nicwa.org/policy), which also tracks current political developments in this area. Recent assessments of the ICWA have been published by Jones, Tilden, and Gaines-Stoner (2008); Simon and Hernandez (2008); Fletcher, Singel, and Fort (2009); Lorillard (2009); Atwood (2010); and Strong (2005), which includes a fuller discussion of the legal context of the ICWA.

In 2008, Canada established a Truth and Reconciliation Commission to investigate the abuse of children in residential boarding schools; for current developments, see the commission's Web site (www.trc.ca/Web sites/ trcinstitution). See also Regan, *Unsettling the Settler Within* (2010); and CBC Radio, "Stolen Children: Truth and Reconciliation" (www.cbc.ca/news/ background/truth-reconciliation). A recent article by A. Simpson (2009) speculates on the impact of Eunice Williams's adoption on Canadian laws regarding Indian and non-Indian status.

For a variety of perspectives on transnational and interracial adoption, see Kennedy, *Interracial Intimacies* (2003); Volkman, *Cultures of Transnational Adoption* (2005); Howell, *The Kinning of Foreigners* (2006); and Gailey, *Blue-Ribbon Babies and Labors of Love* (2010). For boarding school narratives, see Lomawaima, *They Called It Prairie Light* (1994); Adams, *Education for Extinction* (1995); Child, *Boarding School Seasons* (1998); and Trafzer, Keller, and Sisquoc, *Boarding School Blues* (2006). Silko's *Gardens in the Dunes* (1999) is a compelling fictional account of an Indian child's experiences in a California boarding school and in foster care.

Melanson's *Looking for Lost Bird* (1999) offers the personal account of an adopted Jewish woman who discovers that she was stolen from her Navajo family in 1953, shortly after her birth. Like *Indian Killer, Pigs in Heaven,* and *Gardens in the Dunes,* this is a counter-hegemonic captivity tale. So, too, is *The Return of Navajo Boy* (2000), a powerful documentary film about the repatriation of John Wayne Cly, an adopted Navajo infant grown to adulthood.

CHAPTER SEVEN
ON CAPTIVITY AS DIGITAL SPECTACLE

The most prominent and widely circulated visual images from the US wars in Afghanistan and Iraq are, without a doubt, the notorious photographs of the torture of prisoners taken by American soldiers at Saddam Hussein's former prison, Abu Ghraib. One in particular has circulated globally as an icon of the war: the photograph of the hooded prisoner on a box with electrical wires dangling from his outstretched arms. Also instantly recognizable is the photograph of US soldier Lynndie England gloating over a prone male prisoner on a leash. These two images join a constellation of other horrifying images of captivity from the terror-filled "war on terror": footage of the execution of American reporter Daniel Pearl in Pakistan; a photograph of the bound, blindfolded, and naked John Walker Lindh, nicknamed "the American Taliban"; footage of British hostage Margaret Hassan, the humanitarian worker in Iraq, pleading for her life; footage of shackled, manacled, and masked "detainees" being transported to the cage-like prison in the US base at Guantánamo; footage of the bodies of captured American contractors hanging from a bridge in Fallujah, Iraq; footage of Saddam Hussein in captivity, on trial, at his execution by hanging, and deceased.

These and other representations of captivity, torture, and execution have been produced and circulated in various ways. Some were produced by journalists embedded with US forces. Video images of Daniel Pearl, Margaret Hassan, and the American contractors were distributed by their captors. The Guantánamo photos were released by the Department of Defense. The Abu Ghraib photos were taken by soldiers and contractors who circulated them surreptitiously through the Internet before they were revealed to superiors and reproduced through mass media. Once circulated, the images have, of course, taken on a life of their own—as evidence, propaganda, and pornography (Andén-Papadopoulos 2008).

The ethical dimensions of viewing and circulating contemporary images of captivity, torture, and execution have received thoughtful consideration by Susan Sontag (2004), Judith Butler (2004), and others. Regarding Abu Ghraib, Sontag insists that "the photographs are us" because they reveal not an aberration, but "the increasing acceptance of brutality in American life." She writes that "the horror of what is shown in the photographs cannot be separated from the horror that the photographs were taken—with the perpetrators posing, gloating, over their helpless captives." Looking at the Abu Ghraib photos, she is reminded of lynching photos from the US South, "souvenirs of a collective action whose participants felt perfectly justified in what they had done."

Judith Butler (2004) reflects on the beheading of Daniel Pearl, the journalist captured by Al Qaeda in 2002, in the context of a meditation on violence and grieving in the post-9/11 world. "Who counts as human? Whose lives count as lives? And, finally, *What makes for a grievable life?*" she asks (20). Butler contrasts "the nameless Afghans obliterated by United States and European violence" with the *Wall Street Journal* reporter. "Indeed, Daniel Pearl, 'Danny' Pearl, is so familiar to me: he could be my brother or my cousin; he is so easily humanized; he fits the frame, his name has my father's name in it. His last name contains my Yiddish name" (37). She suggests that we have constructed the human in such a way that less familiar lives are less grievable, less acknowledged as a loss.

For both Butler and Sontag, contemporary images of captivity reveal the process of dehumanization and the limits of empathy. How appropriate, then, that these images translate into new media a set of visual tropes—a technology of otherness (Golding 1997)—already familiar from the literature and monuments of settler colonialism. To be sure, the digital production and circulation of these terrible representations set today's representational practices apart from the captivity images of previous eras. In what, following Benjamin (1969) and Debord (1995), we might call "the age of digital spectacle," the means of producing visual images is much more widely dispersed and their circulation considerably broader and swifter than ever before. Nevertheless, it is revealing to view contemporary visual representations of captivity against the background of earlier images of captivity and torture.

In *Captives,* an influential book on British captivity narratives from 1600 to 1850, historian Linda Colley (2002) has offered a reappraisal of the British empire that emphasizes the vulnerabilities and anxieties of imperialism. In British and Anglo-American captivity narratives these vulnerabilities and anxieties are personified by the British colonists and soldiers taken captive in three regions of the empire: North America, North Africa, and India and Afghanistan. Colley's analysis centers on how captivity was central to the British experience and understanding of empire, personalizing overseas events and investing national prestige in the recovery of captives—and, often, in military acts of vengeance against their captors.

Colley argues persuasively that a "culture of captivity" grounded in the Protestant tradition of redemption through suffering was a significant force across the British Empire, not only in North America. As in the North American colonies discussed in Chapter 5, this culture of captivity centers on the figure of a vulnerable British subject whose faith, civility, and national allegiance is tested by captivity among others viewed as savage heathens or brutal infidels. The captive's vulnerability and shame are those of the nation, and the rescue of the captive and subsequent acts of vengeance against the captors are figured as acts of Divine Providence. The British colonial culture of captivity, in short, justifies imperial dominance through representing its violation and restoration; furthermore, this culture of captivity often gains its ideological power through figuring the captive as a vulnerable woman or child who requires rescue by a paternalistic force.

In Chapter 5 we considered this "culture of captivity" as a selective tradition, following Raymond Williams (1977) in recognizing a field of captivity imagery in which particular representations of captivity receive official support while other representations are displaced, distorted, or suppressed. "Tradition is in practice the most evident expression of the dominant and hegemonic pressures and limits," Williams insists, referring to the ways in which the dominant culture asserts positive and negative power over individuals and groups. For him, tradition "is always more than an inert historicized segment; indeed it is the most powerful practical means of incorporation" (115). As a forceful means of social incorporation, then, selective traditions define and shape collective selves (those with whom we identify) and collective others (those whom we view as monstrous, irrational, inhuman). Given the role of selective traditions in social incorporation, it is not surprising to see resonances between the colonial and frontier culture of captivity on the one hand, and the horrifying practices and images emerging from the "global war on terror" on the other.

As we have seen in Figures 7–9, the hegemonic visual representation of captivity features a British or Anglo-American captive cowering under the tomahawk of a Native American warrior. The captive might be John Smith, about to be rescued from execution by the love of Pocahontas, or Jane McCrea, the tragic Tory heroine of John Vanderlyn's famous painting of 1804. Or the captive might be the frontier mother protecting her infant, as depicted in Horatio Greenough's *The Rescue*. In Greenough's representation of the nation's foundational fiction, the warrior's tomahawk is restrained by the hand of a towering male figure in classical garb—clearly the representation of Empire. Here Empire is doubled, with her vulnerability represented by the female captive, and the inevitability of a rightful victory represented by the male redeemer.

The US government and the tightly controlled US media offered up just such a hegemonic representation of captivity in the early days of the invasion of Iraq. The live action footage of Private Jessica Lynch's rescue from captivity by US Special Forces was originally presented as a triumph of US military force after the shock and embarrassment of Lynch's capture and the death of other members of her company. Only after critical examination by independent journalists was it acknowledged that in fact an Iraqi physician disclosed to the US military Lynch's location in an Iraqi hospital, which facilitated the rescue. In contrast to the media circus surrounding Lynch's rescue—which involved embedded television journalists accompanying the rescue party—the more nuanced print stories received relatively little attention. The government and media collaborated on a captivity story modeled on the familiar hegemonic image, with clear lines drawn between a vulnerable captive, her brutal captors, and her righteous rescuers (Kumar 2004). An Iraqi rescuer muddied the picture. As we have seen (Chapter 5), a similar erasing of ambiguities occurred over three centuries before: whereas the Puritan gentlewoman Mary Rowlandson differentiated among individual Algonquian captors—her kind master, her spiteful mistress—the Rev. Increase Mather sharpened the contrast between the pious, civilized Rowlandson and her captors, taken as a collective personification of savagery and evil.

Other clear attempts by the US government and mainstream media to employ captivity imagery for ideological purposes include images of the capture of John Walker Lindh and the capture of Saddam Hussein. In both cases disheveled, disoriented enemies were visually documented soon after they came under US control; in Saddam's case, the extent of his subordination was imparted through releasing images of his teeth being inspected; in Lindh's case, through images of the prisoner's nakedness and utter helplessness. Lindh, a US citizen, was a more ambiguous enemy than Saddam but fit into the familiar mold of the White renegade. As Richard Slotkin has persuasively demonstrated in *Regeneration through Violence* (1973), in American captivity imagery the male captive, much more than the female captive, is viewed as being prone to rejecting civilization and taking up arms against the nation of his birth. Whereas other captives tend to be viewed with sympathy, if some suspicion, renegades evoke a particular horror—revealing, as they do, the fragility and malleability of cultural identity and allegiance. Anguished media discussions about just how a young American like John Walker Lindh could come to be with the Taliban in Afghanistan (Slifkin 2002) demonstrate forcefully what Colley (2002, 277) has called the "imperial anxieties."

As the Abu Ghraib photos demonstrate, military and governmental efforts to control the representation of captivity have proven to be limited in the age of digital spectacle. Although the US government has attempted to control the public's knowledge of battle zones and prisons through the use of embedded reporters, secrecy, denial, and censorship, images of captivity, torture, and execution have nevertheless circulated widely through the Internet, the Web, television, and print media. Footage of captives pleading for their lives and graphic images of execution and severed body parts compromised the US administration's claims of military control in Afghanistan and Iraq, but these could be more or less controlled ideologically through interpreting them as evidence of the brutality of the enemy. It is the self-inflicted wounds, as it were, of the Abu Ghraib photographs that, in their "graphic concreteness" (Andén-Papadopoulos 2008, 11), most thoroughly escape the efforts of the US government to control the representation and interpretation of the war on terror.

One of the key anxieties of empire in the seventeenth through nineteenth centuries was that engaging in warfare against enemies considered savage and brutal would break down carefully constructed barriers between the presumably civilized Self and the savage Other. Just as imperial anxieties over the vulnerability of colonial and frontier settlers resonate with contemporary anxieties, so too do imperial anxieties over barbarous behavior on the part of Americans in the conduct of warfare. Private Lynndie England has her eighteenth-century counterpart in Hannah Dustan (Chapter 5), who tomahawked the entire Native American family who took her captive and brought in their scalps for a bounty payment. In the same way that Specialist England's assertion of dominance over her captive has been met with revulsion, so too did Hannah Dustan's scalping of her captors come to be seen as excessive and shameful. Unlike male renegades who were celebrated for their adoption of Native American modes of warfare, Dustan came to be seen as an example of the decline of feminine virtues on the colonial frontier. In the same vein, England's abuse and humiliation of captive Iraqis have evoked a greater public aversion than similar actions by her male colleagues and superiors.

As different as their experiences of captivity are—one being a captive, the other a captor—Lynndie England shares with Jessica Lynch the dubious distinction of playing a leading female role in the ongoing selective tradition of captivity. England's willingness to be used as a spectacle of sexualized dominance has made her name and image synonymous with US arrogance, brutality, and lawlessness in much of the world and has put her at the center of a debate over whether abusive torture techniques are systemic or the work of individual "bad apples." To this question, I would only note that Tzvetan Todorov (1984) dedicates *The Conquest of America* "to the memory of a Mayan woman devoured by dogs" (iii). The use of dogs to threaten captives and the treatment of captives as if they were dogs connects the abuses at Abu Ghraib not only to systematic torture techniques but also to centuries of violent colonial expansion in the Americas.

Bibliographic Note

In addition to *Precarious Life* (2004), Butler has considered the issues discussed in this chapter in *Frames of War: When Is Life Grievable?* (2010) and "Sexual Politics, Torture, and Secular Time" (2008). Sontag's argument in "Regarding the Torture of Others" (2004) is developed on a broader canvas in *Regarding the Pain of Others* (2003). Scarry's *The Body in Pain* (1987) and Levinson's *Torture: A Collection* (2006) are other essential readings on torture. For the profoundly disturbing Abu Ghraib photos, see *The New Yorker* Web site (Hersh 2004a) and the *Salon* site (*Salon* staff, 2006). For analyses of the images, see Hersh, *Chain of Command* (2004b) and articles by Apel (2005) and Andén-Papadopoulos (2008). Many of the most brutal and degrading Abu Ghraib photos have not been released to the public.

Part Four
Playing Indian

The American practice of "playing Indian" is an important way in which the American imaginary is perpetuated and transmitted from generation to generation. Whether it takes the form of schoolchildren dressing as Pilgrims and Indians for a Thanksgiving pageant, neighborhood children playing "cowboys and Indians," scouts and campers taking on tribal names, or cheerleaders rooting for the local team of "Indians," American youth are socialized through performances of Indianness. Adults also engage in playing Indian, whether as fans performing the "tomahawk chop" at an Atlanta Braves game, vacationers traversing the wilderness in their Cherokee and Winnebago vehicles, or military leaders conflating the killing of Osama bin Laden with the capture of Geronimo. For both children and adults, definitions and performances of collective identity often involve an appropriation of certain elements of Native American culture—names, symbols, costumes—combined with wild imaginings about indigenous realities.

Typically associated with authenticity, freedom, and equality, performances of Indianness date to the Boston Tea Party, as Philip Deloria (1998) discusses in *Playing Indian*. Such performances and embodiments of Indianness remain today an emotionally powerful form of fashioning collective selves and imagining collective others.

It is the affective power of imitating indigeneity that is of central concern in the chapters gathered together in Part Four. Why is it that Americans persist in performing Indianness when other forms of racial mimesis (blackface, for example) have fallen out of favor? How are these performances related to the need for a "nation of immigrants" to legitimate its occupation of the continent and fashion a common identity? Can the desire for belonging characteristic of these representational practices be mobilized in ways consistent with the dignity of all citizens?

Chapter 8, "Crafting American Selves," considers these questions in the context of youth organizations such as the Boy Scouts and Camp Fire. Based on auto-ethnography as well as historical research, this chapter discusses the practices of racial mimesis and cultural appropriation at the foundation of these century-old organizations, as well as contemporary transformations in these practices. "Animated Indians," Chapter 9, is also based on auto-ethnography. This chapter analyzes forms of play associated with two animated films (and their commercial tie-ins) that encourage children to imaginatively identify with Native American figures: Disney's *Pocahontas* and Paramount's *The Indian in the Cupboard*. Racial mimesis in the sports arena is considered in Chapter 10, "The Mascot Slot." Drawing on Michel-Rolph Trouillot's (1991) notion of the "savage slot" and Aihwa Ong's (1996) concept of cultural citizenship, this chapter argues that, far from honoring indigenous people as is often claimed, pseudo-Indian mascots and logos consign Native Americans to a subordinate form of citizenship.

CHAPTER EIGHT
CRAFTING AMERICAN SELVES

American youth organizations and summer camps are generally distinguished by the use of names, symbols, rituals, and attire derived from Native American traditions. Over the past several decades, many of these programs have been forced to reexamine these representational practices. Stung by charges of racist appropriation, individual programs and national organizations such as the Boy Scouts, the YMCA, and Camp Fire have had to confront their historical and current practices, confronting issues of White privilege and representational authority similar to those raised in the academy with respect to ethnographic research and writing (Chapter 1 and Chapter 11); in the sports and corporate arenas with respect to pseudo-Indian mascots, slogans, logos, and trademarks (Chapter 10); and in museums with respect to the display of sacred objects and human remains (Chapter 11 and Chapter 12). The questioning of institutional prerogatives has met resistance in all of these settings, but the issues have been especially difficult for youth organizations, perhaps because the very subjectivities of generations of Americans have been formed through performing indigeneity in childhood. In an age of multiculturalism, "playing Indian" is no longer what it used to be; at the same time, many involved in youth development programs struggle to find alternative practices with an equivalent symbolic resonance and transformative power.

The "situated knowledge" (Haraway 1991) through which I approach this topic is that of a White, middle-class Camp Fire Girl turned ethnographer (not an altogether unique positionality, I have come to learn). My first attempt to examine the representational practices of Camp Fire took the form of an auto-ethnographic essay that achieved critical distance through irony, a tempting stance indeed when one is writing about earnest White, Black, and Asian girls in buckskin and beads singing about the Great Spirit around a ceremonial camp fire (Strong 2006). Since drafting that first essay some years ago, however, I have been involved in ethnographic research among the volunteers and members of Camp Fire USA, the coeducational successor to Camp Fire Girls, and I find my positioning changing to one of respectful engagement in the difficult process of institutional change.

Given the pervasiveness and significance of scouting and other youth development organizations in the United States, there has been surprisingly little ethnographic or auto-ethnographic research on the Boy Scouts, the Girl Scouts, Camp Fire, and the like. A notable exception is Jay Mechling's (2001) ethnography, *On My Honor: Boy Scouts and the Making of American Youth,* which is based on the author's active participation in scouting since he entered Cub Scouts at the age of eight. Mechling, a lifetime Eagle Scout and a member of the Order of the Arrow, remarks in his introduction that he has sometimes found it difficult to establish "the appropriate critical distance for writing about an institution that is so much a part of me" (xxiv). This is a perceptive and revealing statement. Youth organizations are a powerful site for "crafting" and "fashioning" selves, as Kondo (1990) and Greenblatt (1980) have put it in other contexts, and the auto-ethnographer reflects upon his or her experiences with an instrument, the reflecting self, that has itself been shaped by those experiences. Like many auto-ethnographers, Mechling has sought to achieve critical distance through historical and comparative research, as well as through the theoretical framework that he brings to his study, which involves conceiving of the Boy Scouts of America as an institution for the construction of White masculinity. Mechling boldly analyzes homophobia and misogyny as integral to the aggressive masculinity that the Boy Scouts of America fosters and urges the Scouts to adopt a more androgynous style of masculinity. This is admittedly a tall order, although Mechling's recognition of the distance between the ideology of the national organization and the practices of local troops makes his recommendation somewhat less quixotic than it may initially appear.

On My Honor focuses on challenges to the Boy Scouts of America that fall under the rubric of "the three G's": God, gays, and girls (xviii). The ethnography, however, has little to say about race and racism, apart from identifying the troop in which Mechling conducted ethnographic research as predominantly White and middle class. In particular, Mechling does not consider the role that an embodied knowledge of "Indian lore" plays in the Boy Scouts' construction of White masculinity. Though he notes with regret that his boyhood troop's "use of Indian lore somehow mixed a genuine respect for the Native American with a verbal disrespect for real Indians" (xxiv), this very important insight—which parallels his analysis of misogyny and homophobia—is not developed further. To what extent does an emphasis on authentic "Indian lore" actually generate disrespect for living Native people? Although Mechling discusses the romantic interest in Native American traditions that was central to the life of one of the primary founders of the Boy Scouts, naturalist Ernest Thompson Seton, his treatment of Seton's primary legacy, the Order of the Arrow, is limited to a general description of its initiation ritual: "a full Indian pageant, as one might expect, replete with solemn drama, oaths, and symbols of brotherhood" (242). This unusually thin description is disappointing in an ethnography concerned with the construction of a racialized style of masculinity. Exactly what is it that "one might expect," and why are our expectations taken for granted to this extent?

The implications of performing Indianness in the Boy Scouts are treated more fully in other ethnographic and historical accounts. In an earlier publication, Mechling (1980b) himself discusses the "Koshare Indians," a famous troop of non-Indian Explorer Scouts dedicated to the performance of dances from various tribal traditions. Something of a renegade group, the Koshare Scouts and troops like them resisted the national organization's attempt in the 1930s and 1940s to downplay the role of Indian-derived traditions in the Scouts (Powers 1988). Discussing a fascinating 1953 incident in which a Zuni delegation determined that a set of Koshare-made Shalako masks were authentic and claimed them for Zuni Pueblo, Mechling (1980b) blurs the distinction between the Zuni Shalako dancers and the Koshare Scouts, writing that "culture is *never* authentic" (30). I would have to differ with Mechling on this point: the Zuni emissaries to the Boy Scouts effectively asserted control over their own religious representations by claiming the authenticity of the Koshare-made masks, removing them from the realm of touristic performance and recontextualizing them in a sacred realm. This cultural repatriation rests precisely on the Zunis' successful claim to authority not only over material artifacts but also over the very determination of what constitutes authenticity.

The question of authenticity is addressed rather differently in *The Power of Kiowa Song,* an ethnography by anthropologist Luke Lassiter. Lassiter writes that he originally became interested in the Kiowa through completing the "Indian lore" merit badge, which dates to 1911 and emphasizes knowledge and preservation of "authentic" traditions from the past (Lassiter 1998, 22–29; see also Powers 1988). The young Lassiter's interest deepened as he was initiated into the Order of the Arrow, an honorary association of Boy Scouts and adult Scouters featuring ceremonies that aim to reproduce nineteenth-century Plains tribal traditions. From the Order of the Arrow, Lassiter went on to participate in "intertribal" powwows in which Native Americans, Boy Scouts, and White hobbyists (often former Boy Scouts) danced side by side; still later, he learned to sing Kiowa songs and became a powwow singer. Lassiter's encounter with the living tradition of Kiowa song led him to a critical view of the Boy Scouts' and hobbyists' emphasis on the preservation and timeless authenticity of Indian traditions; at the same time, it was Lassiter's participation in an intertribal powwow that acquainted him with the Kiowa singers who welcomed him into their life and art. In this, Lassiter notes, he is not alone; he knows many White males, including historians and other anthropologists, who followed a similar path through Boy Scouts, the Order of the Arrow, and hobbyist performances to social participation in indigenous communities (Lassiter 1998, 239, n. 4).

Lassiter's personal history of intensive, long-term involvement with Kiowa singers is a counterexample to the disregard for living Native Americans that Mechling observed in his boyhood troop, but no doubt the latter's experience is more typical. How regularly do Boy Scouts form social relationships with contemporary Native Americans through their performances of Indianness, learning thereby the nature of specific tribal traditions and their role in shaping and maintaining indigenous communities? How often do they engage in acts of reciprocity that acknowledge the value of the tribal traditions that have been shared with them? On the other hand, how often do these performances lead Boy Scouts to consider themselves experts on "Indian lore," denigrating contemporary Native Americans as "inauthentic" because they do not follow nineteenth-century practices? To what extent does performing Indianness in the Boy Scouts and other organizations teach young American males to feel entitled to masquerade as "braves," "redskins," and "warriors" in other, less respectful settings? How do performances of Indianness differ in girls' organizations, shaping gendered as well as racialized subjectivities? Finally, to what extent does playing Indian in youth programs perpetuate racist stereotypes and hierarchies, precluding rather than facilitating genuine understanding of contemporary Native American lives?

These are the kinds of questions that are at stake in ethnographic research on the role enactments of Indianness play in the socialization of American youth. Performing otherness may be, as it was for Lassiter, a respectful means of bridging difference and creating empathy. However, when it takes the form of a "racist parody"—as Peter Whiteley (1998, 168) rightly describes a performance by a group of White adult "Smokis" impersonating Hopi Snake Dancers—performing otherness becomes a way of enacting and reinforcing racial differences, entitlements, and hierarchies. Most often, perhaps, respect and empathy coexist with entitlement and hierarchy in an ambiguous mélange that resists simple categorization. In analyzing the cultural roots and effects of various performances of Indianness, scholars clearly need a nuanced theoretical apparatus capable of registering the wide range of ways in which non-Indian Americans have, over time, constituted themselves through imitating Native Americans. We also need a theoretical apparatus that takes into account the ways in which some Native Americans have themselves participated in these practices, pursuing their own agendas despite differences in power and influence. The Native American scholar Philip Deloria offers such a sophisticated theory of racial mimesis in his important history, *Playing Indian* (1998), and this theory is useful for ethnographic research as well.

As Deloria demonstrates, although youth organizations such as the Boy Scouts and Camp Fire Girls date to the 1910s, the performance of Indianness in these organizations perpetuates a form of American identity formation that goes back to colonial times. In youth and fraternal organizations, social and political movements, and public performances extending from the Boston Tea Party to Wild West shows to New Age gatherings to professional sports arenas, White Americans—and sometimes others—have adopted costumes and practices they associate with Indians in order to identify with such generalized indigenous qualities as independence, vigor, bravery, loyalty, spiritual power, and closeness to nature. In *Playing Indian* (1998), Deloria demonstrates how in these practices Americans have employed various *mimetic technologies* to imitate Native Americans in ways that are both *positive* and *negative,* meanwhile construing Indians as both *internal* and *external* to American society (95–127). This typology of mimesis, somewhat reminiscent of Todorov's (1984) typology of otherness in *The Conquest of America* (see Chapter 1), allows Deloria to trace shifts in representational practice across time as well as variations within historical eras. Coupled with an attention to shifts in technologies of reproduction, the typology offers a way to situate the embodiment of Indianness in youth organizations alongside other forms of racial mimesis, including those employed by ethnographers such as Lewis Henry Morgan and Luke Lassiter; naturalists such as Ernest Thompson Seton; and Native American authors, performers, and activists "imitating non-Indian imitations of Indians" for White audiences (123). Ultimately, playing Indian should be compared both to highly stigmatized forms of mimesis such as blackface and more revelatory and empathetic forms such as the dramatic performances of Anna Deveare Smith (Dolan 2005).

Looking Backward

The performance of Indianness in American youth development organizations dates to the birth of these organizations in the Progressive Era (1890–1920), when White reformers were intensely concerned with what they saw as the degeneracy and artificiality of modern American urban culture. Looking for a model for revitalizing American youth and reforming their character, these social reformers turned to Native American cultures, which in the tradition of the "noble savage" had long been represented as a repository of natural virtues (see Chapter 1). Together with White ethnographers, environmentalists, and naturalists, some of the Native Americans known as "Red Progressives" served as sources for the nostalgic, antimodernist practices of the Boy Scouts, Camp Fire Girls, YMCA, and other organizations (not including Girl Scouts, which looked elsewhere for its models) (S. Miller 2007). Like other "invented traditions" (Hobsbawm and Ranger 1983), the performance of Indianness in youth organizations was a hybrid of "traditional" practices and modern anxieties and desires. Because primitivist anxieties and desires centered around boys differed from those centered around girls, Native American practices were assimilated into boys' and girls' organizations in rather different ways.

Foremost among the indigenous consultants to the youth development movement was the Santee Sioux physician, author, and lecturer Charles Eastman (Ohiyesa). In a series of popular autobiographical novels, articles, and lectures addressed to American youth and reformers, Eastman recounted his traditional Santee boyhood. In 1914, the articles were gathered together in a single volume, *Indian Scout Talks: A Guide for Boy Scouts and Camp Fire Girls*. Addressed (despite its title) mainly to boys, *Indian Scout Talks* covers "Indian methods of physical training"; hunting and tracking skills; camp craft and woodcraft; canoeing, archery, and other Indian sports; sign language, picture writing, and storytelling; Indian names, dress, and ceremonies; and "training for service."

In its emphasis on physical training, outdoor skills, and service, Eastman's guide—like the scouting and outdoor education movements as a whole—answered concerns that American civilization was declining, its men becoming overly effeminate and its women retreating from their natural reproductive role. "Race suicide" was a commonly articulated fear among "muscular Christians" such as the evolutionary psychologist and eugenicist G. Stanley Hall. These reformers saw indigenous cultures as a repository of virtuous "primitive" practices that could, in Hall's words, help to make "men more manly and women more womanly" (Putney 2001, 37). Luther Gulick, perhaps the most central figure after Hall in the youth development movement, pursued strikingly different physical agendas for boys and girls, introducing basketball and volleyball into the Y's programs for boys while proscribing competitive sports for girls. Eastman (1974 [1914]) differed on this score, reminding his readers that "contrary to popular opinion, our Indian girls and women are not mere drudges, but true feminine athletes, almost as alert as the men and frequently even more muscular" (106). Based on this precedent, Eastman advocated vigorous physical training for Camp Fire Girls, including water lacrosse and a Native American form of field hockey.

Eastman differed from Hall, Gulick, and some of the other founders of American youth organizations in even more fundamental ways. Reinterpreting the evolutionary civilization/savagery dichotomy—which viewed the stage of savagery as intellectually undeveloped, if physically vigorous—Eastman emphasized that the "school of savagery" was systematic, not haphazard, and produced true public servants (188). "Our Indian 'Boy Scouts' are the immediate and unofficial guardians of our safety," he noted (187), explicitly identifying the Boy Scouts of America with the young male scouts appointed to guard a camp circle on the Plains. He urged Boy Scouts and Camp Fire Girls to model their practices after those of Plains Indians, offering separate ceremonies for boys and girls adapted from Sioux rituals, and suggesting that boys' and girls' honors, names, and pictographic signatures might be based directly on those of the Sioux. In recommending that youth organizations adopt an Indian model, Eastman addressed his contemporaries' concern that urban, industrial society had become harmful and meaningless. "Let us have more of this spirit of the American Indian, the Boy Scout's prototype," the guide ends, "to leaven the brilliant selfishness of our modern civilization!" (190).

In his critique of modern "selfishness," Eastman went far beyond the reformers' concern with physical vigor and moral character, allying himself with more radical critics of the excesses of industrial capitalism. As Frederick Hoxie (2001) writes, in his writings and lectures Eastman was "talking back to civilization" (2). His various publications and public addresses offer unfavorable comparisons between Christianity (as practiced) and Indian spirituality, between American economic inequality and Indian generosity, between American material and intellectual development and Indian spiritual values, and between American democratic ideals and the reality of Indian disenfranchisement (75–79, 131–133). In offering Plains Indian practices as a "prototype" for those of the Boy Scouts and, to a lesser extent, the Camp Fire Girls, Eastman was engaged in an ambitious attempt to reform not just American character, but American democracy itself. As in his writings and public lectures, in working with youth development organizations Eastman hoped to increase understanding of indigenous traditions in order to create a more salutary environment for Native people.

On one level Eastman's involvement in Boy Scouts and Camp Fire Girls was an accommodation to the dominant culture that legitimized these organizations' appropriation of elements of Sioux culture. On the other hand, his work shaping these organizations—which included such performances of indigeneity as donning a headdress and demonstrating archery—must be seen as a form of resistance. The same is true for the Dakota linguist and folklorist Ella Deloria, who was closely involved with a local Camp Fire group in New York when she was working with Franz Boas at Columbia University. As Philip Deloria (1998) has emphasized, the racial mimesis of American youth organizations should be understood as neither invented traditions nor cultural appropriations but rather as hybrid traditions resting equally on appropriation and invention.

Of course, no treatment of hybrid cultural forms can ignore asymmetries of power (Kapchan and Strong 1999, 239–253). As important as Eastman's *Indian Scout Talks* and his personal example were in the formation of the Boy Scouts and Camp Fire Girls, two White reformers had considerably more influence: Ernest

Thompson Seton and Luther Gulick. Together with their wives, Grace Gallatin Seton and Charlotte Vetter Gulick, these two men were responsible for founding or shaping an astoundingly large number of organizations and movements in the Progressive Era: the worldwide Woodcraft League, Boy Scouts of America, Brownies, and Cub Scouts in Seton's case; and the Playground Association, YMCA, American Folk Dance Society, and Camp Fire Girls in Gulick's. These organizations all share a commitment to learning through play, which Gulick propounded in a 1920 monograph, *A Philosophy of Play*. Gulick and Seton also imbued these organizations, especially the Camp Fire Girls and the Order of the Arrow, with their strong interest in aesthetic and poetic expression, especially as represented in the indigenous traditions of the Plains.

A Canadian naturalist, illustrator, and amateur ethnologist, Ernest Thompson Seton created the Woodcraft Indians in 1901. Initially aimed at building character in antisocial young men, by 1915 the Woodcraft movement included "tribes" of all ages and both sexes; it ultimately extended to Canada as well as many European countries. Seton's manual, *The Birchbark Rolls of the Woodcraft Indians*, which appeared in a new edition almost every year between 1903 and 1930, influenced the rituals of the Boy Scouts and Camp Fire Girls as well as the Woodcraft Indians. Seton also published the popular *Two Little Savages* (1903), a woodcraft manual in the form of an illustrated autobiographical novel that, like Hall's evolutionary psychology, conflated the "savagery" of children and Indians. Seton's *Sign Talk* (1918), the product of extensive research on the syntax and vocabulary of Plains sign languages, was a major source for the symbolism used in the Boy Scout and Camp Fire movements as well as the Woodcraft Indians.

Like Charles Eastman, Seton (1937) was highly critical of industrial capitalism and urban life. He praised the heroism, communal ownership, physique, spirituality, and tribal orientation of Native Americans, observing that "The Indian was a socialist in the best and literal meaning of the word" (31). Seton's political beliefs and antimilitarism brought him into conflict with others in the Boy Scouts who wished to model the American organization after the military (as Lord Baden-Powell had done in England) or after Daniel Boone and other frontiersmen (the preference of another founder, Daniel Beard). The military model prevailed, and Seton, who chaired the organization's founding committee in 1910, resigned five years later. He subsequently devoted his attention to the Woodcraft movement, which influenced countless summer camps as well as the Order of the Arrow. This honorary brotherhood, which originated in a Philadelphia troop in 1915, was fully incorporated into the national organization in 1948. Through the Order of the Arrow, with its Indian-derived names, symbolism, and performances, Seton's antimodernist approach to youth development has remained an important force in the Boy Scouts.

Seton's colleague Luther Gulick was more conventional in his views and a central member of G. Stanley Hall's circle of evolutionary social reformers. A physician who belonged to a well-known Congregational missionary family, Gulick began working as a physical education specialist for the YMCA in 1887, when that organization was in a period of rapid growth. Gulick, who exhibited a talent for what is today called "branding," was responsible for developing the YMCA's slogan, "Body, Mind, Spirit," and its official seal, an inverted red triangle. After leaving the Y to serve as the physical education director for the New York City public schools, Gulick cofounded the Playground Association of America, which worked to develop public playgrounds in urban areas and stressed the "wholesome use of leisure time" (Putney 1991, 36)—a phrase of Gulick's that captures his preoccupations in a nutshell.

The extended Gulick family—including Luther's sister-in-law, Mrs. E. L. Gulick, and her brother, Dr. C. H. Farnsworth—were pioneers in camping for girls, founding the first three American girls' camps in the first decade of the twentieth century (some thirty years after the first camps for boys). Luther's wife Charlotte was a particularly important leader in this movement, serving as the first president of the National Association of Directors of Girls' Camps. Sebago-Wohelo, the experimental summer camp in Maine operated by Luther and Charlotte Gulick, was the prototype for many of the appropriated traditions of the Camp Fire Girls. Known to Camp Fire Girls by the Arapaho name Hiiteni (Arapaho for "abundant life"), Charlotte was responsible for inventing many of the organization's traditions. She coined the Camp Fire watchword, "Wo-He-Lo" (an acronym for Work, Health, Love); designed many of its hybrid rituals; and published manuals to help Camp Fire Girls choose their "Indian" names and express the names in a pictorial "symbolgram" (see Figure 10). In Camp Fire publications she modeled the ceremonial gown and beaded headband that girls were encouraged to make in order to express their character and mark their achievements. It is largely through Charlotte Gulick's efforts that Camp Fire, quite literally, offered American girls a gender-specific form of both "crafting" and "fashioning" themselves.

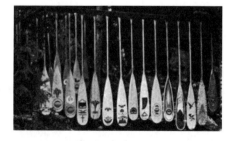

Figure 10. Decorated canoe paddles, captioned "Every Camp fire maiden has a symbol of her own." Adapted from *Sebago-Wohelo Camp Fire Girls* (Rogers 1915).

Camp Fire Girls was founded in 1912, two years after the Boy Scouts and a few months before the Girl Scouts, which initially had less institutional backing. At the time Camp Fire was founded, Luther Gulick was on leave from his position as a "social engineer" and head of the Department of Child Hygiene at the Russell Sage Foundation. Known in Camp Fire by his "Indian" name Timanous (which he translated as "guiding spirit"), Gulick served as the movement's spokesman, articulating an antimodernist view of urban industrial society and new gender roles. Like many of his contemporaries, Gulick deplored the alienation and disenchantment of modern life, particularly in the realm of the workplace, and he worried that the increased employment of women and girls outside the home was destroying the social, emotional, and aesthetic fabric of life. In designing Camp Fire Girls he sought a way, as he put it, to "brush away from the everyday activities of the world the dull gray with which the oil and smoke of this machine age have covered them, to reveal the beauty, romance and adventure of all the common things of life; [to] waken an appreciation of the wonders going on all about us that so many of us fail to see" (Buckler, Fiedler, and Allen 1961, 39). Through ceremonies and other symbolic activities, Gulick hoped to offer American girls a healthy, appealing, and aesthetically satisfying way of life. The emphasis on aesthetics ("seeking beauty," as the Camp Fire Law puts it) was in accord with Gulick's view of the nature of womanhood, and this would come to distinguish Camp Fire from the Boy Scouts and other youth organizations.

Gulick insisted that because of the inherent differences between "womanly" and "manly" virtues and pursuits, it would be "fundamentally evil" for an organization for girls to model itself on the Boy Scouts (Buckler, Fiedler, and Allen 1961, 22). In addition to the Sebago-Wohelo summer camp, Gulick used as a prototype a small group in Vermont already known as the Camp Fire Girls. The original Camp Fire Girls were the creation of William Chauncey Langdon—a poet and consultant for Gulick's department at the Russell Sage Foundation— who had been charged with developing a pageant for the 150th anniversary of the town of Thetford, Vermont. Invented traditions inspired by indigenous rituals and symbols were central to the original Camp Fire Girls, and Ernest Thompson Seton and his first wife, Grace Gallatin Seton, played an important role in their design, just as they did for Sebago-Wohelo. For example, Langdon patterned the ranks through which a girl progresses—Wood Gatherer, Fire Maker, and Torch Bearer—after similar ranks among the Woodcraft "tribes." Likewise, buckskin ceremonial gowns, honor beads, and beaded headbands appeared among Seton's Woodcraft Girls before becoming the distinctive, self-fashioned attire of the Camp Fire Girls.

Despite Gulick's Christian missionary roots, Camp Fire Girls was designed as a nonsectarian organization, and its spirituality reflected its founders' conception of Native American religion. Camp Fire ritual texts make reference to the Great Spirit, sometimes using the Siouan form, Wakonda. This was part of Gulick's attempt to create an organization grounded in universal principles that would have "widespread appeal" (Putney 2001, 158). As one member of the founding circle, John Collier, wrote, Camp Fire sought to help the modern girl "find her own soul and then consciously to enlist that soul in group activity and world service" (Buckler, Fiedler, and Allen 1961, 44). Following G. Stanley Hall's notion that the stages of an individual's life recapitulate human evolutionary history—a theory articulated in the influential 1904 text in which Hall introduced the concept of adolescence—Collier maintained that a "living contact with Indian symbolism and Indian culture" was particularly instrumental in the girl's quest for her soul because it provided "contact with universal life—with life at its fountain source of world-old, world-wide and world-foreseeing adolescent consciousness" (43). Put in more prosaic terms, Collier and other members of the Gulicks' circle considered Native American symbolism particularly appropriate for adolescent girls because they saw indigenous American cultures as themselves at a feminine, adolescent stage of human development—one they associated with creative expression and the discovery of one's authentic nature. As an authentically American form of creativity, indigenous cultural forms could nourish and Americanize adolescent girls, whatever their background—so the thinking went.

Collier himself might be taken as an example of the transformative power of contact with Native American symbolism as mediated through the Camp Fire Girls. First exposed to Native American culture at the Gulick household, Collier became a leader in the movement to reform US Indian policy, eventually launching the "Indian New Deal" as commissioner of Indian Affairs under Franklin D. Roosevelt. In this role he moved the US government away from assimilation policies and toward policies of cultural tolerance and tribal self-determination. Two decades prior to this, Collier wrote one of Camp Fire's central poetic texts, the "Fire Maker's Desire." This text, which a girl recites when she attains the rank of Fire Maker, is an excellent example of Camp Fire's use of metaphor in shaping girls' desires. "As fuel is brought to the fire," she states,

So I purpose to bring
My strength
My ambition
My heart's desire
My joy
And my sorrow
To the fire
Of humankind;
For I will tend
As my fathers have tended

And my fathers' fathers
Since time began
The fire that is called
The love of man for man
The love of man for God. (Camp Fire Girls 1914)

The irony of a girl's rite of passage tying her to her fathers' fathers rather than to a line of women alerts us to the way in which fire symbolism in Camp Fire Girls reinforced patriarchal gender roles. The ceremonial "council fires" of the Camp Fire organization were grounded in a common association in Anglo-American culture between the circle around the campfire and the transfer of sacred or esoteric knowledge (Mechling 1980a; Hinsley 1989). In proposing fire as the Camp Fire Girls' central symbol, however, Luther Gulick reinterpreted the meaning of the fire to fit his gender ideology. "The bearing and rearing of children has always been the first duty of most women," he stated at a 1911 organizational meeting, "and that must always continue to be. This involves service, constant service, self-forgetfulness and always service." Accordingly, Gulick proposed that "the domestic fire—not the wild fire" should be the symbol of Camp Fire, "and that from the first the very meaning of the fire be explained to her, in poetry and the dance" (Buckler, Fiedler, and Allen 1961, 22). In line with this, in Collier's "Fire Maker's Desire" the Camp Fire Girl announces her eagerness to sacrifice herself, like fuel, to the fire of humankind, thus linking herself to all those who, since the beginning, have devoted themselves to tending the flames of community and spiritual love. The pledge evokes in poetic imagery what Gulick described in less mystifying terms as "service, constant service, self-forgetfulness and always service."

During the ritual in which a girl attained the rank of Fire Maker, she was given a bracelet inscribed with the watchword "Wo-He-Lo." The beauty of the bracelet and other Camp Fire honors was as strategic as the use of fire. In the 1911 organizational meeting, following his suggestion that fire be the central symbol of Camp Fire Girls, Gulick continued, "My second point is: show how extensively it is true that beauty has been in the custody of women. Teach the old folk lore, the old folk dances, the old customs, sometimes dancing and singing by night about a fire—have that combined effect upon the senses, and you can make people over in the process and do it pretty quickly" (Buckler, Fiedler, and Allen 1961, 23). Here Gulick the social engineer was speaking in terms that today appear blatantly Foucauldian: employing all the senses, Camp Fire traditions enlisted girls in their own disciplined self-making, using ancient cultural forms to fashion antimodern gendered subjects.

Perhaps Gulick thought that the bourgeois self could be "made over" particularly easily, for he advocated as the next step that the adult Camp Fire "guardian" teach the initiate "the possibility of leading other girls … the factory girls, for instance, the city girls, the mill girls, the country girls" (Buckler, Fiedler, and Allen 1961, 23). All of these girls, Gulick thought, could be instructed and unified through Camp Fire's distinctive practices—and, notably, immigrant girls could be Americanized. In centering Camp Fire around a form of symbolism associated with the nation's history, Gulick and his associates participated in a common form of nationalism that largely excluded the Native American present even while appropriating the Native past (J. O'Brien 2006). The exclusion of contemporary Native Americans proved to be considerably more extreme in Camp Fire than in the Boy Scouts. Though indigenous progressives such as Charles Eastman and Ella Deloria were personally involved with Camp Fire in its early years, as the organization developed, the members' knowledge of indigenous cultures was almost completely mediated through Camp Fire's own generalized traditions. In contrast to common practices in the Order of the Arrow, Camp Fire Girls did not generally participate in powwows, Camp Fire attire did not aspire to tribal specificity, and Camp Fire councils did not regularly adapt the organization's traditions to the region in which they lived. Today, in fact, the organization views its hybrid rituals and symbols as Camp Fire's heritage and makes no claim to ethnographic authenticity (Wallace and Kirby 1996, preface).

Looking Forward

Camp Fire traditions were remarkably stable for the first half century of the organization's existence. When I was a Camp Fire Girl in the 1960s, I participated in practices very similar to those designed by the Gulicks and their circle. My Camp Fire friends and I fashioned ourselves as Indian princesses: we chose or invented "Indian names," designed symbolgrams to visually express those names, sewed our own fringed ceremonial gowns, made beaded headdresses on a handmade loom, and decorated our gowns with strings of colored beads representing our achievements. We participated in ceremonies in which we lit candles using the Wo-He-Lo ritual designed by Charlotte Gulick, and sang a processional in which "Great Wakonda watches o'er." By that time the Camp Fire Law had been altered to include "Worship God" as its first line (an innovation of the 1950s), but otherwise we recited the traditional version: "Give Service, Pursue Knowledge, Be Trustworthy, Be Healthy, Glorify Work, Be Happy."

Nevertheless, as Mechling noted for the Boy Scouts, there was some slippage between Camp Fire traditions and our local practices. I am certain that I did not think of the camp fire as a "domestic fire," as Luther Gulick would have it. Though I remember spending a fair amount of time beading, sewing, and making beeswax candles for the Wo-He-Lo ceremony, it was spending time with my friends and camping in the Colorado mountains that kept me in Camp Fire. The hybrid practices of Camp Fire Girls, which from the beginning embodied contradictory motivations and agendas, lent themselves well to reinterpretation by new generations of girls. My generation was interested in civil rights and women's rights, and some of the traditions of Camp Fire began to be vaguely uncomfortable. The national organization came to share this discomfort: by the 1980s Camp Fire had refashioned itself as a coeducational organization and de-emphasized the indigenous roots of its symbolism. Today's organization, known as Camp Fire USA, is open to youth of both genders regardless of their sexual orientation and spiritual beliefs—policies that differentiate Camp Fire from both the Boy Scouts and the Girl Scouts. Youth are encouraged to draw on their own cultural heritage for their Camp Fire names, pictorial symbols, and ritual attire.

In some ways, then, the contemporary organization has moved sharply away from the central preoccupations of its founding circle. "Worship God" signals a more conventional approach to religion than does an invocation of the Great Spirit. The emphasis on women's reproductive role and re-enchanting domestic life has been replaced by a stress on gender equality and a recognition of diversity in sexual orientation. Always a multiracial organization (although local practices have been affected by housing and schooling patterns), Camp Fire now relies explicitly on a multicultural ideology (which does not mean that all clubs are multicultural; in fact, some are explicitly aimed at members of particular ethnic groups) (Strong and Posner 2010). Finally, in a transformation that echoes Max Weber's (1968) notion of "the routinization of charisma," the romantic primitivism of the founders has, to a large extent, given way to modern bureaucratic forms of organization and management.

It is not particularly surprising to find such changes in an organization that has spanned almost a century. But the movement toward coeducational programs and away from Indian-derived symbolism has posed a significant challenge to Camp Fire. Alumni and the public identify with previous incarnations of Camp Fire—with, for example, the cuteness of the now-retired Bluebirds; the romance of "Indian lore"; and the catchy invitation to "sing around the camp fire, join the Camp Fire girls." In some local councils there remains an attachment to the Indian-derived symbols and rituals, despite an official movement to multiculturalism. At the same time, the antimodernist orientation of Camp Fire continues to speak to young people and families concerned with issues that remain as problematic in the early twenty-first century as they were a century ago: alienation from nature, the social impact of technology, the routinizing of labor, the attenuation of ties to family and community, and controversies regarding gender roles and immigration. In adapting antimodernist practices to meet the challenges of postmodern, postindustrial society, Camp Fire—like other American youth organizations dating to the early twentieth century—is engaged in cultural work at least as complex as that taken on by the founding generation.

Bibliographic Note

Mimesis in performance is discussed in P. Deloria's *Playing Indian* (1998) and Trachtenberg's *Shades of Hiawatha: Staging Indians, Making Americans* (2004). Ziff and Rao's *Borrowed Power* (1997) offers a theory and numerous case studies of cultural appropriation; see also Root, *Cannibal Culture* (1995); Meyer and Royer, *Selling the Indian* (2001); and Berman, "Cultural Appropriation" (2004). Lears, *No Place of Grace* (1981), and Orvell, *The Real Thing* (1989), discuss antimodernism and the concern with authenticity at the time that American youth organizations were founded. Foucault's notion of disciplinary practices is developed in his *History of Sexuality* (1978) and *Discipline and Punish* (1979); for ethnographic applications, see Kondo's *Crafting Selves* (1990) and Lomawaima's "Domesticity in the Federal Indian Schools" (1993), among others. For American youth organizations, see Putney's *Muscular Christianity: Manhood and Sports in Protestant America* (2001) and S. Miller's *Growing Girls: The Natural Origins of Girls' Organizations in America* (2007), in addition to the studies by P. Deloria (1998) and Mechling (2001) discussed extensively in this chapter.

CHAPTER NINE
ANIMATED INDIANS

But if you walk the footsteps of a stranger
You'll learn things you never knew you never knew.
                    —*Pocahontas, in "Colors of the Wind"*

Hollywood has long taken a leading role in shaping the American tradition of "playing Indian." This chapter considers how this tradition is mobilized in two family films released close to the turn of the twenty-first century: Disney's heavily marketed animated film, *Pocahontas* (1995), and the 1995 Columbia/Paramount adaptation of Lynne Reid Banks's popular 1981 children's novel, *The Indian in the Cupboard.* Invoking Donna Haraway's (1991) useful concept once again, I would place my "situated knowledge" of these films and their associated playthings at the intersection of my scholarly interest in representational practices; my childhood experiences of "playing Indian" at school, at summer camp, and in Camp Fire Girls (see Chapter 8); and my experiences raising two daughters (ages seven and ten when the films were released). In other words, this is what Kathleen Stewart (1991) would call a "contaminated" critique, one that is complexly influenced by my participation in the complex cultural phenomena that it analyzes. I write as a pianist who played "Colors of the Wind" (1995), the theme song from *Pocahontas,* so often for my daughters' school choir that it runs unbidden through my mind (see Figure 11). I write as a parent who has spent much of a weekend "playing Indian" on CD-ROM, learning from my younger daughter, Tina, how to "earn symbols" for a computer-generated wampum belt so that we could be inducted as "Friends of the Iroquois." Above all, I write as

Figure 11. The author and her daughters prepare for a performance of "Colors of the Wind" from Disney's *Pocahontas*. Photo © 1997 by Suzanne McEndree.

a cultural critic whose views are influenced both by the insights of my daughters and by my hopes for their generation.

The Miniature: *The Indian in the Cupboard*

As I sit at my computer composing this chapter, a three-inch plastic figurine stands beside the monitor (see Figure 12). He wears a scalp lock, yellow leggings and breechcloth, a yellow knife sheath, and a yellow pouch. Next to him is the case for our videocassette of *The Indian in the Cupboard*, with the cover reversed, as directed, so that the case simulates a weathered wooden cabinet. Beside the cabinet is a plastic skeleton key, almost as large as the figurine, which can be used to open the cabinet. Although it is possible to purchase the figurine and key independently, as well as miniatures of other characters in the film, ours were packaged with the video.

Equipped with the figurine, the cabinet, and the key, I am able to imitate Omri, the nine-year-old American boy whose coming-of-age story is told in the film. Omri, like his English namesake in the novel series (Banks 1981), is given an Indian figurine that comes to life when locked inside a magical cabinet. My figurine does not come to life but nevertheless mocks me as it stands by my computer, underscoring my embeddedness in several traditions—European and Anglo-American, popular and scholarly—that have locked miniature Indians in cabinets, be they late-Renaissance wonder cabinets, children's toy collections, tourists' and collectors' displays, or museum dioramas (Mullaney 1983; Green 1988a; Mechling 1989; Stewart 1993).

If I wish to simulate Omri's mastery over life, I must turn to the CD-ROM version of *The Indian in the Cupboard*, where with my cursor I can animate an Indian figurine—one that, like the figurines at the beginning of the film, appears to be

Figure 12. CD-ROM and video version of *The Indian in the Cupboard*. The cupboard is made by reversing the cover of the video case. The figurine and key were included with the video. Photo © 1997 by Suzanne McEndree.

"antique," made of painted porcelain or wood rather than plastic. The figurine reminds me of a cigar-store Indian or a ship's figurehead, as do the seven other Indian figurines on Omri's shelf. When I move the cursor in order to place the figurine in the cabinet and turn the key, it "comes to life" and begins to talk to me. Like Omri's miniature friend in the film, this animated Indian is named Little Bear. He identifies himself as an Onondaga of the Wolf clan and introduces me to his Ungachis, his "friends" on the toy shelf (Shea 1970 [1860]). He gives me the name of Henuyeha, or "player" (Hewitt 1928, 625). I accompany Little Bear to a promontory overlooking his palisaded village, where his people live in three longhouses.

Descending to the village, I meet the Ungachis, whom I will later bring to life as my guides. I recall the many Native Americans who have made their living as hunting guides or ethnographic consultants. I also think of the participation of my brother and father in a YMCA organization known as Indian Guides (an organization parodied to good effect in the Disney film *Man of the House*). Foremost among my Onondaga "friends" is a clan mother, Gentle Breeze, who will introduce me to Onondaga words, stories, and symbols referring to the ancestors of the clans—Turtle, Bear, Wolf, Snipe, Beaver, Hawk, Deer, and Eel—as well as to the underwater Panther, the Peacemaker, the Tree of Peace, and the Keeper of the Winds and his Spirit Animals. Another Ungachi, a male "chief" named He Knows the Sky, will introduce me to Grandmother Moon, the Path of the Dead, the Bear, the Seven Children, and Star Girl, telling me their stories. ("What I like about the Iroquois," says ten-year-old Katie upon hearing the story of how Star Girl guided the starving people home, "is that it's not only boys and men who do important things.")

An Ungachi named Shares the Songs will teach me to play water drums, a flute, and a variety of rattles, challenging me to remember ever more complex rhythms. Swift Hunter will teach me to recognize and follow animal tracks, while Keeper of the Words will show me how to make a headdress in the style of each of the Six Nations of the League of the Iroquois. Two children will teach me their games: from Blooming Flower, I will learn how to decorate carved templates with beads; from Runs with the Wind, how to play a challenging memory game with seeds of corn, squash, and several varieties of beans.

Succeeding in these various activities requires patience, attentiveness, and a well-developed memory. Each time I succeed I am rewarded with effusive praise and a symbol for my virtual "wampum belt." Upon its completion, a ceremony is held to present me with the completed wampum belt and to name me an Ungachi, a "Friend of the Iroquois." I am feasted with a meal of corn, pumpkin, potatoes, squash, deer, roasted turkey, and cornbread. This concludes what, for me, has been a disconcerting experience of what Taussig (1993) calls "mimetic excess," with a panoply of resonances. I think of Camp Fire Girl "council fires" at which, proudly wearing my deerskin "ceremonial gown" and the beads I had "earned," I paid homage to "Work, Health, and Love" (Chapter 8). I recall lessons and plays about the first Thanksgiving (Chapter 5), and Louis Henry Morgan's activities in the fraternal organization he helped found, the Grand Order of the Iroquois (P. Deloria 1998). I remember the assimilationists at the turn of the twentieth century known as "Friends of the Indian" (Prucha 1973; Hoxie 1984), and Vine Deloria's (1969) caustic dismissal of "anthropologists and other friends" (78–100) in *Custer Died for Your Sins* (see Chapter 1).

Despite my initial discomfort with the power of bringing miniature Onondagas to life—and especially with the power to turn them back into mute "plastic"—I find myself intrigued and charmed by this simulated world. So is Tina, whose favorite game is one in which we bring Euro-Americans to life: the Trading Game, where we barter for trade goods with Spaulding, an English trader. In the process we learn something about Onondaga hunting, farming, manufactures, and desires for trade goods. (The other Euro-American figurine—and the only character drawn from the film besides Little Bear—is the cowardly cowboy Boone, with whom we experience the terrors of Omri's room from the perspective of a person three inches in height.) By the time Tina and I are presented with our wampum belts, we have been introduced to many aspects of Iroquois life in the early eighteenth century: the forest, the river, and the clearing; the powers of various animals; the Onondaga names and legends of the moon, the Milky Way, and several constellations; the architecture and layout of the village; and the Three Sisters (corn, beans, and squash). We have learned about the manufacture of Iroquois goods, the practice of reciprocity, and the importance of clans and clan matrons. We have heard many Onondaga words and learned to recognize a few. With the exception of Spaulding and his trade goods, however, we have encountered no evidence of Iroquois relations with Europeans or with other indigenous peoples.

Little Bear's world is one of order, beauty, and tranquility; it is free of disruptions from warfare, disease, displacement, and Christian evangelism. It serves simultaneously to arouse powerful feelings of nostalgia and nostalgic feelings of power. This is a world under control; a world in which people treat each other with respect; a world pervaded by the soothing, rhythmic music of flutes, rattles, and the non-referential syllables known as vocables. It is a world in which human relationships tend to be dyadic and free of conflict—a world in which, as both the textual and celluloid Omri teaches his friend Patrick, "You can't use people" (Banks 1981, 129). That we enter this world through the conceit of controlling the lives of miniature Indians and "mastering" the knowledge they have to teach us; that in this world the stereotypical Iroquois warrior is replaced by people living outside of history; that we feel we can be "Friends of the Iroquois" without confronting the political and economic claims that friendship would make upon us, whether in 1720—the era in which the CD-ROM is set—or today: these ironies pervade *The Indian in the Cupboard* in all its incarnations (though somewhat differently in each).

Destabilizing stereotypes is tricky, as others easily rush in to fill a void. In Lynne Reid Banks's original series of four novels (1981, 1986, 1989, 1993), Little Bear explicitly unsettles the Plains Indian stereotype, replacing it with a more localized and complexly rendered representation. When he comes to life, Little Bear does not live up to Omri's expectations: he lives in a longhouse rather than a tepee, walks rather than rides a horse, and is unaware of the custom of becoming "blood brothers" (which he adopts from Omri and uses in bidding him good-bye). In other ways, however, Little Bear more than meets expectations: he is a fierce "Iroquois brave" who has taken some thirty scalps; he is volatile, demanding, and interested in "firewater"; he becomes "restive" while watching a Western on television; his English is broken and, early on, mixed with grunts and snarls; he initially thinks of Omri as the Great White Spirit, only to be disillusioned when the boy fails to live up to his expectations of a deity (1981, 20–23, 148). Even so, the most racist typifications are voiced not by the narrator but by "Boohoo" Boone, a humorous cowboy who, when brought to life, denigrates "Injuns" and "redskins" as "ornery," "savage," and "dirty," only to be convinced otherwise by Omri and Little Bear (99–101). These passages and cover illustrations reminiscent of nineteenth-century dime novels have attracted some criticism (Slapin and Seale 1992, 121–122). But the moral of the tale is clear: although Omri at first cherishes his power over Little Bear, calling him "my Indian," he comes to respect Little Bear as an autonomous human being with (as Omri tells Patrick) his own life, times, country, language, and desires (Banks 1981, 70, 82).

Lynne Reid Banks is an Englishwoman who spent the Second World War in Saskatchewan, and the friendship between Omri and Little Bear plays on the alliance between the English and Iroquois in the French and Indian Wars (1754–1763). The historical context of the books, however, is almost completely absent in the film and the CD-ROM, which transpose Omri to New York. Except for a brief vision-like sequence in Little Bear's world, the film takes place completely in Omri's time and place. The film, for this reason, has far less cultural content than the CD-ROM, though what there is has been carefully rendered, following the advice of Onondaga consultants Oren Lyons and Jeanne Shenandoah (Yankowitz 1995, 31). The film is equally nostalgic, however. When Little Bear, preparing to return to his own time, asks whether the Onondaga are always a great people, Omri sadly answers in the affirmative, then reluctantly reveals that "it isn't always so good" for them. While this is indisputable, the scene misses a valuable opportunity to show something of the resiliency and contemporary life of the Onondaga people. Portrayed in the past or in miniature, and without visible descendants, Little Bear is out of place, out of time, and an object of intense longing—as Susan Stewart (1993) suggests is true for miniatures more generally. The film does nothing to help viewers imagine Little Bear's descendants as persons who share a world with Omri even as they share a tradition with Little Bear.

Nevertheless, the film is more successful than the book or CD-ROM in presenting Little Bear as far more than a typification. As played by the Cherokee rap artist Litefoot (Yankowitz 1995), Little Bear dominates the film, even at three inches tall. This Little Bear is not to be patronized, earns Omri's respect, and teaches him to appreciate the awesome responsibility that comes with power over other human beings. Given this, it is jarring to have power over Little Bear, voiced by Litefoot, in the CD-ROM version of *The Indian in the Cupboard*. The CD-ROM encourages the Henuyeha, in the spirit of playful learning, to mimic just what Omri learned not to do—albeit in the service of understanding Little Bear's world. It is doubly disconcerting to possess a plastic figurine of Little Bear. Omri's rejection of objectifying human beings was, predictably, lost on the marketing department—and could easily be lost on some of its young consumers, who could add Little Bear to their collection of *Pocahontas*-related figurines from Burger King. Consider the possibilities: a miniature Little Bear, a miniature Pocahontas, and a magical cupboard. . . .

The Legend: Disney's *Pocahontas*

While the marketing of *The Indian in the Cupboard* and its translation onto CD-ROM undercuts the narrative's critique of objectifying and manipulating human beings, the tensions and contradictions among the message, the medium, and the marketing of Disney's *Pocahontas* are far more blatant. On one level, *Pocahontas* can be dismissed as a commercial product through which Disney's powerful marketing machine has revived and exploited the US public's perennial fascination with playing Indian (P. Deloria 1998), "bringing an American legend to life" (Walt Disney Pictures 1995) in order to hawk beads, baubles, and trinkets to would-be Indian princesses and to those who would seek to please them.

On another level, however, Disney's interpretation of the United States' "foundational romance" (Sommer 1991) makes a serious statement about ethnocentrism, commodification, and exploitation as barriers to the dream of interethnic harmony that Smith and Pocahontas represent—though it stops far short of critiquing settler colonialism. If the film's dialogue and song lyrics are taken seriously, *Pocahontas* attempts (but retreats from) a far broader and more devastating cultural critique than *The Indian in the Cupboard*. The film offers a critique of the commodity form itself—albeit one that is, itself, consummately commodified.

To consider *Pocahontas* in terms of how it meets the challenges posed by its own message is to go beyond an appraisal that would measure it solely against an uncertain and elusive historical reality. Pocahontas may be the first "real-life figure," as the promotional material puts it, to be featured in a Disney film (Walt Disney Pictures 1995), but the pre-Disney Pocahontas was already a highly mythologized heroine known only through colonial representations—from the beginning a product of Euro-American desire. Disney has drawn on various versions of what Rayna Green (1975) calls the "Pocahontas perplex," giving new life and ubiquitous circulation to those deemed resonant with contemporary preoccupations. That is to say, the animated Pocahontas is one of the latest entries in the colonial and neocolonial tradition of noble savagism; the natural virtues she embodies and self-sacrifice she offers are those found in Montaigne and Rousseau, James Fenimore Cooper and *Dances with Wolves*. This is not to imply, to be sure, that Pocahontas is entirely a product of Western colonialism, but that we "know" her only within that arena—which, after all, is tantamount to not knowing her very well at all.

Outside of promotional material, the film's message is articulated most fully in Alan Menken and Stephen Schwartz's "Colors of the Wind," the Academy Award–winning song that the filmmakers believe "best sums up the entire spirit and essence of the film" (Walt Disney Pictures 1995). Responding to Smith's recitation of all that the English can teach the "savages," Pocahontas chides him for thinking "the only people who are people" are those who "look and think" like him. She urges Smith to "walk the footsteps of a stranger," where he will learn things he "never knew" he "never knew" (Disney's *Pocahontas: Illustrated Songbook* 1995, 44). This Pocahontas is, above all, a teacher. Not, as one might expect, a teacher of the Powhatan language and standards of diplomacy, for the time-consuming process of learning to translate across cultural and linguistic borders is finessed through the mystical ability, as another song puts it, to "Listen with Your Heart" (26). Rather, Pocahontas, a veritable child of nature, is a teacher of tolerance and respect for all life.

This is an unfortunate impoverishment of Pocahontas's teachings, one that produces a truly awkward moment in the film, when Pocahontas inexplicably switches from English to the Powhatan language upon first encountering Smith. ("She was just speaking English a moment ago!" observed my daughters when they first saw this scene.) Although a few Powhatan words are sprinkled through the film, and Smith learns how to say "hello" and "good-bye," there is no indication of the intelligence, dedication, and humility needed to "learn things you never knew you never knew." In being figured within the series of Disney heroines that includes Ariel, Belle, and Jasmine (of *The Little Mermaid, Beauty and the Beast,* and *Aladdin,* respectively), this most famous of indigenous cultural mediators is removed from the series of women that includes Malinche, Sacajawea, and Sarah Winnemucca (Karttunen 1994). The ability to "Listen with Your Heart" magically conquers all cultural distance for Pocahontas and John Smith.

This is not to say that it is entirely implausible that Pocahontas teaches Smith tolerance and respect for all life. One of the subtly effective moments in the film is the animated sequence corresponding to the passage in "Colors of the Wind" about walking in the footsteps of a stranger. The footsteps shown are the tracks of a Bear Person, a concept likely to be as unfamiliar to most film viewers as it is to John Smith. "Colors of the Wind" aims to challenge not only ethnocentrism but also anthropocentrism, and the bear scene goes beyond Disney's ordinary anthropomorphizing to open a window onto an animistic view of the world. More often, however, Pocahontas's relationship to animals (for example, to Meeko the raccoon and Flit the hummingbird) is trivialized, appearing not unlike Cinderella's relationship with her friends, the mice and birds, in the Disney film.

In another verse of "Colors of the Wind," Pocahontas contrasts Smith's utilitarian and possessive thinking with her own intimate knowledge of nature. She scolds Smith for seeing the Earth as "just a dead thing you can claim," for she knows that every rock, tree, and creature "has a life, has a spirit, has a name." Then, in the most sensual sequence of the film (or, indeed, of any previous Disney animated feature), Pocahontas entices Smith to run through the forest's hidden trails, taste the Earth's sun-ripened berries, roll in the grasses of the meadows—to enjoy all these riches and "for once, never wonder what they're worth" (Disney's *Pocahontas: Illustrated Songbook* 1995, 44). The seductive and precocious Pocahontas, who stalks Smith like a wildcat and then rolls with him in the grass, is a "free spirit" who embodies the joys of belonging to an uncommodified world. This is not the first time the young Pocahontas has been sexualized—precedents include Smith's own "A True Relation" (1986b [1608]) and "The Generall Historie of Virginia" (1986a [1624]) as well as John Barth's *The Sot-Weed Factor* (1980 [1967])—but it is a startling departure for a Disney children's film. Pocahontas's sensuality no doubt has multiple motivations, but at one level it marks her as an intrinsic part of the natural world—as a "tribal Eve," according to supervising animator Glen Keane (Hochswender 1995, 156).

It is the clear contrast between utilitarian possessiveness and sensual spirituality in scenes and lyrics such as this that earned the Native American activist Russell Means's tribute to *Pocahontas* as "the single finest work ever done on American Indians by Hollywood" by virtue of being "willing to tell the truth" (Walt Disney Pictures 1995). But this critique of capitalist appropriation is enunciated by the same Pocahontas whose licensed image saturated the marketplace—along with that of her father, Powhatan. Even more ironically, Powhatan is modeled after and voiced by the same Russell Means who has demonstrated against the use of pseudo-Indian sports mascots and logos (see Chapter 10). One can only wonder: what is the exotic, sensual, copyrighted Pocahontas if not the mascot for a feminine, earthy, conciliatory New Age spirituality?

An eager and willing student of Pocahontas, John Smith learns to see maize as the true "riches" of Powhatan's land and presents the gold-hungry Governor Ratcliffe with a golden ear of corn. (Like much else, Jamestown's government is simplified in the film, and Ratcliffe is given the role of the obligatory Disney villain.) The play on "golden" makes for an effective scene, but totally excluded from the film is that other sacred American plant, tobacco—which became the salvation of the Virginia economy thanks to John Rolfe, the husband of a mature, Christian, and anglicized Pocahontas never seen in the film. The historical Pocahontas's capture by the English, conversion, transformation into Lady Rebecca Rolfe, and tragic death in London shortly thereafter (Rountree 2006)—true as it might be—does not resonate as well with an Anglo-American audience's expectations as the story of Smith's capture and salvation through the love of a spirited child of nature.

Resonating with expectations, of course, is what creating a "timeless, universal, and uniquely satisfying motion picture experience" is all about (Walt Disney Pictures 1995). In imagining Pocahontas, the filmmakers relied to some extent on consultation with Native people and scholars but more, it seems, on what resonated with their own experiences, desires, and sense of authenticity—so central to the American tradition of playing Indian, as Mechling (1980b) has pointed out. Regarding the composition of "Colors of the Wind," lyricist Stephen Schwartz remarked that "we were able to find the parts of ourselves that beat in synchronicity with Pocahontas," while animator Glen Keane declared, "I'm cast as Pocahontas in the film" (Hochswender 1995, 156). I suppose that this is something like "listening with your heart," but there is a significant tension between this and "walking in the footsteps of a stranger." This is not the Pocahontas we never knew we never knew, but the Pocahontas we knew all along, the Pocahontas whose story is "universal"—that is, familiar, rather than strange and shocking and particular. This is a Pocahontas whose tale—like that of Simba in *The Lion King* or Omri in *The Indian in the Cupboard*—fits into the mold of the Western coming-of-age story; who, yearning to see (as the song goes) "just around the riverbend," grows from youthful irresponsibility to mature self-knowledge through courage and love. It is a Pocahontas who speaks what is known in anthologies as "the wisdom of the elders" (Suzuki and Knudtson 1992) and communes with an animated Grandmother Willow. It is a Pocahontas who—despite a tattoo and garment loosely consistent with sixteenth-century watercolors of other coastal Algonquians—has a Barbie-doll figure, an Asian model's glamour, and an instant attraction to a distinctly Nordic John Smith (Hulton and Quinn 1964; Hochswender 1995). In short, Disney has created a New Age Pocahontas to embody our millennial dreams for wholeness and harmony, while banishing our nightmares of emptiness within and savagery without.

Just as the dream of tolerance and respect for all life is voiced in song, so too are the nightmares of savagery and emptiness. While the dream is figured as feminine and Indian in the lyrical "Colors of the Wind," the nightmare is presented as masculine and universal in the driving and brutal "Savages." Mobilizing stereotypes akin to Boohoo Boone's, but considerably more vicious, the song begins with the English characterizing Pocahontas's people as "vermin," as "filthy little heathens," as "barely even human," as "only good when dead" (Disney's *Pocahontas: Illustrated Songbook* 1995, 50).

This is the ideology of ignoble savagism at its dehumanizing extreme, less typical of the earliest years of the Jamestown colony than of the years after 1622, when Powhatan's kinsman Opechancanough launched a war of resistance against the English (Sheehan 1980; Rountree 2006). In the context of the film, appearing as the English prepare to attack the Powhatan people, it serves to underscore the brutishness of the English colonists rather than the savagery of the "heathen." Earlier, in the opening to "Colors of the Wind," Pocahontas gently challenges the ideology of ignoble savagism by asking Smith why, if it was she who was the "ignorant savage," there was so very much he did not know. Characterized as wise and gentle, if mischievous and spirited, Pocahontas is clearly not an ignorant savage. So the colonists' rhetoric of savagery turns back upon them—at least until Powhatan, advised by a diviner, leads his people in an echoing chorus, calling the "paleface" a soulless, bloodless demon distinguished only by his greed. Now it is the English who are "different from us," who are "barely even human," who are, in short, "savages" (Disney's *Pocahontas: Illustrated Songbook* 1995, 50).

Powhatan's section of "Savages" purports to offer a portrait of the English colonists from a Native point of view. Given what has gone on thus far in the film, and what we know of subsequent history, the accusation strikes home. But this passage, too, ultimately rebounds against those who utter it. John Smith is captured and laid out, the executioner's tomahawk is raised, Smith is about to be mercilessly executed ... and Pocahontas throws her body upon his, successfully pleading with her father for his life. The savagery of fear and intolerance is vanquished through the power of "listening with your heart."

So the foundational fiction goes. It may be that this was all an elaborate adoption ceremony in which Smith became a vassal of Powhatan, who ruled over an expanding collection of villages. It may be that Pocahontas was playing a traditional female role in choosing between life and death for a sacrificial victim (Williamson 1992; Strong 1999; Gleach 2003, 2006; Rountree 2006). It may be that the incident is best understood as part of Smith's imaginative and self-serving fabrication of himself—what Greenblatt (1980) calls "self-fashioning." I would not fault Disney for repeating the rescue as it is commonly known in a film advertised as "An American Legend," but the litany "Savages! Savages!" is another matter. Its ideological work, in the end, is to level the English and the Powhatan people to the same state of ethnocentric brutishness, portraying ignoble savagism as natural and universal rather than having particular cultural and historical roots. Furthermore, when these lyrics are disseminated outside the context of the film, they may have a harmful effect upon a young and impressionable audience. For many Native Americans and other colonized peoples, "savage" is a potent and degrading epithet, comparable in its effects to the word "nigger." I cannot imagine the latter epithet repeated so often, and set to music, in a G-rated film and its soundtrack (which won an Academy Award for best musical score). Is "savage" more acceptable because it is here used reciprocally? Yet viewing ignoble savagism as reciprocal is simply to ignore its role in justifying the extermination and dispossession of indigenous people (Jennings 1975; Berkhofer 1978; Sheehan 1980; Strong 1999).

The filmmakers are aware that they are in risky territory here and characterize the episode as dealing with "one of the most adult themes ever in a Disney film." The theme is described as "the ugliness and stupidity that results when people give in to racism and intolerance" (Walt Disney Pictures 1995), and it is refreshing to have it aired in the open, particularly by a studio with a history, even recently, of racist animation. Even so, a more accurate treatment of the theme would distinguish between English colonialism and Powhatan resistance, and between the English ideology of savagism and Powhatan attitudes toward their own enemies—whom, as Helen Rountree (1989) shows, they generally aimed to politically subordinate and socially incorporate, rather than exterminate and dispossess. This could be done by telling more of Pocahontas's and Powhatan's subsequent dealings with Smith, whom they treated, respectively, as an adopted brother and subordinate ruler (Gleach 1994; Strong 1999; Rountree 2006).

Cultural Critique and Commodification

That *Pocahontas* raises a number of difficult and timely issues is a tribute to its ambition and seriousness of purpose. Indeed, the film begs to be taken as a plea for tolerant, respectful, and harmonious living in a world torn by prejudice, exploitation, ethnic strife, and environmental degradation. This is true, as well, of *The Indian in the Cupboard,* albeit in a more limited fashion. That both films and their associated products and promotions are rife with tensions and ironies exemplifies the limitations of serious cultural critique in an artistic environment devoted to the marketing of dreams. That our children are bombarded with plastic consumables and impoverished caricatures while being admonished to treat other cultures, other creatures, and the land with respect should prompt us to find ways to teach them—and learn from them—the difference between producing and consuming objectified difference on the one hand, and sustaining respectful relationships across difference on the other.

In a society founded on differentiation, objectification, and commercialization, the lesson is a hard one—and one that has characteristically been expressed in an oppositional "Indian" voice. If *Pocahontas* and *The Indian in the Cupboard* can be viewed only with ambivalence because of their own participation in processes of objectification and commodification, the forms of "playing Indian" to which each gives rise may offer genuine possibilities for unlearning these processes and imagining new ones, that is, for learning things we "never knew we never knew."

Katie and Tina have said they love that part of the song, and I agree. We sometimes find ourselves singing Pocahontas's lines, and stop to wonder at the paradoxical form of learning they suggest.

Bibliographic Note

Rountree's *Pocahontas, Powhatan, Opechancanough* (2006) is an excellent and up-to-date introduction to the historical Powhatan and Pocahontas. Tilton, *Pocahontas: The Evolution of an American Narrative* (1994) analyzes the mythical Pocahontas. See also works by Robertson (1996), Gleach (1994, 2003, 2006), and Strong (1999).

Susan Stewart's treatment of nostalgia (1993) and Michael Taussig's concept of "mimetic excess" (1993) are important contributions to theories of representational practice. Discussions of noble and ignoble savagism include H. White's "The Noble Savage Theme as Fetish" (1976); Berkhofer's *The White Man's Indian* (1978); Strong's "Fathoming the Primitive" (1986); Trouillot's "Anthropology and the Savage Slot" (1991); Krech's *The Ecological Indian: Myth and History* (1999); and Ellingson's *The Myth of the Noble Savage* (2001).

The literature on Hollywood Indians is extensive. Newer titles include Rollins and O'Connor, *Hollywood's Indian: The Portrayal of the Native American in Film* (2003), and Aleiss, *Making the White Man's Indian: Native Americans and Hollywood Movies* (2005). An excellent cinematic critique is *Imagining Indians* (1992) by the Hopi filmmaker Victor Masayesva Jr. For more general issues, see Downing and Husband, *Representing 'Race': Racisms, Ethnicities and Media* (2005), and M. Anderson, *Cowboy Imperialism and Hollywood Film* (2007).

Earlier versions of this chapter include more extensive quotations and additional illustrations (Strong 1996, 2003).

CHAPTER TEN
THE MASCOT SLOT

How might we account for the persistence of teams of "Indians," "Redskins," "Braves," "Warriors," and "Chiefs" in the United States, even after several decades of protest and litigation? Why have racist representations of Native Americans proven to be more resistant to critique than those depicting other racial and ethnic groups? Why has progress on this issue been so uneven?

Building on the analysis of the preceding chapters, this chapter addresses these questions through the lens of cultural citizenship. Originally formulated by Aihwa Ong (1996), Renato Rosaldo (1997), and others to analyze the subjective experiences and cultural claims of Asian Americans and Latinos within the United States, analyses of cultural citizenship focus on unequal spaces of national belonging (Dominguez 1996). Extending this concept to Native Americans allows us to see how unequal spaces of belonging are maintained and reproduced when some citizens claim the right to appropriate the representational practices of others, as well as the right to determine for themselves which (if any) practices are respectful and which are demeaning.

Let us begin with two telling examples of what Michael Rogin (1996) calls "racial masquerade." The first is a promotional poster for *Bamboozled* (2000), Spike Lee's satirical film about a millennial revival of the minstrel show. This poster, designed by Art Sims (2000) and now used in marketing the DVD (New Line Cinema 2001), features a highly offensive, stereotypical image of a grinning, watermelon-eating "tar baby" standing in a field of cotton. This is one of two ads that the *New York Times* refused to publish due to its racist content (Goldstein 2000; A. Samuels 2000; Willis 2012). The very same publication, however, routinely prints images of the equally offensive Chief Wahoo, the logo of the Cleveland Indians (see, for example, "Cleveland Indians" 2011).

The striking similarities between Chief Wahoo (see Figure 13) and the censored *Bamboozled* advertisement reveal the extent to which pseudo-Indian mascots and logos perpetuate the otherwise discredited American tradition of minstrelsy (Rogin 1996). Both caricatures use the same palette of black, white, and bright red, and both feature the huge, grinning mouth of the blackface tradition. As Spike Lee demonstrates in *Bamboozled*, the gaping mouth signifies animal instincts and appetites as well as a desperate eagerness to please. Both caricatures also include an iconic feature identifying the figure as a particular kind of primitive "other": the watermelon in the case of the ad, the feathered headband in the case of the sports mascot.

That one image is deemed too offensive to print, even as a satire, while the other is omnipresent reveals how Native Americans are consigned to an allegorical form of cultural citizenship that might be called "the mascot slot." Like the "savage slot" of which it is a part (Trouillot 1991), the mascot slot constitutes difference and inferiority in terms of an exaggerated physicality, evident in pseudo-Indian mascots' (and fans') colorful costumes, exuberant gestures, "war paint," and "war whoops." Though exaggerated physical traits connote strength and virility, they also, as a corollary, tend to connote diminished intellect and self-restraint. This, argues one psychoanalytically inclined scholar, is precisely their appeal: pseudo-Indian mascots, logos, and team names give fans a license to act in the wild, unrestrained manner they attribute to "savages" and children but normally repress in themselves (Ganguly 2006).

For several decades, activists have attempted to persuade sports franchises, school officials, courts of law, the media, and the public that mascots and logos

Figure 13. Cleveland Indians fans at Jacobs Field on October 18, 2007, in Cleveland, Ohio. Photo by Brian Synder-Pool/Getty Images.

such as Chief Wahoo perpetuate harmful stereotypes and constitute racial discrimination (Staurowsky 2001; Harjo 2001, 2005; Baca 2004; Cummings 2008). Much of this work has been educational in nature. An early example of consciousness-raising is a 1987 poster created by a Minnesota group called Concerned American Indian Parents in which a Cleveland Indians' pennant featuring Chief Wahoo was juxtaposed to imaginary pennants for the fictional "Pittsburgh Negroes," "Kansas City Jews," and "San Diego Caucasians." The caption read, "Maybe now you know how Native Americans feel." Perhaps so. But the poster did not picture the four ethnic groups equally, as it lacked visual caricatures of Caucasians and Jews. Subsequent versions of the poster removed human figures from every pennant except that of the actually existing team, the Cleveland Indians (Helmberger 1999). In this case, as is the *Bamboozled* example, the offensiveness of other caricatures was given more recognition than the offensiveness of "redface."

A similar graphic—Tony Auth's 1997 cartoon, "Can You Imagine?"—is more blatant, demonstrating the semiotics of racist stereotyping shared by blackface, war propaganda, and advertising (see Figure 14). The answer to Auth's question is clear: no, we cannot imagine a team, today, called the "Cleveland Africans," the "Cleveland Asians," or the "Cleveland Hispanics." Nor can we imagine contemporary sports logos in which the grinning minstrel's mouth is affixed to a caricature of an Asian, African, or Latino. Still less can we imagine the football team of the nation's capital bearing another color-coded label as derogatory as "Redskins"—a point made forcefully by Ward Churchill (1994) in "Let's Spread the Fun Around," where he proposes, tongue-in-cheek, that teams be named after the full panoply of unmentionable racial slurs.

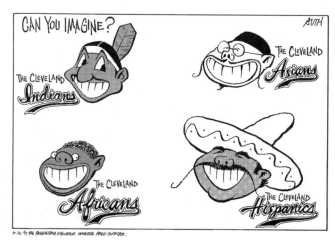

Figure 14. Tony Auth, "Can You Imagine?" (1997). Auth © 1997 The Philadelphia Inquirer. Reprinted with permission of UNIVERSAL UCLIK. All rights reserved.

In this spirit an intramural basketball team at the University of Northern Colorado dubbed itself "The Fighting Whites," adopting a "suit" as its mascot. The multiethnic team took on the name in February 2002 to protest the name and logo of a local high school team, "The Fighting Reds." This protest soon took on national significance, and articles of clothing bearing the Fighting Whites' name and logo (often rendered as "Fighting Whities") became something of a cult item. In one year, the team raised $100,000 for endowed scholarships for Native Americans and other minorities through selling Fighting Whites articles on their Web site (Johansen 2010). But the result of the parody was decidedly mixed. Some conservative commentators thought the ability of Euro-Americans to take the joke indicated that Native Americans should as well; others pointed out the lack of equivalence between the name and logo and many pseudo-Indian names and symbols. Despite local and national attention, including a graduation day rally led by the American Indian Movement activist Russell Means, the Eaton High School Reds continue to use a caricature of a "cross-armed, shovel-nosed, belligerent" Indian as their logo (Fasano 2002; Good 2002; EHS Athletics 2011).

Parodies such as The Fighting Whites, "Can You Imagine?," and "Let's Spread the Fun Around" point to the double standard that prevails when it comes to contemporary racial slurs and masquerades. "Redface" caricatures that would not now be tolerated if they portrayed other racial or ethnic groups are not only tolerated but institutionalized in our school and university systems, youth organizations, sports franchises, and media outlets. They form part of a larger system of commodified representations that are perpetuated by the tourism industry (with its tepees and totem poles), the US military (with its Tomahawk missiles and Apache, Chinook, and Blackhawk helicopters), and the auto industry. As Rosemary Coombe (1998) mordantly notes of the latter, it is "inconceivable that a vehicle could be marketed as 'a wandering Jew,' but North Americans rarely bat an eyelash when a Jeep Cherokee passes them on the road or an advertisement for a Pontiac flashes across their television screen" (78).

As indicated by the documentary film, *In Whose Honor?* (1997), sports teams and their fans often justify their use of pseudo-Indian mascots and logos through what Brenda Farnell (2004) calls the "discourse of honoring." Team owners and fans employing this discourse insist that their use of pseudo-Indian mascots pays respect to the Native American warrior tradition. Because they identify with the invented tradition of Indianness the mascots and logos embody, proponents believe that their intention to honor the Native American warrior tradition carries more weight than the dishonor, disrespect, and discrimination experienced by Native Americans. This "Indians 'R' Us" syndrome, as Churchill (1994) has called it, is grounded in performative practices central to organizations that socialize the young, as we have seen in Chapters 8 and 9. Given this pattern of socialization, many non-Indians come to feel a deep personal investment in pseudo-Indian mascots (Springwood 2004).

Such an emotional investment is a form of White privilege in a settler society (Lipsitz 1998; Staurowsky 2004; Jensen 2005, 2010; Rothenberg 2011). Through "playing Indian" non-Indians may come to feel authorized to use and even to profit from these symbols, regardless of protests from actual Native Americans. Going one step further, proponents of pseudo-Indian mascots often dismiss the objections of Native Americans as mere "political correctness." This rhetoric caricatures those who oppose these representational practices no less than these practices themselves caricature Native Americans. The charge of political correctness trivializes a concern for equality, respect, and social justice by reducing it to humorless oversensitivity. Certain legal commentators suggest that attributions of oversensitivity are significant in the courts as well (Moushegian 2006).

Meaningful progress has been made, to be sure, although legal scholar André Douglas Pond Cummings (2008) is correct in identifying progress as "awkward" and "halting" (316). The 1964 Civil Rights Act and the Fourteenth Amendment equal protection clause have been invoked against mascots in public schools, on the basis that they create a racially hostile and intimidating environment for Native American students (Baca 2004). This argument was cited by the US Commission on Civil Rights (2001) in a statement that called for "an end to the use of Native American images and team names by non-Native schools." The commission labeled pseudo-Indian imagery "insensitive," "disrespectful," "offensive," and contrary to public schools' educational mission in a diverse society (191). According to the Cheyenne/Muscogee activist Suzan Shown Harjo (2010), between 1970 and 2004 some two thousand school and university teams had retired their pseudo-Indian logos and mascots, with less than a thousand remaining, mainly in primary and secondary schools (181).

In a particularly notable development, since 2006, the National Collegiate Athletic Association (NCAA) has banned the use of Native nicknames and logos in its postseason tournaments (Franklin 2006a; Staurowsky 2007). An official of the NCAA noted the influence of the Civil Rights Commission's statement on the association, as well as a statement from the American Psychological Association (2005) citing extensive research on the harmful effects of pseudo-Indian sports symbols on the self-esteem of Native American children, the educational experiences of members of all communities, the preservation of tribal identity, and social relations between Native Americans and other groups. The decision met both official and unofficial resistance, especially from the University of Illinois (Prochaska 2001; Zirin 2010; "Mascot Information" 2011; "Mascots in College Sports" 2012) and the University of North Dakota (Jensen 2010; Associated Press 2011; ICTMN Staff 2011), but the NCAA ban has been generally effective. The Florida Seminoles and the Utes of the University of Utah have been granted exemptions from the NCAA policy because they have secured approval from a "namesake tribe." The NCAA defended this position on the basis of tribal sovereignty (Franklin 2006b), although this argument is not universally accepted (King and Springwood 2001b; Cattelino 2008, 168–169, 247).

Although some educational institutions continue to employ pseudo-Indian names, mascots, logos, and slogans, the trend is clearly away from these representational practices. Professional sports is another matter, however. Teams of "Indians," "Braves," and "Redskins" continue to take the field, and new generations are socialized in their invented traditions. In 2009, the Supreme Court refused to hear a case, *Harjo v. Pro-Football, Inc.*, that challenged trademark protection for the Washington Redskins on the grounds that disparaging trademarks harm the public and are not protected by trademark law. The refusal was based on a technicality, and the merits of the case were not considered (*Harjo v. Pro-Football, Inc.* 2009). Further legal challenges are forthcoming.

Although some argue that the prevalence of pseudo-Indian logos and mascots is not among Native Americans' most pressing concerns, looking at the issue through the framework of cultural citizenship suggests that the demeaning objectification accomplished by racist sports symbols is integral to other forms of subordination and discrimination. As Ong (1996) remarks, the concept of cultural citizenship concerns "how the universalistic criteria of democratic citizenship variously regulate different categories of subjects." As a Foucauldian process of "self-making and being made" within "hierarchical schemes of racial and cultural difference," cultural citizenship defines who does and does not belong within the nation-state and civil society. Differential categories of belonging are reproduced, notes Ong, in "cultural performance" and "everyday ... activities of inclusion and exclusion" (737, 750, 740). The use of pseudo-Indian sports mascots, logos, and rituals are just such normalized performances and activities, ones that exclude contemporary Native Americans from full participatory citizenship by treating them as signs rather than as speakers, as caricatures rather than as agents, as commodities rather than as citizens. Much like "mock Spanish" (Hill 1995) reproduces hegemonic stereotypes of Mexican-American inferiority, so the continued use of pseudo-Indian sports symbols replays colonialist appropriation and reproduces the subordinate place of Native Americans within settler society.

To insist that the "mascot slot" be viewed as a matter of "cultural citizenship" rather than "political correctness" makes a point that extends well beyond the realm of halftime "war dances" and celebrative "tomahawk chops." As several scholars have stressed (Aufderheide 1992; Choi and Murphy 1992; Taylor 1992; Foster and Herzog 1994; Friedman 1995), the charge of "political correctness" is a common way of dismissing claims for recognition on the part of subordinated groups—a way of trivializing their interests, visions, and aspirations while maintaining White privilege. Indeed, charges of political correctness are themselves part of the process that generates subordinated forms of cultural citizenship, what Virginia Dominguez (1996) calls "unequal spaces of belonging to a nation-state" (751). The US Commission on Civil Rights (2001) recognized this in stating,

> The use of American Indian mascots is not a trivial matter. The Commission has a firm understanding of the problems of poverty, education, housing, and health care that face many Native Americans. The fight to eliminate Indian nicknames and images in sports is only one front of the larger battle to eliminate obstacles that confront American Indians. The elimination of Native American nicknames and images as sports mascots will benefit not only Native Americans, but all Americans. The elimination of stereotypes will make room for education about real Indian people, current Native American issues, and the rich variety of American Indian cultures in our country. (192–193)

We might also put it this way: respecting Native American claims to be recognized as persons, citizens, and members of sovereign tribes rather than as sports symbols is central to acknowledging their full humanness and participatory citizenship. Demolishing the "mascot slot" is a prerequisite for the full recognition of indigenous peoples within a transformed, inclusive national imaginary.

Bibliographic Note

Though this chapter employs both Aihwa Ong's (1996) and Renato Rosaldo's (1997) work on cultural citizenship, its perspective is closer to that of Ong, whose approach to contemporary citizenship and sovereignty issues is further developed in *Flexible Citizenship* (1998) and subsequent works.

For a comprehensive sourcebook on the mascot issue, see King, *The Native American Mascot Controversy* (2010). Other useful scholarly works include Spindel, *Dancing at Halftime: Sports and the Controversy over American Indian Mascots* (2000); King and Springwood, *Beyond the Cheers* (2001a) and *Team Spirits* (2001c); and a special issue of the *Journal of Sport and Social Issues* edited by King (2004b). Staurowsky (2007) examines the NCAA decision and its aftermath. Several Web sites track current developments; good places to begin are the Indian Country Today Media Network (http://indiancountrytodaymedianetwork.com), and "Mascots in College Sports" (2012) and "Mascot Information" (2011), both maintained by organizations at the University of Illinois.

In Whose Honor? American Indian Mascots in Sports (1997) is a revealing, if dated, film on the controversy over the University of Illinois's mascot, Chief Illiniwek. It conveys well the possessive investment of White fans in their mascot and the harm that pseudo-Indian mascots and logos cause to Native American students. See Rosenstein (2001) for a discussion of the film.

PART FIVE
INDIGENOUS IMAGINARIES

In spring 2008, a group of visitors toured the campus of the University of Texas at Brownsville, just a few miles north of where the meandering Rio Grande River marks the border between Mexico and the United States. The official who served as our guide said that when he was a boy, he and friends from the Mexican side of the border had roamed around this area on their bicycles. He had seen times change dramatically since then. Under the Secure Fence Act of 2006, the US Department of Homeland Security planned to build an eighteen-foot metal barrier through campus—just one link in a planned security wall of almost 700 miles along the border. Our guide took us to a spot where the planned barrier would bisect the university grounds, divide Brownsville from its sister city of Matamoros, Mexico, and cut off migratory animals from each other and their habitat (Wood 2008; "Texas-Mexico Border Wall" 2011; "Border Fence Information" 2011; Sherif 2011).

The university's president, Juliet Garcia, stood up to the Department of Homeland Security and was taken to court. Not long after our visit, she negotiated an agreement in which the university was allowed to upgrade an existing fence in lieu of the planned wall ("Border Fence Information" 2011). On Valentine's Day, 2009, some 350 campus and community volunteers from Brownsville and Matamoros planted jasmine vines along a ten-foot fence in order to beautify the barrier and demonstrate the existence and strength of the cross-border community. President Garcia (2009) told the crowd, assembled a few weeks after the inauguration of President Obama, that "the border wall ran counter to our very mission as a university," which she described as "to convene the cultures of our community"; "foster an appreciation of the unique heritage of the Lower Rio Grande Valley"; and "provide academic leadership to the intellectual, cultural, social and economic life of the bi-national urban region we serve." She concluded, "Today we will plant vines and seeds of hope—hope that our nation will strengthen its democratic core values during this both difficult and hopeful time in our history."

In calling on the United States to strengthen its commitment to democratic values, President Garcia was pointing to violations of due process on the part of the Department of Homeland Security. Acting under a post-9/11 sense of urgency, the US government had suspended the community and environmental impact statements that might stand in the way of the wall. A working group at the University of Texas School of Law found that the proposed wall disproportionately cut through the property of poor Latino families and indigenous people, while leaving that of wealthy landowners intact (Speed 2008).

For example, the Department of Homeland Security sought condemnation of land owned by the Lipan Apache family of Eloisa García Támez. This land, known as the El Caláboz Ranchería, was granted to García Támez's ancestors in 1763 by the Spanish Crown, and the land grant had heretofore been recognized as valid by the United States. Fighting the condemnation, Eloisa's daughter Margo Támez (2008) argued that "The border wall will not only hinder the health of our requisite ecological habitats for water, birds, plants, mammals, and other wildlife, but it will also increase the already endangered status of our Nde' people, who have suffered great impacts as a result of NAFTA policies in this region" (see also Támez, 2010).

The border wall and the more general militarization of the border pose a serious threat to a number of indigenous nations that straddle the border. These include the Kickapoo in Texas, the Kumeyaay in California, the Yaqui in Arizona, and the Cocopah and Tohono O'odham in Arizona (Luna-Firebaugh 2002; Speed 2008). Tohono O'odham people, for example, live on both sides of the border and have crossed it regularly for family visits, ceremonies, medical care, and other activities. At an intertribal Border Summit in 2006, the Tohono O'odham activists joined with indigenous people from across the United States and Mexico in issuing a number of demands to the US and tribal governments alike. These included a call for the United States to "adopt the UN Declaration on the Rights of Indigenous Peoples and abide by Article 35, which recognizes the rights of indigenous peoples whose lands are separated by international borders and their right to continue their spiritual and cultural practices" (Norrell 2006).

Both proponents and opponents of the border wall realize that its construction simultaneously involves mortar and meaning—that is, both material and representational practices. Through a kind of "cultural work" (Tompkins 1986) that might be called "border work," the Department of Homeland Security represents people on the south side of the Rio Grande as "aliens" and potential terrorists, hardening divisions between them and the US citizens to the north of the border. In contrast, many people in the region view themselves as sharing indigenous and Latino identities that precede US occupation. "The border crossed us" is a statement frequently heard in communities on the border (Luna-Firebaugh 2002). While this is the first time in its history that the United States has attempted to definitively cut itself off from Mexico through the erection of a physical barrier, the representational work of depicting Mexicans as threatening aliens continues the long-standing practice of defining national identity against indigenous others.

Returning to the categories of analysis introduced in Chapter 1, the poetics, politics, economics, and technologies of representation are all manifested in the controversy over the border wall. The poetics of representation involves the deployment of discourses and images of border protection, terrorism, illegality, race, and citizenship on the one hand, against representations of cross-border heritage, community, endangered species, and indigenous rights on the other. These tropes and images are strategically deployed by people, movements, and institutions with different kinds of power (the politics and economics of representation). And they are circulated through a broad array of technologies of representation, ranging from surveys and blueprints to Web sites and jasmine plantings. Identities are created, crossed, and recast as people place themselves, and are placed by others, in relation to the wall. Even President Obama's announcement in December 2010 that the security fence is complete did not end the controversy, as the original plan had been modified in many localities, not only in Brownsville (Farley 2011).

Other forms of border work, past and present, have been considered in the preceding chapters. Part Two explored the inclusions and exclusions created by the tropes of *tribe, discovery,* and *blood.* Part Three considered the crossing of cultural borders in colonial and contemporary captivity narratives, whereas Part Four discussed the mimetic practices found in children's play and in amateur and professional sports, with their complex identifications and oppositions. We turn, in Part Five, to a consideration of the recasting of representational practices in Native, collaborative, and activist ethnographies (Chapter 11) and at indigenously controlled museums (Chapter 12). The development of an indigenous imaginary is central to both cases. This is an increasingly salient representation of history and identity that privileges Native peoples' long-term connections to a local landscape as well as the shared experiences of those across the hemisphere, or even across the globe, who have been subjected to colonial processes of appropriation and subordination (Clifford 2001; de la Cadena and Starn 2007). The ongoing development of an indigenous imaginary is a fluid, expansive form of border work.

The issue of political and cultural sovereignty is also central to the closing chapters. Chapter 11, "Sovereignty, Indigeneity, and Ethnographic Representation," considers contemporary ethnographic research in the context of the decolonization of knowledge, while Chapter 12, "A Native Space on the National Mall," discusses indigenous control over representational practices in the museum context.

CHAPTER ELEVEN
SOVEREIGNTY, INDIGENEITY, AND ETHNOGRAPHIC
REPRESENTATION

In the early twenty-first century, Native North America remains culturally diverse and politically complex. In 2010, there were 565 federally recognized Indian nations, tribes, bands, and organized communities in the United States, including 230 Alaskan Native villages and corporations (Wilkins and Stark 2011, 7). An additional 48 tribes were recognized by states but not by the federal government. More than four million individuals (approximately 1.5 percent of the total US population) identified themselves as American Indian or Alaskan Native on the 2000 census. About two and a half million of these, comprising 1 percent of the total US population, claimed "single race" status; the remainder reported mixed ancestry. The Native American population is growing quickly, with a third of its members in the year 2000 under the age of eighteen. Almost half of those identifying as Native American lived in urban areas (Harvard Project 2008, 6–7, 79, 351).

Native American communities are still recovering from the devastating impact of settler colonialism. Although some Native groups remain in their ancestral lands, many were dispossessed. The 110 million acres held by Native tribes and individuals are often scattered and are under complicated jurisdiction; sacred sites are often outside tribally controlled areas (Nabokov 2006). Economic growth remains uneven, with the median household income of Native Americans in the lower forty-eight states comprising only 58 percent of the overall American median household income. Serious health disparities persist, with elevated rates of depression and high rates of death from liver disease, diabetes, and suicide

(O'Nell 1996, 4–5; Harvard Project 2008, 6–9, 95–111, 219). Though an increasing number of Native Americans are professionals, overall rates of educational attainment remain low compared to those of other ethnic groups (Harvard Project 2008, 199–218). Many Native languages are endangered: only 4 percent of reservation residents reported speaking a Native language in the year 2000, and less than a quarter of the two hundred indigenous languages still spoken in North America had a significant number of young speakers (Goddard 1996, 3–4; Silver and Miller 1997; Harvard Project 2008, 283).

These statistics, however, present an overly bleak picture. Overcoming historical practices of genocide, dispossession, and assimilation, indigenous peoples have demonstrated considerable resiliency and are now reaping the benefits of decades of political activism (Nagel 1996; Johnson, Nagel, and Champagne 1997; Cobb and Fowler 2007). Tribal nations are asserting political and cultural sovereignty; working to reclaim land, artifacts, and sacred sites; building sustainable economies; operating their own educational, judicial, health, and social welfare institutions; and revitalizing their languages and cultures (Jorgensen 2007). Over the past four decades, these efforts have been enabled (if also constrained) by hard-won federal legislation governing Native American civil rights, self-determination, religious freedom, gaming, repatriation (Chapter 12), and child welfare (Chapter 6). The issues of political and cultural sovereignty, cultural property and cultural heritage, cultural and linguistic revitalization, and community and cultural identity are central for indigenous people today, and increasingly indigenous people are conceiving of their identity and their struggles on a global scale.

Many of the issues that are at the center of indigenous life today are also at the center of ethnographic research. In this chapter we will consider contemporary trends in the ethnographic representation of indigenous people—trends that reflect shifts in the production of knowledge, increasing control of indigenous people over the ways in which they are represented, and a new emphasis on indigenous knowledge projects.

Scholarly Knowledge Production

As we have seen (Chapter 1), in response to Vine Deloria's critique of anthropologists in *Custer Died for Your Sins* (1969), together with Dell Hymes's (1972) call to "reinvent anthropology" and the more general critique of ethnographic authority (Clifford 1983), anthropologists and other scholars have worked toward greater accountability to Native peoples (Biolsi and Zimmerman 1997). Ethnographic research has also been affected by the more active role that tribal governments and cultural officials have taken in directing and regulating research as part of intensified claims to political and cultural sovereignty. Some tribal nations—for example, the Navajo—have developed their own institutional review boards, whereas others control ethnographic research through tribal councils, colleges, or research centers (Hernandez 2004; Brugge and Missaghian 2006). Some indigenous groups restrict research on religious topics (Bucko 2004), while many direct researchers toward issues of local concern.

In responding to internal and external critiques, and to changed conditions for research, ethnographers working in Native North America have developed reflexive, collaborative, dialogical, activist, and multisited approaches to research. Reflexive work includes critical analyses of the role that representations of Native peoples, including scholarly representations, have played in colonial and nationalist projects (Chapter 1). Dialogical (Tedlock 1983, 1999) and collaborative approaches (Lassiter 2005) address critiques of the ethnographic authority claimed by outsiders, while activist research responds to demands that anthropologists address issues of concern to Native peoples (Field 2004; Field and Fox 2007). Multisited research (Marcus 1998) allows ethnographers to consider intertribal and transnational phenomena.

Historians of anthropology have pointed to the seeds of current research trends in the Americanist tradition of narrative-based research with indigenous collaborators (Valentine and Darnell 1999; Darnell 2001; Bunzl 2004; Whiteley 2004; Kan and Strong 2006). Other scholars have emphasized disjunctures, pointing to dramatic shifts in ethnographic research and writing as anthropologists have interfaced with the fields of Native American and indigenous studies, ethnic studies, gender studies, and cultural studies—bringing critical race theory, a heightened concern with power and resistance, and what Linda Tuhiwai Smith (1999) calls "decolonizing methodologies" to their ethnographic work (Biolsi and Zimmerman 1997; Bauman and Briggs 2003; Yanagisako 2005; Cattelino 2010).

Collaborative Research, Cultural Property, and Indigenous Knowledge

The power of collaborative research is exemplified in a number of recent ethnographies, for example, *Abalone Tales: Collaborative Explorations of Sovereignty and Identity in Native California* (Field 2008). The product of multiple research partnerships that anthropologist Les Field established with scholars, elders, and leaders of the Ohlone, Pomo, Karuk, Hupa, Yurok, and Wiyot peoples, this book considers cultural, spiritual, economic, and political meanings of the abalone mollusk, both historically and in today's cultural revitalization and tribal recognition efforts. Employing a polyphonic writing style, Field and his coauthors discuss the role of abalone and the spirit being known as Abalone Woman in traditional culture; environmental degradation and cultural extinction; and repatriation, recognition, and cultural recovery efforts. Previously a book such as this might have interpreted abalone as a master symbol or trope of Native identity in Northern California; Field and his collaborators explicitly reject such a totalizing account, offering instead a kaleidoscopic array of interpretations as well as critical reappraisals and appropriations of classic ethnographic research.

Multivocality has proven to be an ideal form for collaborative representations, and even makes its way into the title of Ferguson, Colwell-Chanthaphonh, and Preucel's *History Is in the Land: Multivocal Tribal Traditions in Arizona's San Pedro Valley* (2006). An "archaeological ethnohistory" of the San Pedro Valley, this book contains narratives from tribal researchers from the O'odham, Hopi, Zuni, and Western Apache tribes, all of whom consider the valley an ancestral place. Another collaborative work, *Wiyaxayxt/Wiyaakaa'awn/As Days Go By: Our History, Our Land, Our People—The Cayuse, Umatilla, and Walla Walla,* has a trilingual title (Columbia River Sahaptin, Nez Perce, and English) befitting its agenda of offering "multiple voices, none uniquely authoritative" (Karson 2006, vii). Edited by an anthropologist employed by the Confederated Tribes' cultural center, the book contains sections written by various tribal officials, elders, and scholars as well as non-Indian scholars; the narrative moves from oral traditions to contact history to modern enactments of sovereignty. Like *Abalone Tales* and *History Is in the Land,* this book illustrates how a polyphonic style of representation is ideal for conveying multiple perspectives within and between Native American peoples.

Repatriation is the topic of another important collaborative work, *Blessing for a Long Time: The Sacred Pole of the Omaha Tribe* by Robin Ridington, an anthropologist, and the Omaha historian Dennis Hastings. This book chronicles the repatriation in 1989 of U'mon'hon'ti, or Venerable Man, from the Peabody Museum, where he was deposited a century earlier by the Omaha ethnologist Francis La Flesche and his mentor, Alice Cunningham Fletcher. Like other collaborative efforts, this book has an unusual structure: the authors describe it as a "circle of stories from the life of U'mon'hon'ti" (Ridington and Hastings 1997, xvii) and employ some of the conventions of Native American poetics, such as repetition.

The return of cultural artifacts and human remains is the product of a century-long movement that culminated, in the United States, in the passage of the Native American Graves Protection and Repatriation Act (NAGPRA) in 1990 (Fine-Dare 2002). Important milestones prior to the passage of NAGPRA include the return of Kwakwaka'wakw (Kwakiutl) potlatch artifacts from the National Museum of Canada according to an agreement completed in 1967 (Clifford 1991, 1997, 2004; Jacknis 2002); the repatriation of the Ahayu:da or Twin War Gods from the Smithsonian Institution to Zuni Pueblo in 1987 (Merrill,

Ladd, and Ferguson 1993); and the reclamation of eleven sacred wampum belts by the Six Nations from the National Museum of the American Indian in 1988 (Landsman 1997). These cases and others have been analyzed in accounts that question previous anthropologists' collecting practices while at the same time attending to the complexities of culturally appropriate possession, display, and use within indigenous communities.

The contested ownership of human remains is explored in ethnographic accounts of the controversy over the Ancient One/Kennewick Man and the remains of the Yahi man known as Ishi. The product of activist anthropology, Orin Starn's *Ishi's Brain: In Search of America's Last "Wild" Indian* (2004) tracks the repatriation and reburial of the remains of Ishi, revered as an ancestor by many Native people in California and well known to anthropologists because of his work with A. L. Kroeber and Edward Sapir. Starn's book explores the conflicting demands of science and humanity, as well as conflicting indigenous claims to Ishi's remains. Although Starn's story ends with a reburial, the remains of the Ancient One/Kennewick Man, inadvertently unearthed in 1996 near the Columbia River, rest in a university museum. The Kennewick remains were the subject of a NAGPRA claim by the Confederated Tribes of the Umatilla Indian Reservation and other tribes, a claim that was denied by the Ninth Circuit Court of Appeals (*Bonnichsen v. US* 2004). This case exposed tensions between Native American communities and some archaeologists and physical anthropologists, leading to questions about the adequacy of NAGPRA's provisions for establishing cultural connections between prehistoric remains and contemporary communities (Thomas 2000; Zimmerman 2004; Burke et al. 2008).

The question of ownership goes beyond repatriation and reburial, as Michael Brown (2003) discusses expansively in *Who Owns Native Culture?* This work surveys global disputes over intellectual property, including the copyrighting of indigenous images and ideas (Coombe 1998), the use of indigenous botanical knowledge (Barsh 2001), and the protection of indigenous sacred sites and cultural heritage. Arguing for the notion of a global commons, Brown expresses reservations about the commodifying and essentializing effects of cultural protection policies. Brown's view is contested by others (J. B. Jackson 2006; A. Simpson 2007) including, implicitly, Peter Nabokov, whose 2006 book, *Where the Lightning Strikes: The Lives of American Indian Sacred Places*, offers an analysis of one of the sites Brown discusses, Devils Tower or Bear Butte. The aim of Nabokov's multisited ethnography is to promote greater understanding of and respect for emergence sites, ancestral routes, pilgrimage sites, ceremonial sites, and other sacred places. Adopting the indigenous belief that sacred places are powerful animate beings, Nabokov offers sixteen "biographies" of sacred places, exploring the vulnerability of sites from Maine to Southern California, despite the 1978 passage of the American Indian Religious Freedom Act (AIRFA).

Several other notable ethnographies concern the relationship of indigenous people to the landscape. Although it is a multisited ethnography, Nabokov's book is similar in outlook to Keith Basso's acclaimed *Wisdom Sits in Places: Landscape and Language among the Western Apache* (1996), which demonstrates how indigenous ethical principles are grounded in an intimate knowledge of place-names and stories attached to place. In *Do Glaciers Listen?* Julie Cruikshank (2005) offers a timely exploration of northern Athapaskan narratives about glacial movement and melting. Cruikshank is particularly concerned with the appropriative practice of translating indigenous stories into bureaucratic notions of "traditional ecological knowledge." Among other critiques of subsuming Native environmental knowledges and practices into ecological terms is Shepard Krech's controversial ethnohistory, *The Ecological Indian: Myth and History.* Krech (1999) argues that the contemporary representation of the Indian as a "noble ecologist" (15) is a problematic revival of the myth of the Noble Savage, distorting indigenous cultures and histories (for other views, see Hames 2007; Harkin and Lewis 2007).

Institutional Research Sites, Sovereignty, and the Politics of Identity

The hallmark of traditional ethnographic research—sustained and intensive participant-observation in local communities—remains a significant methodology. Today's ethnographic fieldwork, however, often takes place in institutional settings, including tribal offices, courts, schools, cultural centers, and casinos. This is due in part to indigenous preferences: these tribally controlled institutions have come to serve as "contact zones" (Pratt 1992) between Native communities and the outside world, and they are places in which scholars can contribute to community-based research without intruding on private life. At the same time, tribal institutions are ideal sites for the study of self-determination, economic development, self-representation, and the politics of identity.

Research on contemporary tribal institutions often focuses on the politics of inclusion and exclusion, within tribes and in relation to surrounding communities. Thomas Biolsi's *Deadliest Enemies: Law and the Making of Race Relations on and off Rosebud Reservation* (2001) attributes racial hostility in South Dakota to the adversarial relations between the reservation and surrounding communities established by technologies of governance. *Choctaw Nation: A Story of American Indian Resurgence,* by the Choctaw anthropologist Valerie Lambert (2007), analyzes the increased emphasis on official tribal membership that Choctaw nation-building has entailed. Loretta Fowler's ethnohistory of Cheyenne-Arapaho politics (2002) contrasts the conflict and hegemonic individualism apparent in the tribal government with the cooperative and counter-hegemonic discourse characteristic of powwow activities. And, as we saw in Chapter 4, Circe Sturm's *Blood Politics* (2002) analyzes tribal policies and attitudes regarding the Cherokee Freedmen (descendants of enslaved Africans) through the lens of critical race theory.

Other important ethnographies derive from activist work with tribes seeking federal recognition. The politics of identity in the Mashpee tribal recognition case is well known through the works of James Clifford (1988b) and Jack Campisi (1991). Gerald Sider's (2003) ethnography of the Lumbee and Tuscarora focuses on the processes of social differentiation produced through the struggle for tribal acknowledgment as defined by the federal government (a well-defined tribal roll and territory as well as continuities in culture, history, and identity despite centuries of official policies intended to ensure the opposite). Sara-Larus Tolley's *Quest for Tribal Acknowledgment: California's Honey Lake Maidus* (2006) offers an analysis of the Kafkaesque federal acknowledgment process that is grounded in Foucault's theory of governmentality, Gramsci's theory of resistance, and Maidu theories about the workings of the trickster Coyote.

Tribally controlled schools, museums, and cultural centers are the subject of a number of institutionally based ethnographies. Following monographs on identity formation in an Indian boarding school (Lomawaima 1994) and a tribally controlled community school on the Navajo Nation (McCarty 2002), Tsianina Lomawaima and Teresa McCarty have collaborated on a synthetic account of schooling, citizenship, and sovereignty in *To Remain an Indian: Lessons in Democracy from a Century of Native American Education* (Lomawaima and McCarty 2006). Full-length ethnographies on the tribal museums and cultural centers of the Kwakwaka'wakw (Kwakiutl), Makah, Zuni, and Mashantucket Pequot consider repatriation and cultural revitalization (Jacknis 2002), the representation of identity and authenticity (Bodinger 2007), the politics of knowledge and secrecy (Isaac 2007), conflicts between indigenous museums and other institutions (Erikson 2002), and the redefining and "indigenizing" of the museum (Erikson 2002; Jacknis 2002; Isaac 2007). In addition, as we will see in Chapter 12, a strong body of scholarship is emerging on the National Museum of the American Indian (NMAI). These and other works have been deeply influenced by the research of James Clifford (1997, 2004) and Moira Simpson (2001) on self-representation in tribal museums and cultural centers.

Tribal museums have a long history (Child 2009), but many today are part of gaming and tourism enterprises. As of 2004, twenty-eight states permitted gaming by federally recognized tribes, although only twenty of these permitted casino-style gaming. Gaming brings in substantial revenue—more than $25 billion in 2006—that has led to notable improvements in living conditions, education, and governmental services in many communities. Debates about gaming have centered on social, economic, and environmental impacts; cultural authenticity; the uneven distribution of gaming income across tribes; and the implications for sovereignty of the state restrictions on gaming established in the Indian Gaming Regulatory Act of 1988 (Darian-Smith 2004; Cornell 2008).

One of the few case studies of the impact of gaming on an indigenous community, Jessica Cattelino's *High Stakes: Florida Seminole Gaming and Sovereignty* (2008), tracks Seminole economic development from the first high-stakes bingo parlor to a high-profile Supreme Court case to the ownership of the Hard Rock International corporation. Cattelino uses this case to engage critically with leading theories of political sovereignty and globalization. Following Iris Marion Young's (2001) theory of relational autonomy, Cattelino argues that the Florida Seminoles employ gaming to achieve political and cultural distinctiveness through relations of economic interdependency with surrounding settler communities, the state and federal government, other gaming tribes, and the global economy.

Thomas Biolsi (2005) has recently offered a broad framework for conceptualizing Native American struggles for sovereignty, delineating four ways in which indigenous political space is imagined in the United States: first, the bounded space of the reservation; next, traditional homelands beyond reservation borders, where tribes seek to share sovereignty over sites and resources; third, a national indigenous space in which people claim pan-Indian rights; and, finally, a hybrid political space in which dual citizenship is invoked. Although sovereignty is most often framed in terms of the first spatial imaginary, Natives have confronted the territorial limitations of tribal sovereignty by, for example, asserting off-reservation fishing rights and water rights (Nesper 2002; Lambert 2007) as well as rights to off-reservation sacred sites (Nabokov 2006; Tolley 2006).

But indigenous political space is even more complicated than this model suggests. We need to recognize a fifth space, the global arena, in which indigenous peoples are shaping a common identity and struggle for common rights, as discussed in Ronald Niezen's *The Origins of Indigenism: Human Rights and the Politics of Identity* (2003). Following Cree activists to the international arena, Niezen's research exemplifies the new multisited research on the indigenous rights movement. The emergence of hemispheric or global indigenous identities and their relationship to local identities, on the one hand, and processes of globalization, on the other, is an important research area today (B. Miller 2003; de la Cadena and Starn 2007; Huhndorf 2009; Niezen 2009).

Significant ethnographies on contemporary manifestations of traditional practices continue to appear, but anthropologists are increasingly focusing on border crossing, indigenous alliances, and hybrid expressions of identity. David Samuels (2004) has considered the expression of Western Apache identity in country music, while Anthony Webster (2009) has explored the ethnopoetics of English and bilingual poetry by Navajos. *Native Americans and the Christian*

Right: The Gendered Politics of Unlikely Alliances (2008) by Andrea Smith, a Cherokee scholar in the field of American studies, explores alliances among indigenous evangelicals, feminists, and prison rights advocates. *Native Hubs: Culture, Community, and Belonging in Silicon Valley and Beyond* (2007) by Renya Ramirez, a Winnebago anthropologist, analyzes the ways in which a transnational urban indigenous community creates a sense of belonging in the face of struggles over recognition and citizenship. And a number of anthropologists have studied the experience of indigenous immigrants to the United States, as in Lynn Stephen's *Transborder Lives: Indigenous Oaxacans in Mexico, California, and Oregon* (2007) and Laura Ortiz's *Mixtec Transnational Identity* (2005). Multisited and transnational research methodologies have joined collaboration, reflexivity, and activist anthropology as productive ethnographic approaches to indigenous North America.

Decolonizing Methodologies and the Representation of Indigeneity

In *Decolonizing Methodologies*, Maori studies scholar Linda Tuhiwai Smith (1999) has set an agenda for research on indigenous peoples, enumerating some two dozen "indigenous projects," most of which involve various ways of empowering and healing indigenous communities (142–162). If we take these projects as fairly representative of the projects of Native American communities, it is clear that scholars have made progress in aligning their work with indigenous concerns since Deloria's (1969) critique of "Anthropologists and Other Friends" (78–100). The following list suggests how contemporary ethnographic projects converge with Smith's indigenous projects.

- The projects of *testimony* and *storytelling*: the collecting and analyzing of Native narratives, as in the collaborative ethnography, *Abalone Tales* (Field 2008), or the works of Julie Cruikshank on the Yukon, *Life Lived Like a Story* (1990) and *The Social Life of Stories* (1998).
- *Celebrating survival*: the documentation and analysis of traditional cultural forms such as Kiowa powwow music (Lassiter 1998), Yuchi ceremonialism (J. B. Jackson 2003), or the Lakota sweat lodge (Bucko 1998).
- *Revitalizing* and *remembering*: participation in cultural maintenance and recovery efforts, as in Patricia Erikson's (2002) work with the Makah, or Jennifer Karson's (2006) with the Cayuse, Umatilla, and Walla Walla.
- *Indigenizing, naming*, and *reframing*: scholarship on indigenous languages and worldview, including Keith Basso's *Wisdom Sits in Places* (1996) and Julie Cruikshank's *Do Glaciers Listen?* (2005).

- *Claiming* and *protecting*: scholarship on treaty rights (Nesper 2002), human rights (Niezen 2003), and sacred sites, such as Peter Nabokov's *Where the Lightning Strikes* (2006).
- *Returning, restoring,* and *intervening*: activist works on tribal recognition (Sider 2003; Tolley 2006) or on repatriation, such as Robin Ridington and Dennis Hastings's *Blessing for a Long Time* (1997).
- *Representing* and *creating*: analyses of tribal self-representation and hybrid cultural forms such as cultural centers (Erikson 2002), indigenous film and radio (Klain and Peterson 2000; L. Peterson 2011), popular music (D. Samuels 2004), and bilingual poetry (Webster 2009).
- *Gendering*: scholarship on indigenous expressions and experiences of gender and sexuality, such as Roscoe's *The Zuni Man-Woman* (1992) and recent collaborative works on Navajo women (Schwarz 2003; Lamphere 2007).
- *Democratizing* and *negotiating*: analyses of tribal institutions and their relations with settler society, as in Sturm's *Blood Politics* (2002), Biolsi's *Deadliest Enemies* (2001), and Cattelino's *High Stakes* (2008).
- *Reading* and *writing*: scholarship on indigenous literacies, such as Bender's (2002) ethnography on Cherokee use of Sequoyah's syllabary.
- *Discovery* and *sharing*: works on the production and circulation of indigenous knowledge, for example, Teresa McCarty's (2002) ethnography of the Navajo's Rough Rock demonstration school, and Gwyneira Isaac's (2007) ethnography of the Zuni tribal museum.
- *Envisioning*: scholarship on prophecy (Geertz 1994; Cruikshank 1998) and on strategies for securing the future, such as Cattelino's *High Stakes* (2008).
- *Connecting* and *networking*: investigations of local urban networks, such as *Native Hubs* (Ramirez 2007), and indigenous use of electronic technologies, such as *Native on the Net* (Landzelius 2006), as well as studies of global indigenous movements and identities (Niezen 2003, 2009; B. Miller 2003).

There is, of course, much more to be done in aligning ethnographic scholarship with indigenous realities and concerns. In particular, the developing ethnography of transnational indigenous identities, struggles, networks, and migrations needs to be further developed. But with its strong commitment to collaborative and activist research, multivocal forms of representation, and attentiveness to the particularities of lived experience, ethnographic research continues to play a significant role in the increasingly complex and interdisciplinary field of knowledge about indigenous peoples.

Bibliographic Note

For other discussions of recent ethnographic scholarship, see overviews in Biolsi (2004b), Whiteley (2004), Kan and Strong (2006), Cattelino (2010), A. Simpson (2011), and Starn (2011). The field of Native American and indigenous studies is discussed in Robert Warrior's *Tribal Secrets* (1995), Devon Mihesuah and Angela Cavender Wilson's *Indigenizing the Academy* (2004), Clara Sue Kidwell and Alan Velie's *Native American Studies* (2005), Waziyatawin Angela Wilson and Michael Yellow Bird's *For Indigenous Eyes Only* (2005), Marisol de la Cadena and Orin Starn's *Indigenous Experience Today* (2007), and Chris Anderson's "Critical Indigenous Studies" (2009).

Chapter Twelve
A Native Space on the National Mall

As we have seen, two important developments in Indian Country today are the repatriation of material objects and human remains from non-Native institutions and the concomitant expansion of venues for Native self-representation, including indigenously controlled museums and cultural centers. These are related developments; in fact, the movement for self-representation may itself be considered a way of repatriating knowledge—or, as the Lenape scholar Joanne Barker (2005) puts it, achieving "intellectual sovereignty" (25).

In just a few years of existence, the National Museum of the American Indian (NMAI) in Washington, DC, has come to stand as perhaps "the dominant imaginary of the Indigenous Americas," in the words of the Tuscarora curator and artist Jolene Rickard (2011, 465). Founded by an act of Congress in 1989 as a new branch of the Smithsonian Institution, the NMAI was given a mandate to move toward a majority representation of Native Americans on its board, to inventory all human remains in its collection (and the collection of the Smithsonian as a whole), and to repatriate Native artifacts and human remains at the request of affiliated tribes. This mandate anticipated by a year the passage of the Native American Graves Protection and Repatriation Act (NAGPRA 1990), which instituted a more general process of repatriation (Fine-Dare 2002; Erikson 2008). Both NAGPRA and the National Museum of the American Indian were the culmination of decades of work by indigenous activists trying to regain control over the material and spiritual remains of their ancestors as well as the interpretation of indigenous realities.

The core of the NMAI holdings are more than 800,000 items from indigenous North and South America originally acquired by the New York financier and collector George Gustav Heye. Previously held by the independent Museum of the American Indian in New York, the collections were transferred to the Smithsonian Institution in 1989. Most are held in a storage and research facility in Maryland; exhibition spaces include a museum in a historic building in Manhattan in addition to the new Museum of the American Indian in Washington, DC. After an extensive consultation and planning process, the new museum opened in 2004, under the directorship of Richard West Jr., a Southern Cheyenne attorney (Jacknis 2008; McMullen 2009). The Pawnee attorney Kevin Gover assumed the directorship three years later.

The National Museum of the American Indian, together with more than two hundred tribal museums and cultural centers, exemplifies a postcolonial era in museology (M. Simpson 2001). Often but not always benefitting from repatriation, tribal museums are central to local cultural preservation and revitalization efforts, often serving as a community center and educational facility as well as a storage and display space. Native groups that repatriate artifacts and human remains allocate control over the objects and their interpretation in culturally appropriate ways, which vary according to the type of material and the group in question.

In the case of the National Museum of the American Indian, the culturally appropriate treatment of artifacts is a complicated matter indeed, given the scope of its collections and the breadth of its constituencies. While the NMAI has an extensive program of research and community outreach, it is the permanent exhibitions that have captured the greatest public attention, evoking strong reactions in the museum's audiences. These reactions indicate the challenges that the NMAI's representational practices pose to the expectations of members of the dominant society (Berlo and Jonaitis 2005; Isaac 2007) as well as the intensifying effect of locating the museum in the monumental center of the nation.

As scholars in the field of museum studies have emphasized, museums serve many purposes: they are touchstones for the past, storehouses for the future, and gathering places in the present. Through collected objects, labels and narratives, exhibition design, and architecture, museums select and intensify particular ways of imagining the past, present, and future. Like captivity narratives (Part Three), national museums serve as a selective tradition, a central node in the collective imaginary. Like youth organizations (Part Four), they serve to shape particular kinds of subjectivities.

A key element in the selective intensification of history and culture that museums accomplish is their placement in particular physical and cultural landscapes. Through the choice of a site, the design of space, the display of objects, and the telling of narratives, museums create what Stephen Greenblatt (1991b) has called "resonance" (Bodinger and Strong 2005). Museums are containers in which objects and stories circulate through systems of meaning, deriving power from the resonant qualities of their chambers, which amplify the meanings assigned to their contents. Museums also project their force beyond their walls to participate in ongoing discourses of nation, culture, history, and identity. This is particularly apparent in the case of controversial exhibitions such as *The West as America* (Chapter 3) and convention-defying museums such as the National Museum of the American Indian.

Built on a prominent site on the eastern end of the National Mall, the NMAI is a venue for Native American self-representation that is unprecedented in its visibility and resonance. Housed in a striking building that combines classical and indigenous elements, the museum tempers the strong nationalist resonances of its site with landscaping indigenous to the tidewater region. This is just one of many antinomies the museum deftly negotiates. The cosmopolitan location of the museum contrasts with the dispersed authority of the exhibition's many community curators, while the unified identity of its title—"*the* American Indian"—is refracted in highly localized displays that span the Western Hemisphere. These complex strategies of localization, as we might call them, realize indigenous projects and express indigenous identities on the level of the nation—it is a "national museum," after all—but also on the level of the community, the geographic region, the hemisphere, and the globe.

"Strategies of localization" is a term commonly used to refer to the processes through which global phenomena are adapted to local physical and cultural environments; in the present context it denotes representational practices that produce particular experiences of space. The most obvious strategy of localization at the NMAI is, of course, its privileged site. Established by Congress as a "living memorial" to Native cultures (NMAI Act 1989), the National Museum of the American Indian occupies what is often described as "the last available site" on the Mall, itself widely recognized as a center of national memory (Bloom 2005, 327). Securing this site was a great achievement, for it allows indigenous curators to control the representation of themselves in the national center as well as in the tribal museums dispersed across the country. In this center a "memorial" space becomes a strong statement of indigenous survival and vitality.

The NMAI faces the US Capitol, and from its grounds one can see the Washington Monument at the other end of the mall. The museum's site speaks clearly of the importance of Native peoples in US historical memory, and this is amplified by the renowned Blackfoot architect Douglas Cardinal's design—which from some vantage points echoes the dome of Congress. From the steps of the Capitol one now looks directly down on another dome, that of the National Museum of the American Indian, which has the effect of legitimizing indigenous claims to American space. The NMAI enacts both symbolically and materially a "reclamation of Indian land," as Amanda Cobb (2005) puts it (367).

The NMAI is separated from the mall by a waterfall, a stream, and plants indigenous to the Potomac wetlands that long predate the construction of the US Capitol. The museum arises from the landscape somewhat like a looming limestone cliff. The rough-cut, curvilinear sandstone exterior surfaces give an eroded, ancient quality to the museum that contrasts effectively with the polished marble surface and classical architecture of the Capitol and other buildings and monuments on the Mall (see Figure 15). In fact, the NMAI manages to make these classical buildings appear as European interlopers, an effect that is intensified by the landscaping. The exterior produces a distinctive if hybrid sense of place through blending landscaping evoking the Potomac, architecture evoking the cliff dwellings of the Pueblo Southwest, and boulders brought to the site from the extreme northern and southern points of the hemisphere and as far west as Hawaii. This strategy of blending the local and the hemispheric is also characteristic of the museum's interior, contrasting strongly with the more profoundly local and particularistic representational strategies of tribal museums.

This museum, like much else on the Mall, is meant to be read symbolically, and its message is clearly "We were here before, we're here after, and we'll be here into the future far beyond," as founding director Richard West has put it (Hayden and Lautman 2004, para. 11). The first person plural is omnipresent once one enters the museum, differentiating the NMAI from the typical ethnographic museum. However, the indigenous "we" alternates between the hemispheric "we" invoked by Richard West and the more localized "we" of a particular indigenous community. Despite the unifying emphasis of the museum's name—which follows

Figure 15. The National Museum of the American Indian and the Washington Monument, Washington, DC, 2004. Photo by Chuck Kennedy/MCT via Getty Images.

colonial precedent in putting all indigenous peoples in the hemisphere under a common label—the NMAI, like Native people themselves, shifts between generalizing and particularizing representations of indigenous identity.

Upon entering the museum, the visitor is greeted with a revolving display of words for "welcome" in indigenous languages from North, Central, and South America. From that point on, the visitor is offered multivocal perspectives on indigenous experience in the Western Hemisphere. The hemispheric reach of the NMAI comes across as a highly unusual strategy of localization for a "National Museum" on the National Mall. This strategy was made possible by the breadth of the enormous Heye collection, but it was also an intentional choice aligned with the indigenous rights movement of the period in which the museum was under construction—a movement facilitated by the growth of the Internet, the increasing ease of intercontinental travel, and the development of United Nations' protocols on indigenous rights. This twenty-first-century museum presents a hemispheric indigenous imaginary, one that participates in an increasingly interwoven indigenous future grounded, nevertheless, in a multiplicity of localized experiences.

Beyond the welcome screen, the visitor enters a huge rotunda with a stepped dome ceiling and an opening to the sky that evokes a smoke hole and lets in natural light. The light creates a play of prism-created rainbows on the cantilevered roof. The four directions and a center are marked on the floor of the chamber, creating a sense of sacred space. This somewhat stark, modernist space—designed as a ceremonial hall—is made more intimate by a woven copper screen reminiscent of indigenous basketry (Berlo and Jonaitis 2005, 18).

Elsewhere in the museum, however, the space is cramped rather than expansive. The museum's map shows the display space as following a plan reminiscent of the Southwest's Chaco Canyon, and walking from display area to display area is, indeed, somewhat reminiscent of visiting the small rooms of a Pueblo ruin. Twenty-four display areas have been given over to community curators, eight illustrating each of the themes of the three main exhibitions: *Our Universes* (on traditional knowledges), *Our Peoples* (on Native histories), and *Our Lives* (on contemporary experience and identity). These were designed as rotating exhibits in order to give additional Native communities the opportunity to take their own turns at self-representation in the future. Community curators were asked to choose both the objects they wished to exhibit and the stories they wanted to tell, and in each case the curators are themselves photographed and described.

Here, again, the NMAI is a twenty-first-century institution, employing techniques of community curation and curatorial authorship that are coming to replace the anonymous and authoritative curatorial voice of the traditional museum (Karp, Kreamer, and Lavine 1992; Peers and Brown 2003). This representational strategy, however, is not universally admired; indeed, mainstream critics have found it disorienting and intellectually disappointing. Largely abandoning traditional museological or scholarly categories—be they material technology, culture areas, or linear chronology—the Museum of the American Indian offers a genuinely pluralistic representation of indigenous cultures and histories. One reviewer, Philip Jenkins (2005), labeled the NMAI an "antimuseum" and likened the experience of visiting the museum to taking a "journey without maps."

This is clearly hyperbole. The NMAI is a postcolonial museum that uses strategies of representation, including multivocality and pastiche, that are identified with postmodernism but are also appropriate for representing the diversity of indigenous cultures. At the same time, however, the NMAI uses representational strategies that make it recognizably a museum. There are glass cases, objects, and labels, and the overarching themes of Our Universes, Our Peoples, and Our Lives organize the three display floors. There are dramatic permanent installations in each of the three main exhibitions that offer a common perspective on the theme, such as Jolene Rickard's striking visualization of shifting and mixed indigenous identities in *Our Lives* (see Figure 16). Visitors who feel uncomfortable in the galleries have recourse to the more familiar commercial space of the high-end art gallery and low-end gift shop. The Mitsitam Native Foods Café provides hospitality (the name means "let's eat" in the local Piscataway language). Here the ethnographic "culture area" classification eschewed by the rest of the museum appears as a culinary form, with the Northeast represented by cranberries and maple syrup; the Plains, by buffalo burgers; Mesoamerica, by tamales; and the Northwest, by salmon.

The twenty-four community exhibits are tied together by a celebration of Native "survivance," a term coined by the Anishinaabe scholar Gerald Vizenor

Figure 16. Jolene Rickard (Tuscarora), installation in *Our Lives* exhibit, National Museum of the American Indian, Smithsonian Institution (2005). The installation asks, "What is Native?" Photo by Walter Larrimore.

(1993, 1999, 2009) and glossed at the NMAI as "how we continue to be Native in rapidly changing times." "Five Hundred Years of Survival," the trope that developed during the Columbian Quincentenary as a counterpoint to the dominant narrative of discovery (Chapter 3), has found a prominent home in the NMAI.

As some critics have pointed out, another counter-narrative dating to the quincentenary, "Five Hundred Years of Conquest and Resistance," is downplayed at the NMAI. Hundreds of guns, gold items, and Native American translations of the Bible are given an aesthetic presentation that belies the devastating effect of colonial violence, resource extraction, and religious persecution on Native communities. But this is not primarily a critical history museum; it is, rather, a celebration of indigenous vitality. The NMAI is a strong Native presence on the National Mall, one that serves as a focal point for the gathering and self-representation of indigenous communities from the north to the south of this hemisphere. This is a significant accomplishment indeed. The museum resonates with the joy of having succeeded, at long last, in re-creating a "Native place" on the Potomac River (Blue Spruce 2004). As a gathering place, a venue for self-representation, and a demonstration of multiple indigenous imaginaries, the National Museum of the American Indian shouts survivance loud and clear.

Bibliographic Note

The critiques discussed in this chapter have been taken seriously at the NMAI. In a panel called "NMAI 2.0" at the fourth annual meeting of the Native American and Indigenous Studies Association, three NMAI staff members announced that the museum plans to redesign all its permanent exhibits in order to better communicate with its mainstream audience (Tayac, Smith, and Ash-Milby 2012). It is highly unusual for a museum to undertake such a major transformation, especially so soon after opening. In this, as in so much else, the NMAI is realizing its potential for being what founding director Richard West called a "museum different" (Rothstein 2004).

Two collections of essays explore the NMAI as a product of activism and repatriation, a site for indigenous curatorship and community collaboration, and an imperfect expression of cultural sovereignty, indigenous voice, indigenous historical memory, and multiple indigenous identities (Lonetree and Cobb-Greetham 2008; Sleeper-Smith 2009). The latter volume also contains essays on several tribal museums.

The notion of "resonance" was developed in collaboration with John Bodinger, with whom I organized a panel for the 2005 annual meetings of the American Anthropological Association. Works on Native American self-representation in museums include those of Bodinger (2007), on the Mashantucket Pequot museum and cultural center; Erikson (2002), on the Makah Cultural and Research Center; Jacknis (2002), on the collecting, renaissance, and repatriation of Kwakwaka'wakw (Kwakiutl) art; and Isaac (2007), on a Zuni tribal museum. Moira Simpson (2001), Lawlor (2006), and Cooper (2007) offer comparative discussions of the representation and self-representation of Native Americans in museums. Mihesuah (2000) and Fine-Dare (2002) offer general treatments of repatriation, while Ridington and Hastings (1997) and Jacknis (2002) offer important case studies. *Box of Treasures* (1983) and *The Return of the Sacred Pole* (1988) are excellent documentary films on repatriation.

The field of critical museum studies is expansive. Among the relevant significant works are Ames, *Museums, the Public, and Anthropology* (1986) and *Cannibal Tours and Glass Boxes: The Anthropology of Museums* (1992); Karp and Lavine, *Exhibiting Cultures: The Poetics and Politics of Museum Display* (1991); Hooper-Greenhill, *Museums and the Shaping of Knowledge* (1992); Karp, Kreamer, and Lavine, *Museums and Communities: The Politics of Public Culture* (1992); Moira Simpson, *Making Representations: Museums in the Post-Colonial Era* (2001); Peers and Brown, *Museums and Source Communities* (2003); Hendry, *Reclaiming Culture: Indigenous People and Self-Representation* (2005); and a series of influential essays by James Clifford (1988a, 1988c, 1991, 1997, 2004).

Epilogue

Trickster has accompanied us in our journey through representational space. Whether in the form of Harry Fonseca's shuffling Coyote (see Figure 2) or Gerald Vizenor's tribal striptease, Trickster reminds us of our transformative ability to cast off and recast what Vizenor (2005) calls the "captured images" that serve as a "simulation and ruse of colonial dominance" (181; 1999, vii). In the spirit of Trickster, here's to turning representation against itself in the fight for survivance, for "a new consciousness of coexistence" (1981, x), for a new Turtle Island.

REFERENCES

Print Publications and Manuscripts (Including Online Texts)

"1492: America before Columbus." 1991. Special issue, *National Geographic* (October).

"About *World Song*." n.d. Press release. Columbus, OH: AmeriFlora '92: Celebration of Discovery.

Abu-Lughod, Lila. 1991. "Writing against Culture." In *Recapturing Anthropology: Working in the Present*, edited by Richard G. Fox, 137–162. Santa Fe: School of American Research Press.

Adams, David Wallace. 1995. *Education for Extinction: American Indians and the Boarding School Experience, 1875–1928.* Lawrence: University Press of Kansas.

Albers, Patricia C. 1989. "From Illusion to Illumination: Anthropological Studies of American Indian Women." In *Gender and Anthropology: Critical Reviews for Research and Teaching*, edited by Sandra Morgen, 132–170. Washington, DC: American Anthropological Association.

Aleiss, Angela. 2005. *Making the White Man's Indian: Native Americans and Hollywood Movies.* Westport, CT: Praeger.

Alexie, Sherman. 1996. *Indian Killer.* New York: Atlantic Monthly Press.

Alfred, Taiaiake. 1999a. *Heeding the Voices of Our Ancestors: Kahnawake Mohawk Politics and the Rise of Native Nationalism.* Don Mills, ON: Oxford University Press Canada.

———. 1999b. *Peace, Power, Righteousness: An Indigenous Manifesto.* Don Mills, ON: Oxford University Press Canada.

———. 2002. "Sovereignty." In *A Companion to Native American History*, edited by Philip J. Deloria and Neal Salisbury, 460–474. Malden, MA: Blackwell Publishers.

Allen, Chadwick. 2002. *Blood Narrative: Indigenous Identity in American Indian and Maori Literary and Activist Texts.* Durham, NC: Duke University Press.

Allen, Paula Gunn. 1988. "Selected Poems." In *Harper's Anthology of 20th Century Native American Poetry*, edited by Duane Niatum. New York: HarperCollins.

Alliance for Cultural Democracy. 1991. "500 Years of Resistance." Special issue, *Huracán* (Summer).

"America before Columbus: The Untold Story." 1991. *U.S. News and World Report*, special pull-out section (July 8).

American Psychological Association. 2005. "Resolution Recommending the Immediate Retirement of American Indian Mascots, Symbols, Images, and Personalities by Schools, Colleges, Universities, Athletic Teams, and Organizations." In *The Native American Mascot Controversy: A Handbook*, edited by C. Richard King, 209–216. Lanham, Toronto, and Plymouth, UK: Scarecrow Press, 2010.

Ames, Michael M. 1986. *Museums, the Public, and Anthropology*. Vancouver, BC: University of British Columbia Press.

———. 1992. *Cannibal Tours and Glass Boxes: The Anthropology of Museums*. Seattle: University of Washington Press.

Anaya, James S. 2004. *Indigenous Peoples in International Law*, 2nd ed. New York: Oxford University Press.

Andén-Papadopoulos, Kari. 2008. "The Abu Ghraib Torture Photographs: New Frames, Visual Culture, and the Power of Images." *Journalism* 9 (1): 5–30.

Anderson, Benedict. 1983. *Imagined Communities: Reflections on the Origin and Spread of Nationalism*. London: Verso.

Anderson, Chris. 2009. "Critical Indigenous Studies: From Difference to Density." *Cultural Studies Review* 15 (2): 80–100.

Anderson, Mark Cronlund. 2007. *Cowboy Imperialism and Hollywood Film*. New York: Peter Lang Publishers.

Apel, Dora. 2005. "Torture Culture: Lynching Photographs and the Images of Abu Ghraib." *Art Journal* 64 (2): 88–100.

Associated Press. 1992. "Squabble Spoils U.S. Pavilion Opening/Indian 'Princess' Kept out of Expo '92 after Native Credentials Questioned." *Houston Chronicle*, April 21. http://www.chron.com/CDA/archives/archive.mpl/1992_1050402/squabble-spoils-u-s-pavilion-opening-indian-prince.html.

———. 2011. "Fighting Mad: North Dakota School, Political Leaders Meet with NCAA about Nickname." *Washington Post*, August 12. http://www.washingtonpost.com/sports/north-dakota-school-political-leaders-meet-with-ncaa-about-fighting-sioux-nickname/2011/08/12/gIQAz59RBJ_story.html.

Atwood, Barbara. 2010. *Children, Tribes, and States: Adoption and Custody Conflicts over American Indian Children*. Durham: Carolina Academic Press.

Aufderheide, Patricia, ed. 1992. *Beyond PC: Toward a Politics of Understanding*. St. Paul: Graywolf Press.

Axtell, James. 1981. *The European and the Indian*. Oxford: Oxford University Press.

———. 1985. *The Invasion Within: The Contest of Cultures in Colonial North America*. Oxford: Oxford University Press.

———. 1988. *After Columbus: Essays in the Ethnohistory of Colonial North America*. Oxford: Oxford University Press.

———. 1992. *Beyond 1492: Encounters in Colonial North America*. Oxford: Oxford University Press.

———. 2001. *Natives and Newcomers: The Cultural Origins of North America*. Oxford: Oxford University Press.

Baca, Lawrence R. 1988. "The Legal Status of American Indians." In *Handbook of North American Indians*, edited by William C. Sturtevant, vol. 4: *History of Indian-White Relations*, edited by Wilcomb E. Washburn, 230–237. Washington, DC: Smithsonian

Institution, for sale by the US Government Printing Office, Superintendent of Documents.

———. 2004. "Native Images in Schools and the Racially Hostile Environment." *Journal of Sport and Social Issues* 28 (1): 71–78.

Baker, Marie Annharte. 1990. "Cheeky Moon." *Gatherings: The En'owkin Journal of First North American Peoples* 1 (Fall): 38. Also in Marie Annharte Baker, *Being on the Moon*. Winlaw, BC: Polestar Press, 1990.

Bakhtin, Mikhail. 1984. *The Dialogical Principle*. Minneapolis: University of Minnesota Press.

Banks, Lynn Reid. 1981. *The Indian and the Cupboard*. New York: Doubleday.

———. 1986. *The Return of the Indian*. New York: Doubleday.

———. 1989. *The Secret of the Indian*. New York: Doubleday.

———. 1993. *The Mystery of the Cupboard*. New York: William Morrow.

Barker, Joanne. 2005. "For Whom Sovereignty Matters." In *Sovereignty Matters: Locations of Contestation and Possibility in Indigenous Struggles for Self-Determination*, edited by Joanne Barker, 1–31. Lincoln: University of Nebraska Press.

Barreiro, José, ed. 1990. "View from the Shore: American Indian Perspectives on the Quincentenary." Special Columbus Quincentenary edition, *Northeast Indian Quarterly* 7 (3).

Barsh, Russel Lawrence. 2001. "Who Steals Indigenous Knowledge?" In *Proceedings of the 95th Annual Meeting of the American Society of International Law*, 153–161. http://www.jstor.org/stable/25659474.

Barth, John. 1980 [1967]. *The Sot-Weed Factor*. Toronto: Bantam Books.

Basso, Keith H. 1979. *Portraits of "The Whiteman": Linguistic Play and Cultural Symbols among the Western Apache*. Cambridge: Cambridge University Press.

———. 1996. *Wisdom Sits in Places: Landscape and Language among the Western Apache*. Albuquerque: University of New Mexico Press.

Bataille, Gretchen M., ed. 2001. *Native American Representations: First Encounters, Distorted Images, and Literary Appropriations*. Lincoln: University of Nebraska Press.

Bauman, Richard, and Charles L. Briggs. 2003. *Voices of Modernity: Language Ideologies and the Politics of Inequality*. Cambridge: Cambridge University Press.

Bender, Margaret. 2002. *Signs of Cherokee Culture: Sequoyah's Syllabary in Eastern Cherokee Life*. Chapel Hill: University of North Carolina Press.

Benjamin, Walter. 1969. "The Work of Art in the Age of Mechanical Reproduction." In *Illuminations*, edited by Hannah Arendt, 217–253. New York: Schocken Books.

Bercovitch, Sacvan. 1978. *The American Jeremiad*. Madison: University of Wisconsin Press.

Berkhofer, Robert F., Jr. 1978. *The White Man's Indian: Images of the American Indian from Columbus to the Present*. New York: Alfred A. Knopf.

Berlo, Janet Catherine, and Ruth B. Phillips. 1992. "'Vitalizing the Things of the Past': Museum Representations of Native North American Art in the 1990s." *Museum Anthropology* 16 (1): 29–43.

Berlo, Janet Catherine, and Aldona Jonaitis. 2005. "'Indian Country' on Washington's Mall—The National Museum of the American Indian: A Review Essay." *Museum Anthropology* 28 (2): 17–30.

Berman, Tressa. 2004. "Cultural Appropriation." In *A Companion to the Anthropology of American Indians*, edited by Thomas Biolsi, 383–397. Malden, MA: Blackwell Publishers.

Bieder, Robert E. 1986. *Science Encounters the Indian, 1820–1880: The Early Years of American Ethnology*. Norman: University of Oklahoma Press.

———. 2000. "The Representations of Indian Bodies in Nineteenth-Century American Anthropology." In *Repatriation Reader: Who Owns American Indian Remains?*, edited by Devon Mihesuah, 19–36. Lincoln: University of Nebraska Press.

Bigelow, Bill, and Bob Peterson, eds. 1991. "Rethinking Columbus." Special issue, *Rethinking Schools*. Milwaukee: Rethinking Schools Ltd., in collaboration with the Network of Educators on the Americas.

———. 1998. *Rethinking Columbus: The Next 500 Years*. Milwaukee: Rethinking Schools Ltd.

Biolsi, Thomas. 1995. "The Birth of the Reservation: Making the Modern Individual among the Lakota." *American Ethnologist* 22 (1): 28–54.

———. 2001. *Deadliest Enemies: Law and the Making of Race Relations on and off Rosebud Reservation*. Berkeley: University of California Press.

———. 2004a. "Political and Legal Status ('Lower 48' States)." In *A Companion to the Anthropology of American Indians*, edited by Thomas Biolsi, 231–247. Malden, MA: Blackwell Publishers.

———, ed. 2004b. *A Companion to the Anthropology of American Indians*. Malden, MA: Blackwell Publishers.

———. 2005. "Imagined Geographies: Sovereignty, Indigenous Space, and American Indian Struggle." *American Ethnologist* 32 (2): 239–259.

Biolsi, Thomas, and Larry Zimmerman, eds. 1997. *Indians and Anthropologists: Vine Deloria Jr. and the Critique of Anthropology*. Tucson: University of Arizona Press.

Bird, S. Elizabeth, ed. 1996. *Dressing in Feathers: The Construction of the Indian in American Popular Culture*. Boulder, CO: Westview Press.

Bloom, John. 2005. "Exhibition Review: National Museum of the American Indian." Special issue: Indigenous Peoples of the United States, *American Studies* 46 (3–4, Fall–Winter): 327–338. Published jointly with *Indigenous Studies Today* 1 (Fall 2005/Spring 2006).

Blu, Karen. 1980. *The Lumbee Problem: The Making of an American Indian People*. New York: Cambridge University Press.

Blue Spruce, Duane. 2004. *Spirit of a Native Place: Building the National Museum of the American Indian*. Washington, DC: National Geographic Society.

Bodinger de Uriarte, John J. 2007. *Casino and Museum: Representing Mashantucket Pequot Identity*. Tucson: The University of Arizona Press.

Bodinger de Uriarte, John J., and Pauline Turner Strong. 2005. "Museum Resonance: Representing the Past of the Present and Future." Panel introduction, annual meetings, American Anthropological Association, Washington, DC (November).

Bodnar, John. 1993. *Remaking America: Public Memory, Commemoration, and Patriotism in the Twentieth Century*. Princeton, NJ: Princeton University Press.

Boldt, Menno, and Anthony Long. 1985. *The Quest for Justice: Aboriginal Peoples and Aboriginal Rights*. Toronto: University of Toronto Press.

"Border Fence Information." 2011. The University of Texas at Brownsville and Texas Southmost College. http://www.utb.edu/newsinfo/Pages/BorderFence.aspx.

Bordewich, Fergus M. 1996. *Killing the White Man's Indian: Reinventing Native Americans at the End of the Twentieth Century*. New York: Doubleday.

Bragdon, Kathleen J. 2001. *The Columbia Guide to American Indians of the Northeast*. New York: Columbia University Press.

Briggs, Charles L. 1996. "The Politics of Discursive Authority in Research on the 'Invention of Tradition.'" *Cultural Anthropology* 11 (4): 435–469.

Brightman, Robert A. 2006. "Culture and Culture Theory in Native North America." In *New Perspectives on Native North America: Cultures, Histories and Representations*, edited by Sergei A. Kan and Pauline Turner Strong, 351–394. Lincoln: University of Nebraska Press.

Brooks, James F. 2002. *Captives and Cousins: Slavery, Kinship, and Community in the Southwest Borderlands*. Chapel Hill: University of North Carolina Press.

Brown, Jennifer S. H. 1996. *Strangers in Blood: Fur Trade Company Families in Indian Country*. Norman: University of Oklahoma Press.

Brown, Michael F. 2003. *Who Owns Native Culture?* Cambridge, MA: Harvard University Press.

Brugge, Doug, and Mariam Missaghian. 2006. "Protecting the Navajo People through Tribal Regulation of Research." *Science and Engineering Ethics* 12 (3): 491–507.

Buckler, Helen, Mary F. Fiedler, and Martha F. Allen. 1961. *Wo-He-Lo: The Story of the Camp Fire Girls, 1910–1960*. New York: Holt, Rinehart and Winston.

Bucko, Raymond A. 1998. *The Lakota Ritual of the Sweat Lodge*. Lincoln: University of Nebraska Press.

———. 2004. "Religion." In *A Companion to the Anthropology of American Indians*, edited by Thomas Biolsi, 171–195. Malden, MA: Blackwell Publishers.

Bunch, Lonnie. 1992. "Embracing Controversy: Museum Exhibitions and the Politics of Change." *The Public Historian* 14 (3, Summer): 63–65.

Bunzl, Matti. 2004. "Boas, Foucault, and the 'Native Anthropologist': Notes toward a Neo-Boasian Anthropology." *American Anthropologist* 106 (3): 435–442.

Burke, Heather, Claire Smith, Dorothy Lippert, Joe Watkins, and Larry Zimmerman. 2008. *Kennewick Man: Perspectives on the Ancient One*. Walnut Creek, CA: Left Coast Press.

Burnham, Michelle. 1997. *Captivity and Sentiment: Cultural Exchange in American Literature, 1682–1861*. Hanover, NH: Dartmouth University Press.

Butler, Judith. 2004. *Precarious Life: The Power of Mourning and Violence*. London: Verso.

———. 2008. "Sexual Politics, Torture, and Secular Time." *The British Journal of Sociology* 59 (1): 1–23.

———. 2010. *Frames of War: When Is Life Grievable?* London: Verso.

Calloway, Colin. 1992. *North Country Captives: Selected Narratives of Indian Captivity from Vermont and New Hampshire*. Hanover, NH: University Press of New England.

Camp Fire Girls. 1914. *The Book of the Camp Fire Girls*. 5th ed., revised. New York: National Headquarters.

Campisi, Jack. 1991. *The Mashpee Indians: Tribe on Trial*. Syracuse, NY: Syracuse University Press.

Canneto, Stephen. 1992. Promotional materials for *Navstar '92*. Columbus, Ohio. Author's collection.

Carriere, Jeanne Louise. 1994. "Representing the Native American: Culture, Jurisdiction, and the Indian Child Welfare Act." *Iowa Law Review* 79: 587–652.

Carsten, Janet. 2001. "Substantivism, Antisubstantivism, and Anti-Antisubstantivism." In *Relative Values: Reconfiguring Kinship Studies*, edited by Sarah Franklin and Susan McKinnon, 29–53. Durham, NC: Duke University Press.

Carter, Clarence E., ed. 1934–1962. *The Territorial Papers of the United States*. 26 vols. Washington, DC: US Government Printing Office.

Castiglia, Christopher. 1996. *Bound and Determined: Captivity, Culture-Crossing, and White Womanhood from Mary Rowlandson to Patty Hearst*. Chicago: University of Chicago Press.

Castile, George Pierre, and Robert L. Bee, eds. 1992. *State and Reservation: New Perspectives on Federal Indian Policy*. Tucson: University of Arizona Press.

Cattelino, Jessica R. 2008. *High Stakes: Florida Seminole Gaming and Sovereignty*. Durham, NC: Duke University Press.

———. 2010. "Anthropologies of the United States." *Annual Review of Anthropology* 39: 275–292.

CBC Radio. 2012. "Stolen Children: Truth and Reconciliation." http://www.cbc.ca/news/background/truth-reconciliation.

Ceci, Lynn. 1975. "Fish Fertilizer: A Native North American Practice?" *Science* 188 (4): 26–30.

———. 1990. *The Effect of European Contact and Trade on the Settlement Pattern of Indians in Coastal New York, 1524–1665*. New York: Garland.

Cheyfitz, Eric. 1997. *The Poetics of Imperialism: Translation and Colonization from "The Tempest" to "Tarzan."* Philadelphia: University of Pennsylvania Press.

Chiapelli, Fredi, Michael J. B. Allen, and Robert L. Benson, eds. 1976. *First Images of America*. 2 vols. Berkeley: University of California Press.

Child, Brenda. 1998. *Boarding School Seasons: American Indian Families, 1900–1949*. Lincoln: University of Nebraska Press.

———. 2009. "Creation of the Tribal Museum." In *Contesting Knowledge: Museums and Indigenous Perspectives*, edited by Susan Sleeper-Smith, 251–256. Lincoln: University of Nebraska Press.

Choi, Jung Min, and John W. Murphy. 1992. *The Politics and Philosophy of Political Correctness*. Westport, CT: Praeger.

Churchill, Ward. 1994. "Let's Spread the Fun Around." In *Indians Are Us? Cultures and Genocide in Native North America*, 65–72. Monroe, ME: Common Courage Press.

Clergy and Laity Concerned. 1991. *Rediscover the History of the Americas: 1492–1992*. CALC Report. Decatur, GA: CALC.

"Cleveland Indians." 2011. Web index to articles in the *New York Times*. http://topics.nytimes.com/top/news/sports/baseball/majorleague/clevelandindians/index.html.

Clifford, James. 1983. "On Ethnographic Authority." *Representations* 1: 118–146.

———. 1988a. "Histories of the Tribal and the Modern." In *The Predicament of Culture: Twentieth-Century Ethnography, Literature, and Art*, 189–214. Cambridge, MA: Harvard University Press.

———. 1988b. "Identity in Mashpee." In *The Predicament of Culture: Twentieth-Century Ethnography, Literature, and Art*, 277–346. Cambridge, MA: Harvard University Press.

———. 1988c. "On Collecting Art and Culture." In *The Predicament of Culture: Twentieth-Century Ethnography, Literature, and Art*, 215–251. Cambridge, MA: Harvard University Press.

———. 1988d. *The Predicament of Culture: Twentieth-Century Ethnography, Literature, and Art*. Harvard: University Press Cambridge.

———. 1991. "Four Northwest Coast Museums: Travel Reflections." In *Exhibiting Cultures: The Poetics and Politics of Museum Display*, edited by Ivan Karp and Steven D. Lavine, 212–254. Washington, DC: Smithsonian Institution Press.

———. 1997. *Routes: Travel and Translation in the Late Twentieth Century.* Cambridge, MA: Harvard University Press.

———. 2001. "Indigenous Articulations." *The Contemporary Pacific* 13 (2): 467–490.

———. 2004. "Looking Several Ways: Anthropology and Native Heritage in Alaska." *Current Anthropology* 45 (1): 5–29.

———. 2011. "Response to Orin Starn: 'Here Come the Anthros (Again): The Strange Marriage of Anthropology and Native America.'" *Cultural Anthropology* 26 (2): 218–224.

Clifford, James, and George Marcus, eds. 1986. *Writing Culture: The Politics and Poetics of Ethnography.* Berkeley: University of California Press.

Clifton, James A. 1989. *Being and Becoming Indian: Biographical Studies of North American Frontiers.* Chicago: The Dorsey Press.

———, ed. 1990. *The Invented Indian: Cultural Fictions and Government Policies.* New Brunswick, NJ: Transaction Publishers.

Cobb, Amanda J. 2005. "The National Museum of the American Indian: Sharing the Gift." Special Issue: The National Museum of the American Indian, *American Indian Quarterly* 29 (3–4): 361–383.

Cobb, Daniel M., and Loretta Fowler. 2007. *Beyond Red Power: American Indian Politics and Activism since 1900.* Santa Fe: School of Advanced Research.

Colley, Linda. 2002. *Captives: The Story of Britain's Pursuit of Empire and How Its Soldiers and Civilians Were Held Captive by the Dream of Global Supremacy, 1600–1850.* New York: Pantheon.

Conklin, Beth A., and Laura R. Graham. 1995. "The Shifting Middle Ground: Amazonian Indians and Eco-Politics." *American Anthropologist*, new series, 97 (4): 695–710.

Cook, Curtis, and Juan D. Lindau, eds. 2000. *Aboriginal Rights and Self-Government: The Canadian and Mexican Experience in North American Perspective.* Montreal: McGill-Queen's University Press.

Coombe, Rosemary J. 1998. *The Cultural Life of Intellectual Properties: Authorship, Appropriation, and the Law.* Durham, NC: Duke University Press.

Cooper, Karen Coody. 2007. *Spirited Encounters: American Indians Protest Museum Policies and Practices.* Lanham, MD: Altamira Press.

Cornell, Stephen. 2008. "The Political Economy of American Indian Gaming." *Annual Review of Law and Social Science* 4: 63–82.

Crosby, Alfred W. 1972. *The Columbian Exchange: Biological and Cultural Consequences of 1492.* Westport, CT: Greenwood Press.

———. 1978. "God ... Would Destroy Them, and Give Their Country to Another People ..." *American Heritage* 29 (6): 38–43.

———. 1987. *The Columbian Voyages, the Columbian Exchange, and Their Historians: Essays on Global and Comparative History.* Washington, DC: American Historical Association.

Crosby, Alfred W., and Helen Nader. 1989. *The Voyages of Columbus: A Turning Point in World History.* ERIC Clearinghouse for Social Studies/Social Science Education. Bloomington: Social Studies Development Center, Indiana University.

Cruikshank, Julie. 1998. *The Social Life of Stories: Narrative and Knowledge in the Yukon Territory.* Lincoln: University of Nebraska Press.

———. 2005. *Do Glaciers Listen? Local Knowledge, Colonial Encounters, and Social Imagination.* Vancouver: University of British Columbia Press.

Cruikshank, Julie, with A. Sidney, K. Smith, and A. Ned. 1990. *Life Lived Like a Story: Life Stories of Three Yukon Native Elders*. Lincoln: University of Nebraska Press.

Cultural Survival. 2010. "Victory! U.S. Endorses UN Declaration on the Rights of Indigenous Peoples." December 16. http://www.culturalsurvival.org/news/united-states/victory-us-endorses-un-declaration-rights-indigenous-peoples.

Cummings, André Douglas Pond. 2008. "Progress Realized? The Continuing American Indian Mascot Quandary." *Marquette Sports Law Review* 18: 309–335.

Darian-Smith, Eve. 2004. *New Capitalists: Law, Politics, and Identity Surrounding Casino Gaming on Native American Land*. Belmont, CA: Wadsworth/Thomson.

———. 2010. "Environmental Law and Native American Law." *Annual Review of Law and Social Science* 6: 359–386.

Darnell, R. 2001. *Invisible Genealogies: A History of Americanist Anthropology*. Lincoln: University of Nebraska Press.

Davis, F. James. 1995. "The Hawaiian Alternative to the One-Drop Rule." In *American Mixed Race: The Culture of Microdiversity*, edited by Naomi Zack, 115–131. Lanham, MD: Rowman and Littlefield.

Debord, Guy. 1995. *The Society of Spectacle*. New York: Zone Books.

de la Cadena, Marisol, and Orin Starn. 2007. *Indigenous Experience Today*. Oxford: Berg Publishers.

Deloria, Ella Cara. 1988. *Waterlily*. Lincoln: University of Nebraska Press.

Deloria, Philip J. 1998. *Playing Indian*. New Haven, CT: Yale University Press.

———. 2004. *Indians in Unexpected Places*. Lawrence: University of Kansas Press.

Deloria, Philip J., and Neal Salisbury, eds. 2002. *A Companion to American Indian History*. Malden, MA: Blackwell Publishers.

Deloria, Vine. 1969. *Custer Died for Your Sins: An Indian Manifesto*. New York: Macmillan.

———. 1970. *We Talk, You Listen: New Tribes, New Turf*. New York: Macmillan.

———. 1971. *Of Utmost Good Faith*. New York: Bantam Books.

———. 1974. *Behind the Trail of Broken Treaties: An Indian Declaration of Independence*. New York: Delacorte Press.

———. 1998. "Comfortable Fictions and the Struggle for Turf: An Essay Review of *The Invented Indian: Cultural Fictions and Government Policies*." In *Natives and Academics: Researching and Writing about American Indians*, edited by Devon Mihesuah, 65–83. Lincoln: University of Nebraska Press.

Deloria, Vine, and Clifford M. Lytle. 1983. *American Indians, American Justice*. Austin: University of Texas Press.

———. 1984. *The Nation Within: The Past and Future of American Indian Sovereignty*. New York: Pantheon Books.

Demos, John. 1994. *The Unredeemed Captive: A Family Story from Early America*. New York: Alfred A. Knopf.

Denlinger, Ken. 1992. "Protest of 'Redskins' Draws 2,000 at Stadium." *Washington Post*, January 27, final edition, C18.

Derounian-Stodola, Kathryn Zabelle, and James Arthur Levernier. 1993. *The Indian Captivity Narrative, 1550–1900*. New York: Twayne Publishers.

Dickinson, Jonathan. 1977 [1699]. "God's Protecting Providence Man's Surest Help and Defence ... Evidenced in the Remarkable Deliverance of Divers Persons, from the Devouring Waves of the Sea ... and Also from the More Cruelly Devouring Jawes of the Inhumane Canibals of Florida ..." In *Narratives of North American Indian Captivities*, vol. 4, edited by Wilcomb E. Washburn. Philadelphia: Reiner Jansen.

Dilworth, Leah. 1996. *Imagining Indians in the Southwest: Persistent Visions of a Primitive Past*. Washington, DC: Smithsonian Institution Press.

Dippie, Brian W. 1982. *The Vanishing American: White Attitudes and U.S. Indian Policy*. Middletown, CT: Wesleyan University Press.

Dolan, Jill. 2005. "Finding Our Feet in One Another's Shoes: Multiple-Character Solo Performance." In *Utopia in Performance: Finding Hope at the Theater*, 63–88. Ann Arbor: University of Michigan Press.

Dominguez, Virginia. 1996. "Comment on Ong: Cultural Citizenship as Subject-Making." *Current Anthropology* 37: 751–752.

Dor-Ner, Zvi. 1991. *Columbus and the Age of Discovery*. New York: William Morrow.

Dorst, John. 2000. *Postcolonial Encounters: Narrative Constructions of Devils Tower National Monument in Post-colonial America*, edited by C. Richard King, 303–320. Urbana: University of Illinois Press.

Dowd, Gregory Evans. 1992. *A Spirited Resistance: The North American Indian Struggle for Unity, 1745–1815*. Baltimore: Johns Hopkins University Press.

Downing, John, and Charles Husband. 2005. *Representing 'Race': Racisms, Ethnicities and Media*. Thousand Oaks, CA: Sage Publications.

Drinnon, Richard. 1980. *Facing West: The Metaphysics of Indian-Hating and Empire-Building*. Norman: University of Oklahoma Press.

Eastman, Charles A. 1974 [1914]. *Indian Scout Craft and Lore*. [Indian Scout Talks: A Guide for Boy Scouts and Camp Fire Girls]. New York: Dover Publications.

Ebersole, Gary L. 1995. *Captured by Texts: Puritan to Postmodern Images of Indian Captivity*. Charlottesville: University of Virginia Press.

Edmunds, R. David. 2002. "Native Americans and the United States, Canada, and Mexico." In *A Companion to American Indian History*, edited by Philip J. Deloria and Neal Salisbury, 397–421. Malden, MA: Blackwell Publishers.

Egan, Timothy. 1998. "An Indian Without Reservations." *New York Times Magazine*, January 18: 16–19.

EHS Athletics. 2011. "Athletics Home Page, Eaton School District, Eaton, Colorado." https://sites.google.com/a/eaton.k12.co.us/ath-ehs/.

Ellingson, Terry Jay. 2001. *The Myth of the Noble Savage*. Berkeley: University of California Press.

Elliott, Jan. 1989/90. "Exhibiting Ideology: A Review of *First Encounters: Spanish Explorations in the Caribbean and the United States, 1492–1570*." *Akwesasne Notes* (Midwinter): 6–21.

Erikson, Patricia. 2008. "Decolonizing the 'Nation's Attic': The National Museum of the American Indian and the Politics of Knowledge-Making in a National Space." In *The National Museum of the American Indian: Critical Conversations*, edited by Amy Lonetree and Amanda J. Cobb-Greetham, 43–83. Lincoln: University of Nebraska Press.

Erikson, Patricia, with Helma Ward and Kirk Wachendorf. 2002. *Voices of a Thousand People: The Makah Cultural Research Center*. Lincoln: University of Nebraska Press.

Expo '92 Sevilla. 1992. Seville: Centro de Prensa/Press Center. (April). Press packet.

Fabian, Johannes C. 1983. *Time and the Other: How Anthropology Makes Its Object*. New York: Columbia University Press.

Fanshel, David. 1972. *Far from the Reservation: The Transracial Adoption of American Indian Children*. Metuchen, NJ: Scarecrow Press.

Faris, James S. 1996. *Navajo and Photography: A Critical History of the Representation of an American People*. Albuquerque: University of New Mexico Press.

Farley, Robert. 2011. "Obama Says the Border Fence Is 'Now Basically Complete.'" *St. Peters-burg Times*, May 16. http://www.politifact.com/truth -o -meter/ statements/2011/ may/16/barack-obama/obama-says-border-fence-now-basically-complete/.

Farnell, Brenda. 2004. "The Fancy Dance of Racializing Discourse." *Journal of Sport and Social Issues* 28 (1): 30–55.

———. 2009. *Do You See What I Mean? Plains Indian Sign Talk and the Embodiment of Action*. Lincoln: University of Nebraska Press.

Fasano, T. M. 2002. "In Eaton, Fightin' Reds Mascot Has Come under Fire." *Greeley Tribune*, January 20. www.greeleytribune.com/article/20020120/SPORTS/101200007.

Feest, Christian F. 1987. "Pride and Prejudice: The Pocahontas' Myth and the Pamunkey." *European Review of Native American Studies* 1 (1): 5–12.

Ferguson, T. J., Roger Anyon, and Edmund J. Ladd. 2000. "Repatriation at the Pueblo of Zuni: Diverse Solutions to Complex Problems." In *Repatriation Reader: Who Owns American Indian Remains?*, edited by Devon Mihesuah, 239–265. Lincoln: University of Nebraska Press.

Ferguson, T. J., Chip Colwell-Chanthaphonh, and Robert W. Preucel. 2006. *History Is in the Land: Multivocal Tribal Traditions in Arizona's San Pedro Valley*. Tucson: University of Arizona Press.

Fernandez, James W. 1986. *Persuasions and Performances: The Play of Tropes in Culture*. Bloomington: Indiana University Press.

Field, Les W. 2004. "Beyond 'Applied' Anthropology." In *A Companion to the Anthropology of American Indians*, edited by Thomas Biolsi, 472–489. Malden, MA: Blackwell Publishers.

Field, Les W., with Cheryl Seidner, Julian Lang, Rosemary Cambra, Florence Silva, Vivien Hailstone, Darlene Marshall, Bradley Marshall, Callie Lara, Merv George Sr., and the Cultural Committee of the Yurok Tribe. 2008. *Abalone Tales: Collaborative Explorations of Sovereignty and Identity in Native California*. Durham, NC: Duke University Press.

Field, Les W., and Richard G. Fox, eds. 2007. *Anthropology Put to Work*. Oxford: Berg.

Fienup-Riordan, Ann. 1990. *Eskimo Essays: Yup'ik and How We See Them*. New Brunswick, NJ: Rutgers University Press.

———. 1995. *Freeze-Frame: Alaskan Eskimos in Movies*. Seattle: University of Washington Press.

Fine-Dare, Kathleen S. 2002. *Grave Injustice: The American Indian Repatriation Movement and NAGPRA*. Lincoln: University of Nebraska Press.

Fixico, Donald. 1986. *Termination and Relocation: Federal Indian Policy, 1945–1960*. Albuquerque: University of New Mexico Press.

———. 2002. "Federal and State Policies and American Indians." In *A Companion to American Indian History*, edited by Philip J. Deloria and Neal Salisbury, 379–396. Malden, MA: Blackwell Publishers.

Fleischner, Jennifer. 1994. "A Conversation with Barbara Kingsolver." In *A Reader's Guide to the Fiction of Barbara Kingsolver*, 13–18. New York: HarperCollins.

Fleming, E. McClung. 1965. "The American Images as Indian Princess, 1765–1783." *Winterthur Portfolio* 2: 65–81.

———. 1967. "From Indian Princess to Greek Goddess in the American Image, 1783–1815." *Winterthur Portfolio* 3: 37–66.

Fletcher, Matthew L., Wenona T. Singel, and Kathryn E. Fort. 2009. *Facing the Future: The Indian Child Welfare Act at 30*. East Lansing: Michigan State University Press.

Flores, Richard R. 2002. *Remembering the Alamo: Memory, Modernity, and the Master Symbol*. Austin: University of Texas Press.

Fogelson, Raymond D. 1985. "Interpretations of the American Psyche: Some Historical Notes. Social Contexts of American Ethnology, 1840–1984." *Proceedings of the American Ethnological Society*, edited by June Helm, 4–27. Washington, DC: American Anthropological Association.

———. 1991. "The Red Man in the White City." In *Columbian Consequences*, vol. 3, edited by David H. Thomas, 73–90. Washington, DC: Smithsonian Institution Press.

———, ed. 2004. *Southeast*, vol. 14, *Handbook of North American Indians*, edited by William C. Sturtevant. Washington, DC: Smithsonian Institution, for sale by the US Government Printing Office, Superintendent of Documents.

Foley, Doug. 1995. *The Heartland Chronicles*. Philadelphia: University of Pennsylvania Press.

Forbes, Jack D. 1987. "Shouting Back to the Geese." In *I Tell You Now: Autobiographical Essays by Native American Writers*, edited by Brian Swann and Arnold Krupat, 111–126. American Indian Lives Series. Lincoln: University of Nebraska Press.

Foster, Lawrence, and Patricia Herzog, eds. 1994. *Defending Diversity: Contemporary Philosophical Perspectives on Pluralism and Multiculturalism*. Amherst: University of Massachusetts Press.

Foster, Michael K., Jack Campisi, and Marianne Mithun, eds. 1984. *Extending the Rafters: Interdisciplinary Approaches to Iroquoian Studies*. Albany: State University of New York Press.

Foster, Morris W. 1992. *Being Comanche: The Social History of an American Indian Community*. Tucson: University of Arizona Press.

Foucault, Michel. 1978. *History of Sexuality, vol. 1: An Introduction*. Robert Hurley, trans. New York: Random House.

———. 1979. *Discipline and Punish: The Birth of the Prison*. Alan Sheridan, trans. New York: Vintage Books.

———. 1988. *Technologies of the Self*, edited by Luther H. Martin, Huck Gutman, and Patrick H. Hutton. Boston: University of Massachusetts Press.

Fowler, Loretta. 2002. *Tribal Sovereignty and the Historical Imagination: Cheyenne-Arapaho Politics*. Lincoln: University of Nebraska Press.

Francis, Daniel. 1992. *The Imaginary Indian: The Image of the Indian in Canadian Culture*. Vancouver: Arsenal Pulp Press.

Franklin, Bernard M. 2006a. "Challenges of the Indian Mascot Policy—Association's Position Backed by Research and Deliberation." *National Collegiate Athletic Association News Archive*, March 27. http://fs.ncaa.org/Docs/NCAANewsArchive/2006/Editorial/challenges%2Bof%2Bthe%2Bindian%2Bmascot%2Bpolicy%2B-%2Bassociation_s%2Bposition%2Bbacked%2Bby%2Bresearch%2Band%2Bdeliberation%2B-%2B3-27-06%2Bncaa%2Bnews.html.

———. 2006b. Statement, Hearing on "An Examination of the NCAA's Relationship with Member Institutions." Committee on Education and the Workforce. 109th Congress, December 15. http://archives.republicans.edlabor.house.gov/archive/hearings/109th/fc/ncaa121506/franklin.htm.

Franklin, Sarah, and Susan McKinnon, eds. 2001. *Relative Values: Reconfiguring Kinship Studies*. Durham, NC: Duke University Press.

Franklin, Sarah, and Helena Ragoné, eds. 1998. *Reproducing Reproduction: Kinship, Power, and Technological Innovation*. Philadelphia: University of Pennsylvania Press.

Friedman, Marilyn. 1995. "Codes, Canons, Correctness, and Feminism." In *Political Correctness: For and Against*, edited by Marilyn Friedman and Jan Narveson, 1–45. Lanham, MD: Rowman and Littlefield.

Gailey, Christine Ward. 2010. *Blue-Ribbon Babies and Labors of Love: Race, Class, and Gender in U.S. Adoption Practice*. Austin: University of Texas Press.

Ganguly, Keya. 2006. "Of Totems and Taboos: An Indian's Guide to Indian Chiefs and Other Objects of Fan Fascination." *South Atlantic Quarterly* 105 (2): 373–390.

Garcia, Juliet V. 2009. "Planting Seeds of Hope." Speech, February 14. http://blue.utb.edu/newsandinfo/BorderFence%20Issue/Planting_Seeds_of_HopeDrGarciaSpeech.htm.

Garoutte, Eva Marie. 2003. *Real Indians: Identity and the Survival of Native America*. Berkeley: University of California Press.

Geertz, Armin. 1994. *The Invention of Prophecy: Continuity and Meaning in Hopi Indian Religion*. Berkeley: University of California Press.

Gibson, Arell M. 1988. *Indian Land Transfers*, edited by Wilcomb E. Washburn. Washington, DC: Smithsonian Institution Press.

Gidley, Mick. 1998. *Edward S. Curtis and the North American Indian, Inc*. Cambridge: Cambridge University Press.

Gill, Sam. 1987. *Mother Earth: An American Story*. Chicago: University of Chicago Press.

Ginsburg, Faye D. 1991. "Indigenous Media: Faustian Contact or Global Village?" *Cultural Anthropology* 6: 92–112.

———. 1993. "Aboriginal Media and the Australian Imaginary." *Public Culture* 5 (2): 557–578.

———. 2002. "Screen Memories: Resignifying the Traditional in Indigenous Media." In *Media Worlds: Anthropology on New Terrain*, edited by Faye D. Ginsburg, Lila Abu-Lughod, and Brian Larkin, 39–57. Berkeley: University of California Press.

Ginsburg, Faye D., and Rayna Rapp, eds. 1995. *Conceiving the New World Order: The Global Politics of Reproduction*. Berkeley: University of California Press.

Gleach, Frederic W. 1994. "Pocahontas and Captain John Smith Revisited." In *Actes du vingt-cinquième congrès des Algonquinistes*, edited by William Cowen, 167–186. Ottawa: Carleton University.

———. 2003. "Controlled Speculation and Constructed Myths: The Saga of Pocahontas and Captain John Smith." In *Reading Beyond Words: Contexts for Native History*, edited by Jennifer S. H. Brown and Elizabeth Vibert, 39–74. Peterborough: Broadview Press.

———. 2006. "Pocahontas: An Exercise in Mythmaking and Marketing." In *New Perspectives on Native North America: Cultures, Histories, and Representations*, edited by Sergei A. Kan and Pauline Turner Strong, 433–455. Lincoln: University of Nebraska Press.

Goddard, Ives. 1996. "Introduction." In *Handbook of North American Indians*, edited by William C. Sturtevant, vol. 17: *Languages*, edited by Ives Goddard, 1–16. Washington, DC: Smithsonian Institution, for sale by the US Government Printing Office, Superintendent of Documents.

Golding, Sue, ed. 1997. *The Eight Technologies of Otherness*. London: Routledge.

Goldstein, Joseph, Anna Freud, and Albert J. Solnit. 1973. *Beyond the Best Interest of the Child*. New York: Free Press.

Goldstein, Patrick. 2000 "Doing the Right Thing? Not Yet." *The Los Angeles Times*, September 10. http://articles.latimes.com/2000/sep/10/entertainment/ca-18435.

Good, Owen S. 2002. "School's Nickname Fuels Fury; American Indians March against 'Reds' Moniker." *Rocky Mountain News*, May 20. http://www.highbeam.com/doc/1G1-87931623.html.

Gordon, Avery, and Christopher Newfield. 1994. "White Philosophy." *Critical Inquiry* 20: 737–757.

Gramsci, Antonio. 1972. *Selections from the Prison Notebooks*, edited by Quintin Hoare and Geoffrey Nowell Smith. New York: International Publishers.

Green, Rayna D. 1975. "The Pocahontas Perplex: The Image of Indian Women in American Culture." *Massachusetts Review* 16: 698–714.

———. 1988a. "The Indian in Popular Culture." In *Handbook of North American Indians*, edited by William C. Sturtevant, vol. 4: *History of Indian-White Relations*, edited by Wilcomb E. Washburn, 587–606. Washington, DC: Smithsonian Institution, for sale by the US Government Printing Office, Superintendent of Documents.

———. 1988b. "The Tribe Called Wannabee: Playing Indian in America and Europe." *Folklore* 99: 30–55.

———. 1992. *Women in American Indian Society*. New York: Chelsea House Publishers.

———. 1996. "'We Never Saw These Things Before': Southwest Indian Laughter and Resistance to the Invasion of the Tse va ho." In *The Great Southwest of the Fred Harvey Company and the Santa Fe Railway*, edited by Marta Weigle and Barbara A. Babcock, 201–206. Phoenix: The Heard Museum.

Greenblatt, Stephen J. 1980. *Renaissance Self-Fashioning: From More to Shakespeare*. Chicago: University of Chicago Press.

———. 1991a. *Marvelous Possessions: The Wonder of the New World*. Chicago: University of Chicago Press.

———. 1991b. "Resonance and Wonder." In *Exhibiting Cultures: The Poetics and Politics of Museum Display*, edited by Ivan Karp and Steven D. Lavine, 42–56. Washington, DC: Smithsonian Institution Press.

Gulick, Luther. 1920. *A Philosophy of Play*. New York: Charles Scribner's Sons.

Gutmann, Amy, ed. 1994. *Multiculturalism: Examining the Politics of Recognition*. Princeton, NJ: Princeton University Press.

Gyles, John. 1977 [1736]. "Memoirs of Odd Adventures, Strange Deliverances andc. in the Captivity of John Gyles, Esq.: Commander of the Garrison on St. George's River." Facsimile. In *Narratives of North American Indian Captivities*, vol. 6, compiled by Wilcomb E. Washburn. Boston: S. Kneeland and T. Green.

Haefeli, Evan, and Kevin Sweeney. 2003. *Captors and Captives: The 1704 French and Indian Raid on Deerfield*. Boston: University of Massachusetts Press.

Hager, C. Steven, with Tina Law. 1997. *Handbook on the Indian Child Welfare Act*, edited by Colline Meek and Michael Snyder. Oklahoma City: Oklahoma Indian Legal Services.

Haig-Brown, Celie. 1992. "Choosing Border Work." *Canadian Journal of Native Education* 19 (1): 96–116.

Hale, Charles R. 2002. "Does Multiculturalism Menace? Governance, Cultural Rights and the Politics of Identity in Guatemala." *Journal of Latin American Studies* 34: 485–534.

Hall, G. Stanley. 1904. *Adolescence and Its Psychology and Its Relations to Physiology, Anthropology, Sociology, Sex, Crime, Religion, and Education.* 2 vols. New York: Appleton-Century-Crofts.

Hall, Stuart, ed. 1997. *Representation: Cultural Representations and Signifying Practices.* London: Sage Publications, for The Open University.

Hambrick-Stowe, Charles E. 1982. *The Practice of Piety: Puritan Devotional Disciplines in Seventeenth-Century New England.* Chapel Hill: University of North Carolina Press.

Hames, Raymond. 2007. "The Ecologically Noble Savage Debate." *Annual Review of Anthropology* 36: 177–190.

Hamilton, Annette. 1990. "Fear and Desire: Aborigines, Asians, and the National Imaginary." *Australian Cultural History* 19: 14–35.

Hammell, George R. 1987. "Mythical Realities and European Contact in the Northeast during the Sixteenth and Seventeenth Centuries." *Man in the Northeast* 33: 67–87.

Handler, Richard. 1988. *Nationalism and the Politics of Culture in Quebec.* Madison: University of Wisconsin Press.

———. 1992. "On the Valuing of Museum Objects." *Museum Anthropology* 16 (1): 21–28.

Handler, Richard, and Eric Gable. 1997. *The New History in an Old Museum: Creating the Past at Colonial Williamsburg.* Durham, NC: Duke University Press.

Handler, Richard, and Jocelyn Linnekin. 1984. "Tradition, Genuine and Spurious." *Journal of American Folklore* 97 (385): 273–290.

Hanson, Elizabeth. 1977 [1728]. "God's Mercy Surmounting Man's Cruelty, Exemplified in the Captivity and Redemption of Elizabeth Hanson ..." Facsimile. In *Narratives of North American Indian Captivities*, vol. 6, compiled by Wilcomb E. Washburn. New York: Garland.

Haraway, Donna. 1989. *Primate Visions: Gender, Race, and Nature in the World of Modern Science.* New York: Routledge.

———. 1991. "Situated Knowledges: The Science Question in Feminism and the Privilege of Partial Perspective." In *Simians, Cyborgs, and Women: The Reinvention of Nature*, 183–201. New York: Routledge.

Harjo, Suzan Shown. 2001. "Fighting Name-Calling: Challenging 'Redskins' in Court." In *Team Spirits: Essays on the History and Significance of Native American Mascots*, edited by C. Richard King and Charles F. Springwood, 189–207. Lincoln: University of Nebraska Press.

———. 2005. "Just Good Sports: The Impact of 'Native' References in Sports on Native Youth and What Some Decolonizers Have Done about It." In *For Indigenous Eyes Only: A Decolonization Handbook*, edited by Waziyatawin Angela Wilson and Michael Yellow Bird, 31–52. Santa Fe: School of American Research.

———. 2010. "Note to Congress: Stop Shielding 'Indian' Mascots and Start Defending Indian People." In *The Native American Mascot Controversy: A Handbook*, edited by C. Richard King, 179–182. Lanham, MD: Scarecrow Press.

Harjo v. Pro-Football (09-326). 2011. Supreme Court Home, Native American Rights Fund. http://www.narf.org/sct/caseindexes/current/harjo.html.

Harkin, Michael E., and David Rich Lewis. 2007. *Native Americans and the Environment: Perspectives on the Ecological Indian.* Lincoln: University of Nebraska Press.

Harmon, Alexandra. 2002. "Wanted: More Histories of Indian Identity." In *A Companion to American Indian History*, edited by Philip J. Deloria and Neal Salisbury, 248–265. Malden, MA: Blackwell Publishers.

Harring, Sidney L. 1994. *Crow Dog's Case: American Indian Sovereignty, Tribal Law, and United States Law in the Nineteenth Century.* Cambridge: Cambridge University Press.

———. 2002. "Indian Law, Sovereignty, and State Law: Native People and the Law." In *A Companion to Native American History,* edited by Philip J. Deloria and Neal Salisbury, 441–459. Malden, MA: Blackwell Publishers.

Harvard Project on American Indian Economic Development. 2008. *The State of the Native Nations: Conditions under U.S. Policies of Self-Determination.* Oxford: Oxford University Press.

Hayden, Thomas, and Robert Lautman. 2004. "National Museum of the American Indian: By the People." *Smithsonian* 35 (6): 50–57.

Helmberger, Pat Stave. 1999. *Indians as Mascots in Minnesota Schools.* Golden Valley, MN: Friends of the Bill of Rights Foundation.

Hendry, Joy. 2005. *Reclaiming Culture: Indigenous People and Self-Representation.* New York: Palgrave Macmillan.

Hernandez, Juan Avila. 2004. "Blood, Lies, and Indian Rights: TCUs Become Gatekeepers for Research." *Tribal College Journal* 16 (2). http://tribalcollegejournal.org/themag/backissues/winter2004/winter2004hernandez.html.

Hersh, Seymour M. 2004a. "Annals of National Security: Torture at Abu Ghraib." *The New Yorker,* May 10. http://www.newyorker.com/archive/2004/05/10/040510fa_fact.

———. 2004b. *Chain of Command: The Road from 9/11 to Abu Ghraib.* New York: HarperCollins.

Hewitt, J. N. B. 1928. *Iroquoian Cosmology, Second Part. 43rd Annual Report of the Bureau of American Ethnology, 1925–26.* Washington, DC: US Government Printing Office.

Hill, Jane. 1995. "Mock Spanish: A Site for the Indexical Reproduction of Racism in American English." *Language and Culture: Symposium 2,* Binghamton University. http://language-culture.binghamton.edu/symposia/2/part1/index.html.

Hinsley, Curtis M. 1981. *Savages and Scientists: The Smithsonian Institution and the Development of American Anthropology, 1846–1910.* Washington, DC: Smithsonian Institution Press.

———. 1989. "Zunis and Brahmins: Cultural Ambivalence in the Gilded Age." In *Romantic Motives: Essays on Anthropological Sensibility,* edited by George W. Stocking Jr., 169–207. Madison: University of Wisconsin Press.

Hobhouse, Henry. 1987. *Seeds of Change: Five Plants That Transformed Mankind.* New York: Harper and Row.

Hobsbawm, Eric, and Terence Ranger, eds. 1983. *The Invention of Tradition.* Cambridge: Cambridge University Press.

Hochswender, Woody. 1995. "Pocahontas: A Babe in the Woods." *Harpers Bazaar* (June): 154–157.

Hogan, Linda. 1987. "The Two Lives." In *I Tell You Now: Autobiographical Essays by Native American Writers,* edited by Brian Swann and Arnold Krupat, 231–249. American Indian Lives Series. Lincoln: University of Nebraska Press.

Honour, Hugh. 1975. *The New Golden Land: European Images of America from the Discoveries to the Present Time.* New York: Pantheon.

Hooper-Greenhill, Eilean. 1992. *Museums and the Shaping of Knowledge.* New York: Routledge.

Howell, Signe. 2006. *The Kinning of Foreigners: Transnational Adoption in a Global Perspective*. New York: Berghahn Books.

Hoxie, Frederick E. 1984. *A Final Promise: The Campaign to Assimilate the Indians, 1880–1920*. Lincoln: University of Nebraska Press.

———. 1992. "Crow Leadership amidst Reservation Oppression." In *State and Reservation: New Perspectives on Federal Indian Policy*, edited by George Pierre Castile and Robert L. Bee, 38–60. Tucson: University of Arizona Press.

———. 2001. *Talking Back to Civilization: Indian Voices from the Progressive Era*. Boston: Bedford/St. Martin's.

Hughes, Langston. 1953. *Simple Takes a Wife*. New York: Simon and Schuster.

Hughte, Phil. 1994. *A Zuni Artist Looks at Frank Hamilton Cushing*. Zuni, NM: Pueblo of Zuni Arts and Crafts.

Huhndorf, Shari M. 2001. *Going Native: Indians in the American Cultural Imagination*. Ithaca, NY: Cornell University Press.

———. 2009. *Mapping the Americas: The Transnational Politics of Contemporary Native Culture*. Ithaca, NY: Cornell University Press.

Hulton, Paul, and David Beers Quinn. 1964. *The American Drawing of John White, 1577–1590*. Chapel Hill: University of North Carolina Press.

Humins, John H. 1987. "Squanto and Massasoit: A Struggle for Power." *New England Quarterly* 60: 54–70.

Hymes, Dell, ed. 1972. *Reinventing Anthropology*. New York: Pantheon.

ICTMN Staff. 2011. "Fighting Sioux Nickname One Step Closer to Being Retired." *Indian Country Today Media Network*, August 13. http://indiancountrytodaymedianetwork.com/2011/08/fighting-sioux-nickname-one-step-closer-to-being-retired/.

Isaac, Gwyneira. 2007. *Mediating Knowledges: Origins of a Zuni Tribal Museum*. Tucson: University of Arizona Press.

Jacknis, Ira. 2002. *The Storage Box of Tradition: Kwakiutl Art, Anthropologists, and Museums, 1881–1981*. Washington, DC: Smithsonian Institution Press.

———. 2008. "A New Thing? The National Museum of the American Indian in Historical and Institutional Context." In *The National Museum of the American Indian: Critical Conversations*, edited by Amy Lonetree and Amanda J. Cobb-Greetham, 3–42. Lincoln: University of Nebraska Press.

Jackson, Jason Baird. 2003. *Yuchi Ceremonial Life: Performance, Meaning and Tradition in a Contemporary American Indian Community*. Lincoln: University of Nebraska Press.

———. 2006. "Review: *Who Owns Native Culture?* by Michael F. Brown." *Journal of American Folklore* 119: 492–493.

Jackson, Jean E. 1989. "Is There a Way to Talk about Making Culture without Making Enemies?" *Dialectical Anthropology* 14: 127–143.

———. 1995. "Culture, Genuine and Spurious: The Politics of Indianness in the Vaupés, Colombia." *American Ethnologist* 22 (1): 3–27.

Jaimes, M. Annette, ed. 1992. *The State of Native America: Genocide, Colonization, and Resistance*. Boston: South End Press.

Jenkins, Philip. 2005. "The Antimuseum: Indian History without a Guide." *Christian Century*, February 8.

Jennings, Francis. 1975. *The Invasion of America: Indians, Colonialism, and the Cant of Conquest*. Chapel Hill: University of North Carolina Press.

———. 1984. *The Ambiguous Iroquois Empire: The Covenant Chain Confederation of Indian Tribes with English Colonies from Its Beginnings to the Lancaster Treaty of 1744.* New York and London: Norton.

———. 1988. *Empire of Fortune.* New York: Norton.

Jennings, Francis, William N. Fenton, Mary A. Druke, and David R. Miller, eds. 1995. *The History and Culture of Iroquois Diplomacy: An Interdisciplinary Guide to the Treaties of the Six Nations and Their League.* Syracuse, NY: Syracuse University Press.

Jensen, Robert. 2005. *The Heart of Whiteness: Confronting Race, Racism, and White Privilege.* San Francisco: City Lights Books.

———. 2010. "What the 'Fighting Sioux' Tells Us about White People." In *The Native American Mascot Controversy: A Handbook,* edited by C. Richard King, 33–40. Lanham, MD: Scarecrow Press.

Johansen, Bruce E. 2010. "Putting the Moccasin on the Other Foot: A Media History of the 'Fighting Whities.'" In *The Native American Mascot Controversy: A Handbook,* edited by C. Richard King, 163–178. Lanham, MD: Scarecrow Press.

Johnson, Troy R., ed. 1991. *The Indian Child Welfare Act: Indian Homes for Indian Children.* National Conference Proceedings, 1. Los Angeles: American Indian Studies Center, University of California at Los Angeles.

Johnson, Troy R., Joane Nagel, and Duane Champagne. 1997. *American Indian Activism: Alcatraz to the Longest Walk.* Champaign: University of Illinois Press.

Jolivette, Andrew. 2006. *Cultural Representation in Native America.* Lanham, MD: Altamira Press.

Jones, B. J. 1995. *The Indian Child Welfare Act Handbook: A Legal Guide to the Custody and Adoption of Native American Children.* Chicago: Section of Family Law, American Bar Association.

Jones, B. J., Mark Tilden, and Kelly Gaines-Stoner. 2008. *The Indian Child Welfare Act Handbook: A Legal Guide to the Custody and Adoption of Native American Children,* 2nd ed. Chicago: Section of Family Law, American Bar Association.

Jones, Dorothy V. 1988. "British Colonial Indian Treaties." In *Handbook of North American Indians,* edited by William C. Sturtevant, vol. 4: *History of Indian-White Relations,* edited by Wilcomb E. Washburn, 185–194. Washington, DC: Smithsonian Institution, for sale by the US Government Printing Office, Superintendent of Documents.

Jorgensen, Miriam, ed. 2007. *Rebuilding Native Nations: Strategies for Governance and Development.* Tucson: University of Arizona Press.

Kammen, Michael G. 1993. *Mystic Chords of Memory: The Transformation of Tradition in American Culture.* New York: Vintage Books.

Kan, Sergei, ed. 2001. *Strangers to Relatives: The Adoption and Naming of Anthropologists in Native North America.* Lincoln: University of Nebraska Press.

Kan, Sergei, and Pauline Turner Strong. 2006. "Introduction." In *New Perspectives on Native North America: Cultures, Histories, Representations,* edited by Sergei Kan and Pauline Turner Strong, xi–xlii. Lincoln: University of Nebraska Press.

Kapchan, Deborah A., and Pauline Turner Strong, eds. 1999. "Theorizing the Hybrid." Special issue, *Journal of American Folklore* 112 (445).

Karp, Ivan, and Steven D. Lavine, eds. 1991. *Exhibiting Cultures: The Poetics and Politics of Museum Display.* Washington, DC: Smithsonian Institution Press.

Karp, Ivan, Christine Mullen Kreamer, and Steven Lavine, eds. 1992. *Museums and Communities: The Politics of Public Culture.* Washington, DC: Smithsonian Books.

Karson, Jennifer. 2006. *Wiyaxayxt/Wiyaakaa'awn/As Days Go By: Our History, Our Land, Our People—the Cayuse, Umatilla, and Walla Walla.* Portland: Oregon Historical Society Press.

Karttunen, Frances. 1994. *Between Worlds: Interpreters, Guides, and Survivors.* New Brunswick, NJ: Rutgers University Press.

Kauanui, Khaulani J. 2008. *Hawaiian Blood: Colonialism and the Politics of Sovereignty and Indigeneity.* Durham, NC: Duke University Press.

Kelly, Lawrence C. 1983. *The Assault on Assimilation: John Collier and the Origins of Indian Reform.* Albuquerque: University of New Mexico Press.

Kennedy, Randall. 2003. *Interracial Intimacies: Sex, Marriage, Identity, and Adoption.* New York: Pantheon Books.

Kidwell, Clara Sue, and Alan Velie. 2005. *Native American Studies.* Edinburgh: Edinburgh University Press.

Kincaid, Jamaica. 1990. *Lucy.* New York: Farrar, Straus and Giroux.

King, C. Richard. 2004a. "This Is Not an Indian: Situating Claims about Indianness in Sporting Worlds." *Journal of Sport and Social Issues* 28 (1): 3–10.

———, ed. 2004b. "Re/claiming Indianness: Critical Perspectives on Native American Mascots." Special issue, *Journal of Sport and Social Issues* 28 (1): 3–87.

———. 2010. *The Native American Mascot Controversy: A Handbook.* Plymouth, UK: Scarecrow Press.

King, C. Richard, and Charles Fruehling Springwood. 2001a. *Beyond the Cheers: Race as Spectacle in College Sport.* New York: State University of New York Press.

———. 2001b. "The Best Offense ... : Dissociation, Desire, and the Defense of the Florida State University Seminoles." In *Team Spirits: The Native American Mascots Controversy,* edited by C. Richard King and Charles Fruehling Springwood, 129–156. Lincoln: University of Nebraska Press.

———, eds. 2001c. *Team Spirits: The Native American Mascots Controversy.* Lincoln: University of Nebraska Press.

Kingsolver, Barbara. 1988. *The Bean Trees.* New York: HarperCollins.

———. 1993. *Pigs in Heaven.* New York: HarperCollins.

Klain, Bennie, and Leighton C. Peterson. 2000. "Native Media, Commercial Radio, and Language Maintenance: Defining Speech and Style for Navajo Broadcasters and Broadcast. Navajo." *Texas Linguistic Forum* 43: 117–127.

Klein, Kerwin Lee. 1997. *Frontiers of Historical Imagination: Narrating the European Conquest of Native America, 1890–1990.* Berkeley: University of California Press.

Koehler, Lyle. 1980. *A Search for Power: The "Weaker Sex" in Seventeenth-Century New England.* Urbana: University of Illinois Press.

Kolodny, Annette. 1984. *The Land before Her: Fantasy and Experience of the American Frontiers, 1630–1860.* Chapel Hill: University of North Carolina Press.

———. 1992. "Discovery, Encounter, Conquest: Competing Paradigms and Volatile Historical Truths." Biennial Conference of the European Association for American Studies, Universidad de Sevilla (April 4).

Kondo, Dorinne. 1990. *Crafting Selves: Power, Gender, and Discourses of Identity in a Japanese Workplace.* Chicago: University of Chicago Press.

Krech, Shepard, III. 1999. *The Ecological Indian: Myth and History.* New York: Norton.

Kroeber, Karl. 1990. Comment. In Gerald Vizenor, *Crossbloods: Bone Courts, Bingo, and Other Reports,* jacket. Minneapolis: University of Minnesota Press.

Krupat, Arnold. 1989. *The Voice in the Margin: Native American Literature in the Canon.* Berkeley: University of California Press.

Kuhn, Thomas. 1962. *The Structure of Scientific Revolutions.* Chicago: University of Chicago Press.

Kumar, Deepa. 2004. "War Propaganda and the (Ab)use of Women: Media Constructions of the Jessica Lynch Story." *Feminist Media Studies* 4 (3): 297–313.

Lambert, Valerie. 2007. *Choctaw Nation: A Story of American Indian Resurgence.* Lincoln: University of Nebraska Press.

Lamphere, Louise, with Eva Price, Carole Cadman, and Valerie Darwin. 2007. *Weaving Women's Lives: Three Generations in a Navajo Family.* Albuquerque: University of New Mexico Press.

Landsman, Gail H. 1997. "Informant as Critic: Conducting Research on a Dispute between Iroquoianist Scholars and Traditional Iroquois." In *Indians and Anthropologists: Vine Deloria, Jr., and the Critique of Anthropology,* edited by Thomas Biolsi and Larry J. Zimmerman, 160–176. Tucson: University of Arizona Press.

Landsman, Gail H., and Sara Cikorski. 1992. "Representation and Politics: Contesting Histories of the Iroquois." *Cultural Anthropology* 7 (4): 425–447.

Landzelius, Kyra, ed. 2006. *Native on the Net: Indigenous and Diasporic Peoples in the Virtual Age.* New York: Routledge.

Lassiter, Luke E. 1998. *The Power of Kiowa Song: A Collaborative Ethnography.* Tucson: University of Arizona Press.

———, ed. 2005. *The Chicago Guide to Collaborative Ethnography.* Chicago: University of Chicago Press.

Lawlor, Mary. 2006. *Public Native America: Tribal Self-Representation in Museums, Pow-wows, and Casinos.* New Brunswick, NJ: Rutgers University Press.

Lears, T. J. Jackson. 1981. *No Place of Grace: Antimodernism and the Transformation of American Culture, 1880–1920.* New York: Pantheon Books.

Lepore, Jill. 1999. *The Name of War: King Philip's War and the Origins of American Identity.* New York: Vintage Books.

Levenson, Jay A., ed. 1991. *Circa 1492: Art in the Age of Exploration.* New Haven, CT: Yale University Press.

Levinson, Sanford. 2006. *Torture: A Collection.* Oxford: Oxford University Press.

Lewis, Randolph. 2006. *Alanis Obomsawin: The Vision of a Native Filmmaker.* Lincoln: University of Nebraska Press.

Limerick, Patricia. 1987. *The Legacy of Conquest.* New York: Norton.

———. 2000. *Something in the Soil: Legacies and Reckonings in the New West.* New York: Norton.

Linenthal, Edward T. 2001. *Preserving Memory: The Struggle to Create America's Holocaust Museum.* New York: Columbia University Press.

———. 2003. *The Unfinished Bombing: Oklahoma City in American Memory.* Oxford: Oxford University Press.

Linenthal, Edward T., and Tom Engelhardt. 1996. *History Wars: The "Enola Gay" and Other Battles for the American Past.* New York: Henry Holt and Company.

Lipsitz, George. 1998. *The Possessive Investment in Whiteness: How White People Profit from Identity Politics.* Philadelphia: Temple University Press.

Littlefield, Alice. 2004. "Education." In *A Companion to the Anthropology of American Indians,* edited by Thomas Biolsi, 321–337. Malden, MA: Blackwell Publishers.

Lomawaima, K. Tsianina. 1993. "Domesticity in the Federal Indian Schools: The Power of Authority over Mind and Body." *American Ethnologist* 20: 227–240.

———. 1994. *They Called It Prairie Light: The Story of Chilocco Indian School.* Lincoln: University of Nebraska Press.

———. 2002. "American Indian Education: By Indians versus for Indians." In *A Companion to Native American History,* edited by Philip J. Deloria and Neal Salisbury, 422–440. Malden, MA: Blackwell Publishers.

Lomawaima, K. Tsianina, and Teresa L. McCarty. 2006. *To Remain an Indian: Lessons in Democracy from a Century of Native American Education.* New York: Teachers College Press.

Lonetree, Amy, and Amanda J. Cobb-Greetham, eds. 2008. *The National Museum of the American Indian: Critical Conversations.* Lincoln: University of Nebraska Press.

Lorillard, Christine Metteer. 2009. "Retelling the Stories of Indian Families: Judicial Narratives That Determine the Placement of Indian Children under the Indian Child Welfare Act." *Whittier Journal of Child and Family Advocacy* 8 (2): 191–236.

Luna-Firebaugh, Eileen M. 2002. "The Border Crossed Us: Border Crossing Issues of the Indigenous Peoples of the Americas." *Wicazo Sa Review* 17 (1): 159–181.

Lunenfeld, Marvin, ed. 1991. *Discovery, Invasion, Encounter: Sources and Interpretations.* Lexington, MA: D.C. Heath.

Macpherson, Crawford Brough. 1962. *The Political Theory of Possessive Individualism: Hobbes to Locke.* Oxford: Oxford University Press.

Marcus, George. 1998. "Ethnography in/of the World System: The Emergence of Multi-Sited Ethnography." In *Ethnography through Thick and Thin.* Princeton, NJ: Princeton University Press.

Marcus, George, and Michael Fischer. 1986. *Anthropology as Cultural Critique: An Experimental Moment in the Human Sciences.* Chicago: University of Chicago Press.

"Mascot Information." 2011. American Indian Studies, University of Illinois, Champagne Urbana. http://www.ais.illinois.edu/mascot/.

"Mascots in College Sports." 2012. LibGuides @ University of Illinois Library. http://uiuc.libguides.com/mascots.

Mather, Cotton. 1977 [1702]. *Magnalia Christi Americana: or, The Ecclesiastical History of New-England....* 7 vols. London. Annotated edition, vols. 1–2, edited by Kenneth B. Murdock, with the assistance of Elizabeth W. Miller. Cambridge, MA: Belknap Press.

———. 1977 [1697]. "Humiliations Follow'd with Deliverances.... Accompanied and Accommodated with a Narrative, of a Notable Deliverance Lately Received by Some English Captive, from the Hands of Cruel Indians...." Facsimile. *Garland Library of Narratives of North American Indian Captivities,* vol. 1, compiled by Wilcomb Washburn. New York: Garland.

———. 1978 [1699]. "Decennium Luctuosum." Facsimile. *Garland Library of Narratives of North American Indian Captivities,* vol. 3, compiled by Wilcomb Washburn. New York: Garland.

———. 1981 [1697]. "Humiliations Follow'd with Deliverances." Excerpted in *Puritans Among the Indians: Accounts of Captivity and Redemption, 1676–1724,* edited by Alden T. Vaughan and Edward W. Clark. Cambridge, MA: Harvard University Press.

McCarthy, Theresa L. 2008. "Iroquoian and Iroquoianist: Anthropologists and the Haudenosaunee at Grand River." *Histories of Anthropology* 4: 135–171.

McCarty, Teresa L. 2002. *A Place to Be Navajo: Rough Rock and the Struggle for Self-Determination in Indigenous Schooling*. Mahwah, NJ: Lawrence Erlbaum.

McGuire, Randall. 1997. "Why Have Archaeologists Thought That the Real Indians Were Dead and What Can We Do about It?" In *Indians and Anthropologists: Vine Deloria, Jr., and the Critique of Anthropology*, edited by Thomas Biolsi and Larry Zimmerman, 63–91. Tucson: University of Arizona Press.

McMaster, Gerald, and Lee-Ann Martin, eds. 1992. *Indigena: Contemporary Native Perspectives*. Vancouver: Douglas and McIntyre.

McMillan, Alan. 1988. *Native Peoples and Cultures of Canada: An Anthropological Overview*. Vancouver: Douglas and McIntyre.

McMullen, Ann. 2009. "Reinventing George Heye: Nationalizing the Museum of the American Indian and Its Collections." In *Contesting Knowledge: Museums and Indigenous Perspectives*, edited by Susan Sleeper-Smith, 65–105. Lincoln: University of Nebraska Press.

McNeill, William H. 1976. *Plagues and Peoples*. New York: Doubleday.

McNickle, D'Arcy. 1970. "American Indians Who Never Were." *Indian History* 3 (3): 4–7.

———. 1973. *Native American Tribalism: Indian Survivals and Renewals*. New York: Oxford University Press.

Mechling, Jay. 1980a. "The Magic of the Boy Scout Campfire." *Journal of Folklore* 93: 35–56.

———. 1980b. "'Playing Indian' and the Search for Authenticity in Modern White America." *Prospects* 5: 17–33.

———. 1989. "Banana Cannon and Other Folk Traditions between Humans and Nonhuman Animals." *Western Folklore* 48: 312–323.

———. 2001. *On My Honor: Boy Scouts and the Making of American Youth*. Chicago: University of Chicago Press.

Medicine, Beatrice. 1972. "The Anthropologist as the Indian's Image Maker." In *The American Indian Reader: Anthropology*, edited by Jeanette Henry, 23–28. San Francisco: Indian Historian Press.

———. 2001. *Learning to Be an Anthropologist and Remaining "Native": Selected Writings*. Urbana: University of Illinois Press.

Melanson, Yvette, with Claire Safran. 1999. *Looking for Lost Bird: A Jewish Woman Discovers Her Navajo Roots*. New York: Avon.

Merrill, William L., and Richard E. Ahlborn. 1997. "Zuni Archangels and the Ahayu:da: A Sculpted Chronicle of Power and Identity." In *Exhibiting Dilemmas: Issues of Representation at the Smithsonian*, edited by Amy Henderson and Adrienne L. Kaeppler, 176–205. Washington, DC: Smithsonian Institution Press.

Merrill, William L., Edmund J. Ladd, and T. J. Ferguson. 1993. "The Return of the Ahayu:da: Lessons for Repatriation from Zuni Pueblo and the Smithsonian Institution." *Current Anthropology* 34: 523–567.

Metteer, Christine. 1996. "*Pigs in Heaven*: A Parable of Native American Adoption under the Indian Child Welfare Act." *Arizona State Law Journal* 28 (2): 589–628.

Meyer, Carter Jones, and Diana Royer, eds. 2001. *Selling the Indian: Commercializing and Appropriating American Indian Cultures*. Tucson: University of Arizona Press.

Mihesuah, Devon Abbott. 1996. *American Indians: Stereotypes and Realities*. Atlanta, GA: Clarity.

———, ed. 2000. *Repatriation Reader: Who Owns American Indian Remains?* Lincoln: University of Nebraska Press.

Mihesuah, Devon Abbott, and Angela Cavender Wilson, eds. 2004. *Indigenizing the Academy: Transforming Scholarship and Empowering Communities*. Lincoln: University of Nebraska Press.

Milanich, Jerald T., and Susan Milbrath, eds. 1989. *First Encounters: Spanish Explorations in the Caribbean and the United States, 1492–1570*. Gainesville, FL: Florida Museum of Natural History and University of Florida Press.

Milbrath, Susan, and Jerald Milanich. 1991. "Columbian Conflict." *Museum News*, September/October, 34–37.

Miller, Bruce Granville. 2003. *Invisible Indigenes: The Politics of Non-Recognition*. Lincoln: University of Nebraska Press.

Miller, Jay. 2002. "Kinship, Family Kindreds, and Community." In *A Companion to Native American History*, edited by Philip J. Deloria and Neal Salisbury, 139–153. Malden, MA: Blackwell Publishers.

Miller, Susan A. 2007. *Growing Girls: The Natural Origins of Girls' Organizations in America*. New Brunswick, NJ: Rutgers University Press.

Mintz, Sidney. 1986. *Sweetness and Power: The Place of Sugar in Modern History*. New York: Penguin.

Mitchell, Timothy. 1988. *Colonizing Egypt*. Cambridge: Cambridge University Press.

Modell, Judith S. 1994. *Kinship with Strangers: Adoption and Interpretations of Kinship in American Culture*. Berkeley: University of California Press.

———. 1998. "Rights to the Children: Foster Care and Social Reproduction in Hawai'i." In *Reproducing Reproduction*, edited by Sarah Franklin and Helena Ragoné, 156–172. Philadelphia: University of Pennsylvania Press.

Momaday, N. Scott. 1969. *The Way to Rainy Mountain*. Albuquerque: University of New Mexico Press.

———. 1974. "I Am Alive." In *The World of the American Indian*, edited by Jules B. Billiard, 11–27. Washington, DC: National Geographic Society.

Monsivais, Jose. 1997. "A Glimmer of Hope: A Proposal to Keep the Indian Child Welfare Act of 1978 Intact." *American Indian Law Review* 22 (1): 1–36.

Moore, John H. 1992. "The Enduring Reservations of Oklahoma." In *State and Reservation: New Perspectives on Federal Indian Policy*, edited by George Pierre Castile and Robert L. Bee, 92–109. Tucson: University of Arizona Press.

Morgan, Edmund Sears. 1980. *The Puritan Family: Religion and Domestic Relations in Seventeenth-Century New England*. Westport, CT: Greenwood Press.

Morrison, Howard Alexander. 1992. *American Encounters: A Companion to the Exhibition at the National Museum of American History, Smithsonian Institution*. Washington, DC: National Museum of American History Press.

Morrison, Kenneth M. 1979. "Towards a History of Intimate Encounters: Algonkian Folklore, Jesuit Missionaries, and Kiwakwe, the Cannibal Giant." *American Indian Culture and Research Journal* 3 (4): 51–80.

Moushegian, Brian R. 2006. "Native American Mascots' Last Stand—Legal Difficulties in Eliminating Public University Use of Native American Mascots." *Villanueva Sports and Entertainment Law Journal* 13: 465–492.

Mullaney, Steven. 1983. "Strange Things, Gross Terms, Curious Customs: The Rehearsal of Cultures in the Late Renaissance." *Representations* 3: 40–67.

Mullin, Molly M. 2001. *Culture in the Marketplace: Gender, Art, and Value in the American Southwest*. Durham, NC: Duke University Press.

Myers, Joseph A., ed. 1981. *They're Young Once but Indian Forever: A Summary and Analysis of Investigative Hearings on Indian Child Welfare*. Oakland, CA: American Indian Lawyer Training Program.

Myers, Raquelle, Nancy Thorington, and Joseph Myers, eds. 1998. *Significant Ties Exception to the ICWA: Judicial Decision-Making or Incorporating Bias into Law?* Petaluma, CA: National Indian Justice Center, Inc.

Nabokov, Peter. 2002. *A Forest of Time: American Indian Ways of History*. New York: Cambridge University Press.

———. 2006. *Where the Lightning Strikes: The Lives of American Indian Sacred Places*. New York: Penguin Books.

Nagel, Joane. 1996. *American Indian Ethnic Renewal: Red Power and the Resurgence of Identity and Culture*. New York: Oxford University Press.

Namias, June. 1993. *White Captives: Gender and Ethnicity on the American Frontier*. Chapel Hill: University of North Carolina Press.

Nash, Gary B., Charlotte Crabtree, and Ross E. Dunn. 2000. *History on Trial: Culture Wars and the Teaching of the Past*. New York: Vintage Books.

Nash, Roderick. 1982. *Wilderness and the American Mind*. New Haven, CT: Yale University Press.

National Council of Catholic Bishops. 1991a. *Encounters with Faith: A Handbook for the Observance of the Fifth Centenary of Evangelization in the Americas*. Washington, DC: United States Catholic Conference.

———. 1991b. *Heritage and Hope: Evangelization in the United States/Pastoral Letter on the Fifth Centenary of Evangelization in the Americas*. Washington, DC: United States Catholic Conference.

———. 1992. *1992: A Time for Remembering, Reconciling, and Recommitting Ourselves as People/Pastoral Reflections on the Fifth Centenary and Native American People*. Washington, DC: United States Catholic Conference.

National Council of the Churches of Christ in the U.S.A. 1990. "A Faithful Response to the 500th Anniversary of the Arrival of Christopher Columbus" (May 17). New York: National Council of Churches.

National Council for the Social Studies. 1991. *The Columbian Quincentenary: An Educational Opportunity*. Washington, DC.

Nelson, Diane A. 1999. *A Finger in the Wound: Body Politics in Quincentennial Guatemala*. Berkeley: University of California Press.

Nesper, Larry. 2002. *The Walleye War: The Struggle for Ojibwe Spearfishing and Treaty Rights*. Lincoln: University of Nebraska Press.

New Line Cinema. 2001. DVD cover, *Bamboozled*. www.newline.com/properties/bamboozled.html.

Niezen, Ronald. 2003. *The Origins of Indigenism: Human Rights and the Politics of Identity*. Berkeley: University of California Press.

———. 2009. *The Rediscovered Self: Indigenous Identity and Cultural Justice*. Montreal: McGill-Queen's University Press.

Norrell, Brenda. 2006. "Indigenous Border Summit Opposes Border Wall and Militarization." *Citizen Action in the Americas Profile*, October 31. Silver City, NM: International Relations Center. http://americas.irc-online.org/amcit/3648.

O'Brien, Jean. 2003. *Dispossession by Degrees: Indian Land and Identity in Natick, Massachusetts, 1650–1790*. Lincoln: University of Nebraska Press.

————. 2006. "'Vanishing' Indians in the Nineteenth-Century New England: Local Historians' Erasure of Still-Present Indian Peoples." In *New Perspectives on Native North America: Cultures, Histories, Representations*, edited by Sergei Kan and Pauline Turner Strong, 413–432. Lincoln: University of Nebraska Press.

————. 2010. *Firsting and Lasting: Writing Indians Out of Existence in New England*. Minneapolis: University of Minnesota Press.

O'Brien, Sharon. 1990. *American Indian Tribal Governments*. Norman: University of Oklahoma Press.

Olick, Jeffrey K., Vered Vinitzky-Seroussi, and Daniel Levy, eds. 2011. *The Collective Memory Reader*. Oxford: Oxford University Press.

Olsen, Evelyn Guard. 1967. *Indian Blood*. Parsons, WV: McClain Printing Co.

O'Nell, Theresa Deleane. 1996. *Disciplined Hearts: History, Identity, and Depression in an American Indian Community*. Berkeley: University of California Press.

Ong, Aihwa. 1996. "Cultural Citizenship as Subject-Making: Immigrants Negotiate Racial and Cultural Boundaries in the United States." *Current Anthropology* 37: 737–762.

————. 1998. *Flexible Citizenship: The Cultural Logics of Transnationality*. Durham, NC: Duke University Press.

Orians, George Harrison, ed. 1970. *Days of Humiliation, Times of Affliction and Disaster: Nine Sermons for Restoring Favor with an Angry God, 1696–1727*. Gainesville, FL: Scholars' Facsimiles and Reprints.

Ortiz, Alfonso. 1970. "American Indian Philosophy and Its Relation to the Modern World." In *Indian Voices: The First Convocation of American Indian Scholars*, edited by Rupert Costo et al., 9–47. San Francisco: Indian Historian Press.

————. 1977. "Some Concerns Central to the Writing of 'Indian' History." *Indian Historian* 10 (1): 17–22.

Ortiz, Laura Velasco. 2005. *Mixtec Transnational Identity*. Tucson: University of Arizona Press.

Orvell, Miles. 1989. *The Real Thing: Imitation and Authenticity in American Culture, 1880–1940*. Chapel Hill: University of North Carolina Press.

Owens, Louis. 1992. *Other Destinies: Understanding the American Indian Novel*. Norman: University of Oklahoma Press.

Pearce, Roy Harvey. 1965 [1953]. *Savagism and Civilization: A Study of the Indian and the American Mind*. [The Savages of America]. Baltimore: John Hopkins Press.

Peers, Laura, and Alison K. Brown. 2003. *Museums and Source Communities: A Routledge Reader*. New York: Routledge.

Pelotte, Donald. 1992. Remarks. Symposium on the Columbian Quincentenary, George Warren Brown School of Social Work, Washington University, St. Louis, MO (March 19).

Perdue, Theda, and Michael D. Green. 2001. *The Columbia Guide to American Indians of the Southeast*. New York: Columbia University Press.

Perry, Richard J. 1996. *From Time Immemorial: Indigenous Peoples and State Systems*. Austin: University of Texas Press.

Peterson, Jacqueline. 1991. "Sacred Encounters: Ethnohistory for a Museum Audience." Annual Meetings of the American Historical Association, Chicago (December 28).

Peterson, Jacqueline, and Jennifer S. H. Brown. 1985. *The New Peoples: Being and Becoming Métis in North America*. Winnipeg: University of Manitoba Press.

Peterson, Leighton. 2011. "'Reel Navajo': The Linguistic Creation of Indigenous Screen Memories." *American Indian Culture and Research Journal* 35 (2): 111–134.

Philips, Sloan. 1997. "The Indian Child Welfare Act in the Face of Extinction." *American Indian Law Review* 20 (2): 351–364.

Phillips, Carla Rahn, and David J. Weber, eds. 1991. *Essays on the Columbian Encounter.* Washington, DC: The American Historical Association.

Povinelli, Elizabeth A. 2002. *The Cunning of Recognition: Indigenous Alterities and the Making of Australian Multiculturalism.* New Haven, CT: Yale University Press.

Powers, William K. 1988. "The Indian Hobbyist Movement in North America." In *Handbook of North American Indians,* edited by William C. Sturtevant, vol. 4: *History of Indian-White Relations,* edited by Wilcomb E. Washburn, 557–561. Washington, DC: Smithsonian Institution, for sale by the US Government Printing Office, Superintendent of Documents.

Pratt, Mary Louise. 1992. *Imperial Eyes: Travel Writing and Transculturation.* London: Routledge.

Prins, Harald E. L. 2002. "Visual Media and the Primitivist Perplex: Colonial Fantasies, Indigenous Imagination, and Advocacy in North America." In *Media Worlds,* edited by Faye D. Ginsburg, Lila Abu-Lughod, and Brian Larkin, 58–74. Berkeley: University of California Press.

———. 2004. "Visual Anthropology." In *A Companion to the Anthropology of American Indians,* edited by Thomas Biolsi, 506–525. Malden, MA: Blackwell Publishers.

Prochaska, David. 2001. "At Home in Illinois: Presence of Chief Illiniwek, Absence of Native Americans." In *Team Spirits: Essays on the History and Significance of Native American Mascots,* edited by C. Richard King and Charles F. Springwood, 157–185. Lincoln: University of Nebraska Press.

Prucha, Francis Paul, ed. 1973. *Americanizing the American Indians: Writings by the "Friends of the Indian," 1880–1900.* Cambridge, MA: Harvard University Press.

———, ed. 2000. *Documents of United States Indian Policy.* 3rd edition. Lincoln: University of Nebraska Press.

Putney, Clifford. 2001. *Muscular Christianity: Manhood and Sports in Protestant America, 1880–1920.* Cambridge, MA and London: Harvard University Press.

Ramirez, Renya. 2007. *Native Hubs: Culture, Community, and Belonging in Silicon Valley and Beyond.* Durham, NC: Duke University Press.

Regan, Paulette. 2010. *Unsettling the Settler Within: Indian Residential Schools, Truth Telling, and Reconciliation in Canada.* Vancouver: University of British Columbia Press.

Resnick, Judith. 1989. "Dependent Sovereigns: Indian Tribes, States, and the Federal Courts." *University of Chicago Law Review* 56: 671–759.

Revard, Carter. 1987. "Walking among the Stars." In *I Tell You Now: Autobiographical Essays by Native American Writers,* edited by Brian Swann and Arnold Krupat, 65–84. Lincoln: University of Nebraska Press.

Richardson, Valerie. 2010. "Obama Adopts U.N. Manifesto on Rights of Indigenous Peoples." *Washington Times,* December 16. http://www.washingtontimes.com/news/2010/dec/16/obama-adopts-un-manifesto-on-rights-of-indigenous-/.

Richter, Daniel K. 1983. "War and Culture: The Iroquois Experience." *William and Mary Quarterly* 40 (4): 528–559.

———. 1992. *The Ordeal of the Longhouse: The Peoples of the Iroquois League in the Era of European Colonization.* Chapel Hill: University of North Carolina Press.

———. 2003. *Facing East from Indian Country.* Cambridge, MA: Harvard University Press.

Rickard, Jolene. 2011. "Visualizing Sovereignty in the Time of Biometric Sensors." *South Atlantic Quarterly* 110 (2): 465–482.

Ridington, Robin, and Dennis Hastings. 1997. *Blessing for a Long Time: The Sacred Pole of the Omaha Tribe*. Lincoln: University of Nebraska Press.

Ringle, Ken. 1991. "Rediscovering America: Reaping New History from *Seeds of Change*." *Washington Post*, October 27.

Rizo, Chris. 2009. "U.S. Supreme Court Rejects Redskins Mascot Challenge." *Legal NewsLine.com*, November 16. http://www.legalnewsline.com/news/224048-u.s. -supreme-court-rejects-redskins-mascot-challenge.

Robertson, Karen. 1996. "Pocahontas at the Masque." *Signs* 21: 551–583.

Rodham, Hillary. 1973. "Children under the Law." *Harvard Educational Review* 43 (4): 487–514.

Rogers, Ethel. 1915. *Sebago-Wohelo Camp Fire Girls*. Battle Creek, MI: Good Health Publishing.

Rogin, Michael. 1996. *Blackface, White Noise: Jewish Immigrants in the Hollywood Melting Pot*. Berkeley: University of California Press.

Rollins, Peter C., and John E. O'Connor, eds. 2003. *Hollywood's Indian: The Portrayal of the Native American in Film*, expanded edition. Lexington: University Press of Kentucky.

Root, Deborah. 1995. *Cannibal Culture: Art, Appropriation, and the Politics of Attire*. Boulder, CO: Westview Press.

Rosaldo, Renato. 1997. "Cultural Citizenship, Inequity, and Multiculturalism." In *Latino Cultural Citizenship: Claiming Identity, Space and Rights*, edited by William V. Flores and Rina Benmayor, 26–38. Boston: Beacon Press.

Roscoe, Will. 1992. *The Zuni Man-Woman*. Albuquerque: University of New Mexico Press.

Rosenstein, Jay. 2001. "In Whose Honor? Mascots and Media." In *Team Spirits: Essays on the History and Significance of Native American Mascots*, edited by C. Richard King and Charles F. Springwood, 241–256. Lincoln: University of Nebraska Press.

Ross, Brian, Rhonda Schwartz, Lee Ferran, and Avni Patel. 2011. "Top Secret Stealth Helicopter Program Revealed in Osama Bin Laden Raid: Experts, May 4, 2011." *ABC News*. http://abcnews.go.com/Blotter/top-secret-stealth -helicopter-program-revealed-osama-bin/story?id=13530693.

Rothenberg, Paula. 2011. *White Privilege: Essential Readings on the Other Side of Racism*. 4th ed. New York: Worth Publishers.

Rothstein, Edward. 2004. "Museum Review; Museum with an American Indian Voice." *New York Times*, September 21. http://www.nytimes.com/2004/09/21/arts/ design/21muse.html?_r=1.

Rountree, Helen C. 1989. *The Powhatan Indians of Virginia: Their Traditional Culture*. Norman: University of Oklahoma Press.

———. 2006. *Pocahontas, Powhatan, Opechancanough*. Charlottesville: University of Virginia Press.

Ruble, Erin, and Gerald Torres. 2004. "Perfect Good Faith." *Nevada Law Journal* 5 (1): 93–125.

Rushing, W. Jackson. 1993. "Contingent Histories, Aesthetic Politics." *New Art Examiner* (March): 14–20.

Rydell, Robert W. 1984. *All the World's a Fair: Visions of Empire at American International Expositions, 1876–1916*. Chicago: University of Chicago Press.

Sahlins, Marshall. 1981. *Historical Metaphors and Mythical Realities*. Ann Arbor: University of Michigan Press.

———. 1985. *Islands of History*. Chicago: University of Chicago Press.

Said, Edward. 1978. *Orientalism*. New York: Random House.

Sale, Kirkpatrick. 1990. *The Conquest of Paradise: Christopher Columbus and the Columbian Legacy*. New York: Alfred A. Knopf.

Salisbury, Neal. 1981. "Squanto: Last of the Patuxets." In *Struggle and Survival in Colonial America*, edited by David G. Sweet and Gary B. Nash, 228–246. Berkeley: University of California Press.

———. 1982. *Manitou and Providence: Indians, Europeans, and the Making of New England, 1500–1643*. Oxford: Oxford University Press.

———, ed. 1997. *The Sovereignty and Goodness of God: With Related Documents (by Mary Rowlandson)*. Boston: Bedford/St. Martin's.

Salon staff. 2006. "Collection: The Abu Ghraib Files." March 14. http://www.salon.com/news/abu_ghraib/2006/03/14/introduction.

Samuels, Allison. 2000. "Spike's Minstrel Show." *Newsweek*, October 1. http://magazine-directory.com/Newsweek.htm.

Samuels, David. 1999. "The Whole and the Sum of the Parts, or, How Cookie and His Cupcakes Told the Story of Apache History in San Carlos." *Journal of American Folklore* 112 (445): 467–476.

———. 2004. *Putting a Song on Top of It: Expression and Identity of the San Carlos Apache*. Tucson: University of Arizona Press.

Sanders, Ronald. 1978. *Lost Tribes and Promised Lands: The Origins of American Racism*. New York: Perennial.

Satz, Ronald N. 2002 [1975]. *American Indian Policy in the Jacksonian Era*. Norman: University of Oklahoma Press.

Sayre, Gordon M. 1997. *"Les Sauvage Américains": Representations of Native Americans in French and English Literature*. Chapel Hill: University of North Carolina Press.

———, ed. 2000. *American Captivity Narratives*. Boston: Houghton Mifflin Company.

Scarry, Elaine. 1987. *The Body in Pain: The Making and Unmaking of the World*. Oxford: Oxford University Press.

Scheckel, Susan. 1998. *The Insistence of the Indian*. Princeton, NJ: Princeton University Press.

Schneider, David M. 1980. *American Kinship: A Cultural Account*, 2nd ed. Ann Arbor: University of Michigan Press.

———. 1984. *A Critique of the Study of Kinship*. Ann Arbor: University of Michigan Press.

Schutz, Alfred. 1964–1973. *Collected Papers, vol. 1: The Problem of Social Reality*, 4th ed., edited by Maurice Natanson. *vol. 2: Studies in Social Theory*, edited by Arvid Brodelsen. The Hague: M. Niihoff.

Schwarz, Maureen Trudelle. 2003. *Blood and Voice: Navajo Women Ceremonial Practitioners*. Tucson: University of Arizona Press.

Seaver, James Everett. 1995 [1824]. "A Narrative of the Life of Mrs. Mary Jemison …" Facsimile. In *Narratives of North American Indian Captivities*, vol. 41, edited by Wilcomb E. Washburn. New York: Garland.

Segal, Daniel A. 1988. "Nationalism, Comparatively Speaking." *Journal of Historical Sociology* 1 (3): 301–321.

———, ed. 1996. Resisting Identities. Theme issue, *Cultural Anthropology* 11 (4).

———. 2000. "'Western Civ' and the Staging of History in American Higher Education." *American Historical Review* 105 (3): 770–805.

Segal, Daniel A., and Richard Handler. 1992. "How European Is Nationalism?" *Social Analysis* 32: 1–15.

Seton, Ernest Thompson. 1903. *Two Little Savages*. Garden City, NY: Doubleday.

———. 1903–1932. *The Birchbark Rolls of the Woodcraft Indians, Containing Their Constitution, Laws, Games, and Deeds*. 30 editions. Philadelphia, PA: Curtis Publishing Company; New York: A. S. Barnes.

———. 1918. *Sign Talk*. Garden City, NY: Doubleday.

Seton, Ernest Thompson, and Julia M. Seton, comps. 1937. *The Gospel of the Redman*. Commemorative edition. Foreword by Paul Goble. Introduction by Dee Seton Barber. Bloomington: World Wisdom.

Shapiro, Leonard. 1991. "Princess Pale Moon Draws Special Note; AIM 'Totally Opposed' to Her Anthem Role." *Washington Post*, November 3. http://www.highbeam.com/doc/1P2-1093380.html.

Shea, John Gilmary. 1970 [1860]. *A French-Onondaga Dictionary, from a Manuscript of the Seventeenth Century*. Reprint. New York: AMS Press.

Sheehan, Bernard W. 1980. *Savagism and Civility: Indians and Englishmen in Colonial Virginia*. Cambridge: Cambridge University Press.

Sheridan, Diana, ed. 1992. "Women Speak to Colonization, Conquest, Columbus." *CSWS Review: Annual Magazine of the Center for the Study of Women in Society*. Eugene: University of Oregon Press.

Sherif, Maurice. 2011. "The American Wall: From the Pacific Ocean to the Gulf of Mexico" (excerpt). Courtesy of the University of Texas Press. *Texas Monthly* Web exclusive, March. http://www.texasmonthly.com/2011-03-01/book_excerpt.php.

Sider, Gerald M. 2003. *Living Indian Histories: The Lumbee and Tuscarora People in North Carolina*. Chapel Hill: University of North Carolina Press.

Sider, Gerald M., and Gavin Smith, eds. 1997. *Between History and Histories: The Making of Silences and Commemorations*. Toronto: University of Toronto Press.

Siebert, Monika. 2006. "Atanarjuat and the Ideological Work of Contemporary Indigenous Filmmaking." *Public Culture* 18: 531–550.

Silko, Leslie Marmon. 1999. *Gardens in the Dunes*. New York: Simon and Schuster.

Silver, Shirley, and Wick R. Miller, eds. 1997. *American Indian Languages: Cultural and Social Contexts*. Tucson: University of Arizona Press.

Silverman, Kenneth. 1984. *The Life and Times of Cotton Mather*. New York: Harper and Row.

Simmons, Leo W., ed. 1942. *Sun Chief: The Autobiography of a Hopi Indian*. New Haven, CT: Yale University Press.

Simmons, William. 1986. *Spirit of the New England Tribes: Indian History and Folklore, 1620–1984*. Hanover and London: University Press of New England.

Simon, Rita J., Howard Alstein, and Marygold S. Melli. 1994. *The Case for Transracial Adoption*. Washington, DC: American University Press.

Simon, Rita J., and Sarah Hernandez. 2008. *Native American Transracial Adoptees Tell Their Stories*. Lanham, MD: Lexington Books.

Simpson, Audra. 2007. "On the Logic of Discernment." *American Quarterly* 59 (2): 479–491.

———. 2009. "Captivating Eunice: Membership, Colonialism, and Gendered Citizenships of Grief." *Wicazo Sa Review* 24 (2): 105–129.

———. 2011. "Settlement's Secret." *Cultural Anthropology* 26 (2): 205–217.

Simpson, Moira G. 2001. *Making Representations: Museums in the Post-Colonial Era*, rev. ed. New York: Routledge.

Sims, Art. 2000. Promotional poster for *Bamboozled*. 11:24 Design. http://spikeleeposters.com/posters/1.html.

Singer, Beverly R. 2001. *Wiping the War Paint off the Lens: Native American Film and Video*. Minneapolis: University of Minnesota Press.

Slapin, Beverly, and Doris Seale. 1992. *Through Indian Eyes: The Native Experience in Books for Children*. Philadelphia: New Society Publishers.

Sleeper-Smith, Susan, ed. 2009. *Contesting Knowledge: Museums and Indigenous Perspectives*. Lincoln: University of Nebraska Press.

Slifkin, Anne R. 2002. "John Walker Lindh." *South Atlantic Quarterly* 101 (2): 417–424.

Slotkin, Richard. 1973. *Regeneration through Violence: The Mythology of the American Frontier, 1600–1860*. Middletown, CT: Wesleyan University Press.

Smith, Andrea. 2008. *Native Americans and the Christian Right: The Gendered Politics of Unlikely Alliances*. Durham, NC: Duke University Press.

Smith, John. 1986a [1624]. "The Generall Historie of Virginia...." In *The Complete Works of Captain John Smith (1580–1631)*, edited by Philip L. Barbour. Chapel Hill: University of North Carolina Press.

———. 1986b [1608]. "A True Relation...." In *The Complete Works of Captain John Smith (1580–1631)*, edited by Philip L. Barbour. Chapel Hill: University of North Carolina Press.

Smith, Linda Tuhiwai. 1999. *Decolonizing Methodologies: Research and Indigenous Peoples*. London: Zed Books.

Smith, Marian W. 1951. "American Indian Warfare." *Transactions of the New York Academy of Science* 12: 348–365.

Smith, Paul Chaat. 2009. *Everything You Know about Indians Is Wrong*. Minneapolis: University of Minnesota Press.

Smith, Sherry L. 2000. *Reimagining Indians: Native Americans through Anglo Eyes, 1880–1940*. Oxford: Oxford University Press.

Snyder, Christina. 2010. *Slavery in Indian Country: The Changing Face of Captivity in Early America*. Cambridge, MA: Harvard University Press.

Sommer, Doris. 1991. *Foundational Fictions: The National Romances of Latin America*. Berkeley: University of California Press.

Sontag, Susan. 2003. *Regarding the Pain of Others*. New York: Farrar, Straus and Giroux.

———. 2004. "Regarding the Torture of Others." *New York Times*, May 23.

Speed, Shannon. 2008. "Human Rights and the Border Wall." *Anthropology News* 49 (9): 25.

Spindel, Carol. 2000. *Dancing at Halftime: Sports and the Controversy over American Indian Mascots*. New York: New York University Press.

Spivak, Gayatri Chakravorty. 1988. "Can the Subaltern Speak?" In *Marxism and the Interpretation of Culture*, edited by Cary Nelson and Lawrence Grossberg, 271–313. Urbana: University of Illinois Press.

———. 1993. *Outside in the Teaching Machine*. New York: Routledge.

Springwood, Charles Fruehling. 2004. "'I'm Indian Too!': Claiming Native American Identity, Crafting Authority in Mascot Debates." *Journal of Sport and Social Issues* 28: 56–70.

Starn, Orin. 2004. *Ishi's Brain: In Search of America's Last "Wild" Indian.* New York: Norton.

———. 2011. "Here Come the Anthros (Again): The Strange Marriage of Anthropology and Native America." *Cultural Anthropology* 26: 179–204.

Starna, William A., and Ralph Watkins. 1991. "Northern Iroquoian Slavery." *Ethnohistory* 38 (1): 34–53.

Staurowsky, Ellen J. 2001. "Sockalexis and the Making of the Myth at the Core of Cleveland's 'Indian' Image." In *Team Spirits: Essays in the History and Significance of Native American Mascots,* edited by C. Richard King and Charles F. Springwood, 82–106. Lincoln: University of Nebraska Press.

———. 2004. "Privilege at Play: On the Legal and Social Fictions That Sustain American Indian Sport Imagery." *Journal of Sport and Social Issues* 28 (1): 11–29.

———. 2007. "'You Know, We Are All Indian': Exploring White Power and Privilege in Reactions to the NCAA Native American Mascot Policy." *Journal of Sport and Social Issues* 31 (1): 61–76.

Stedman, Raymond William. 1982. *Shadows of the Indian: Stereotypes in American Culture.* Norman: University of Oklahoma Press.

Stephen, Lynn. 2007. *Transborder Lives: Indigenous Oaxacans in Mexico, California, and Oregon.* Durham, NC: Duke University Press.

Sternecky, Neal. 1992. "Pogo." *Los Angeles Times Syndicate,* January 7.

Stewart, Kathleen. 1991. "On the Politics of Cultural Theory: A Case for 'Contaminated' Cultural Critique." *Social Research* 58: 395–412.

Stewart, Susan. 1993. *On Longing: Narratives of the Miniature, the Gigantic, the Souvenir, the Collection.* Durham, NC: Duke University Press.

Stiffarm, Lenore A., with Phil Lane Jr. 1992. "The Demography of Native North America: A Question of American Indian Survival." In *The State of Native America: Genocide, Colonization, and Resistance,* edited by M. Annette Jaimes, 23–53. Boston: South End Press.

Stocking, George W., Jr., ed. 1985. *Objects and Others: Essays on Museums and Material Culture.* Madison: University of Wisconsin Press.

———. 1987. *Victorian Anthropology.* New York: The Free Press.

———, ed. 1991. *Colonial Situations: Essays on the Contextualization of Ethnographic Knowledge.* Madison: University of Wisconsin Press.

Strathern, Marilyn. 1992. *After Nature: English Kinship in the Late Twentieth Century.* Cambridge: Cambridge University Press.

Strong, Pauline Turner. 1986. "Fathoming the Primitive: Australian Aborigines in Four Explorers' Journals, 1697–1845." *Ethnohistory* 33 (2): 175–194.

———. 1991. "Reinterpreting Images of the Frontier: Controversial Art Exhibit Portrays Destruction Wrought by Westward Expansion." *St. Louis Post-Dispatch,* September 30, Commentary Page.

———. 1992. Unpublished field notes: Seville, Spain; Ottawa, Canada; Columbus, Ohio; Denver, Colorado; Minneapolis, Minnesota; St. Louis and Kansas City, Missouri; Washington, DC.

———. 1996. "Animated Indians: Critique and Contradiction in Commodified Children's Culture." *Cultural Anthropology* 11: 405–424.

———. 1997. "Exclusive Labels: Indexing the National 'We' in Commemorative and Oppositional Exhibitions." *Museum Anthropology* 21: 42–56.

———. 1999. *Captive Selves, Captivating Others: The Politics and Poetics of Colonial American Captivity Narratives.* Boulder, CO: Westview Press/Perseus Books.

———. 2002. "Transforming Outsiders: Captivity, Adoption, and Slavery Reconsidered." In *A Companion to American Indian History*, edited by Philip J. Deloria and Neal Salisbury, 339–356. Malden, MA: Blackwell Publishers.

———. 2003. "Playing Indian in the 1990s: *Pocahontas* and *The Indian in the Cupboard*." In *Hollywood's Indian: The Portrayal of the Native American in Film*, 2nd ed., edited by Peter C. Rollins and John E. O'Connor, 187–205. Lexington: University Press of Kentucky.

———. 2005. "What Is an Indian Family? The Indian Child Welfare Act and the Renascence of Tribal Sovereignty." Special issue: Indigenous Peoples of the United States. *American Studies* 46 (3–4, Fall–Winter): 205–231. Published jointly with *Indigenous Studies Today* 1 (Fall 2005/Spring 2006).

———. 2006. "'To Light the Fire of Our Desire': Primitivism in the Camp Fire Girls." In *New Perspectives on Native North America: Cultures, Histories and Representations*, edited by Sergei Kan and Pauline Turner Strong, 474–488. Lincoln: University of Nebraska Press.

Strong, Pauline Turner, and Laurie Posner. 2010. "Selves in Play: Sports, Scouts, and American Cultural Citizenship." *International Review for the Sociology of Sport* 45 (2): 390–409.

Strong, Pauline Turner, and Barrik Van Winkle. 1996. "'Indian Blood': Reflections on the Reckoning and Refiguring of Native North American Identity." *Cultural Anthropology* 11: 547–576.

Sturken, Marita. 1997. *Tangled Memories: The Vietnam War, the AIDS Epidemic, and the Politics of Remembering*. Berkeley: University of California Press.

Sturm, Circe D. 2002. *Blood Politics: Race, Culture, and Identity in the Cherokee Nation of Oklahoma*. Berkeley: University of California Press.

Sturtevant, William C., ed. 1978–2008. *Handbook of North American Indians*, 15 volumes. Washington, DC: Smithsonian Institution, for sale by the US Government Printing Office, Superintendent of Documents.

Sturtevant, William C., and David B. Quinn. 1999 [1987]. "This New Prey: Eskimos in Europe in 1567, 1576, and 1577." In *Indians and Europe: An Interdisciplinary Collection of Essays*, edited by Christian F. Feest, 61–140. Lincoln: University of Nebraska Press. [Aachen, Germany: Edition Herodot.]

Suzuki, David, and Peter Knudtson. 1992. *Wisdom of the Elders: Sacred Native Stories of Nature*. New York: Bantam.

Támez, Margo. 2008. "Open Letter to Cameron County Commission." June 3. http://www.utexas.edu/law/academics/centers/humanrights/borderwall/communities/tamezfamily.html.

———. 2010. "Restoring Lipan Apache Women's Laws, Lands, and Strength in El Calaboz Ranchería at the Texas-Mexico Border." *Signs* 35 (3): 558–569.

Tapper, Melbourne. 2001. "Blood/Kinship, Governmentality, and Cultures of Order in Colonial Africa." In *Relative Values: Reconfiguring Kinship Studies*, edited by Sarah Franklin and Susan McKinnon, 329–354. Durham, NC: Duke University Press.

Taussig, Michael. 1993. *Mimesis and Alterity: A Particular History of the Senses*. New York: Routledge.

Tayac, Gabrielle, Paul Chaat Smith, and Kathleen Ash-Milby. 2012. "NMAI 2.0: Redirecting the National Museum of the American Indian." Panel, annual meeting, Native American and Indigenous Studies Association, Uncasville, CT (June).

Taylor, Charles. 1992. "Multiculturalism and 'The Politics of Recognition.'" In *Multiculturalism and "The Politics of Recognition,"* edited by Amy Gutmann, 25–74. Princeton, NJ: Princeton University Press.

Tedlock, Dennis. 1983. *The Spoken Word and the Work of Interpretation.* Philadelphia: University of Pennsylvania Press.

———. 1999 [1974]. *Finding the Center: The Art of the Zuni Storyteller (from Live Performances in Zuni by Andrew Peynetsa and Walter Sanchez).* Lincoln: University of Nebraska Press.

Tenorio-Trillo, Mauricio. 1996. *Mexico at the World's Fairs: Crafting a Modern Nation.* Berkeley: University of California Press.

"The Texas-Mexico Border Wall." 2011. UT Working Group on Human Rights and the Border Wall, University of Texas School of Law. http://www.utexas.edu/law/academics/centers/humanrights/borderwall.

Thomas, David Hurst. 2000. *Skull Wars: Kennewick Man, Archaeology, and the Battle for Identity.* New York: Basic Books.

Thornton, Russell. 1987. *American Indian Holocaust and Survival.* Norman: University of Oklahoma Press.

Tilton, Robert S. 1994. *Pocahontas: The Evolution of an American Narrative.* Cambridge: Cambridge University Press.

Todorov, Tzvetan. 1984. *The Conquest of America: The Question of the Other.* Richard Howard, trans. New York: Harper and Row.

Tolley, Sara-Larus. 2006. *Quest for Tribal Acknowledgment: California's Honey Lake Maidus.* Norman: University of Oklahoma Press.

Tompkins, Jane P. 1986. *Sensational Designs: The Cultural Work of American Fiction, 1790–1860.* New York: Oxford University Press.

Trachtenberg, Alan. 2004. *Shades of Hiawatha: Staging Indians, Making Americans, 1880–1930.* New York: Hill and Wang.

Trafzer, Clifford E., Jean A. Keller, and Lorene Sisquoc, eds. 2006. *Boarding School Blues: Revisiting American Indian Educational Experiences.* Lincoln: Bison Books.

Trigger, Bruce G., ed. 1978. *Northeast,* vol. 15, *Handbook of North American Indians,* edited by William C. Sturtevant, Washington, DC: Smithsonian Institution, for sale by the US Government Printing Office, Superintendent of Documents.

Trouillot, Michel-Rolph. 1991. "Anthropology and the Savage Slot: The Poetics and Politics of Otherness." In *Recapturing Anthropology,* edited by Richard G. Fox, 17–44. Santa Fe: School of American Research Press.

———. 1995. *Silencing the Past: Power and the Production of History.* Boston: Beacon Press.

Truettner, William H. 1991a. "The West and the Heroic Ideal: Using Images to Interpret History." *Chronicles of Higher Education,* November 20, B1–B2.

———, ed. 1991b. *The West as America: Reinterpreting Images of the Frontier.* Washington, DC: Smithsonian Institution Press.

Ulrich, Laurel Thatcher. 1982. *Good Wives: Image and Reality in the Lives of Women in Northern New England, 1650–1750.* New York: Alfred A. Knopf.

Unger, Steven, ed. 1977. *The Destruction of American Indian Families.* New York: Association on American Indian Affairs, Inc.

"University, Community Come Together to Plan 'Seeds of Hope.'" 2009. The University of Texas at Brownsville and Texas Southmost College. http://blue.utb.edu/newsandinfo/BorderFence%20Issue/UpdateBorderFenceIssue.htm.

US Commission on Civil Rights. 2001. "Statement on the Use of Native American Images and Nicknames as Sports Symbols." Reprinted in *The Native American Mascot Controversy: A Handbook*, edited by C. Richard King, 191–194. Lanham, MD: Scarecrow Press, 2010.

Valentine, Lisa P., and Regna Darnell, eds. 1999. *Theorizing the Americanist Tradition.* Toronto: University of Toronto Press.

Vaughan, Alden T. 1983. "Narratives of North American Indian Captivity: A Selective Bibliography." *Garland Reference Library of the Humanities,* vol. 370. New York: Garland.

Vaughan, Alden T., and Edward W. Clark, eds. 1981. *Puritans among the Indians: Accounts of Captivity and Redemption, 1676–1724.* Cambridge, MA: Belknap Press of Harvard University Press.

Vaughan, Alden T., and Daniel K. Richter. 1980. "Crossing the Cultural Divide: Indians and New Englanders, 1605–1763." *Proceedings of the American Antiquarian Society* 90, part 1.

Viola, Herman J., and Carolyn Margolis, eds. 1991. *Seeds of Change: A Quincentennial Commemoration.* Washington, DC: Smithsonian Institution Press.

Vizenor, Gerald. 1981. *Earthdivers: Tribal Narratives on Mixed Descent.* Minneapolis: University of Minnesota Press.

———. 1987. "Crows Written on the Poplars: Autocritical Autobiographies." In *I Tell You Now: Autobiographical Essays by Native American Writers,* edited by Brian Swann and Arnold Krupat, 99–110. Lincoln: University of Nebraska Press.

———. 1990. *Crossbloods: Bone Courts, Bingo, and Other Reports.* Minneapolis: University of Minnesota Press.

———. 1993. "The Ruins of Representation: Shadow Survivance and the Literature of Dominance." *American Indian Quarterly* 17 (1): 7–30.

———. 1994. *Shadow Distance: A Gerald Vizenor Reader.* Middletown, CT: Wesleyan.

———. 1999. *Manifest Manners: Narratives on Postindian Survivance.* Lincoln: University of Nebraska Press.

———. 2005. *The Trickster of Liberty: Tribal Heirs to a Wild Baronage.* Minneapolis: University of Minnesota Press.

———. 2009. *Native Liberty: Natural Reason and Cultural Survivance.* Lincoln: University of Nebraska Press.

Vogel, Susan, ed. 1988. *ART/artifact.* New York: The Center for African Art.

Voigt, Lisa. 2008. *Writing Captivity in the Early Modern Atlantic: Circulations of Knowledge and Authority in the Iberian and English Imperial Worlds.* Chapel Hill: University of North Carolina Press.

Volkman, Toby, ed. 2005. *Cultures of Transnational Adoption.* Durham, NC: Duke University Press.

Wallace, Frances Loomis, and Earlleen Kirby. 1996. *Your Symbol Book.* Kansas City: Camp Fire Boys and Girls.

Wallach, Alan. 1992. "Revisionism Has Transformed Art History, but Not Museums." *Chronicle of Higher Education,* January 22, B2–B3.

———. 1998. *Exhibiting Contradictions: Essays on the Art Museum in the United States.* Boston: University of Massachusetts Press.

Walt Disney Pictures Presents "Pocahontas." 1995. Press Information. Burbank, CA: Walt Disney Pictures.

Warrior, Robert Allen. 1995. *Tribal Secrets: Recovering American Indian Intellectual Traditions.* Minneapolis: University of Minnesota Press.

———. 1998. "Literature and Students in the Emergence of Native American Studies." In *Studying Native America: Problems and Prospects,* edited by Russell Thornton, 111–129. Madison: University of Wisconsin Press.

Washburn, Wilcomb E., comp. 1977–1980. *Narratives of North American Indian Captivities.* 111 volumes. New York: Garland.

———, ed. 1988. *History of Indian-White Relations,* vol. 4, *Handbook of North American Indians,* ed. William C. Sturtevant. Washington, DC: Smithsonian Institution, for sale by the US Government Printing Office, Superintendent of Documents.

Weber, Max. 1968. *Economy and Society: An Outline of Interpretive Sociology,* edited by Guenther Roth and Claus Wittich. Berkeley: University of California Press.

Webster, Anthony K. 2009. *Explorations in Navajo Poetry and Poetics.* Albuquerque: University of New Mexico Press.

Weston, Kath. 2001. "Kinship, Controversy, and the Sharing of Substance: The Race/Class Politics of Blood Transfusion." In *Relative Values: Reconfiguring Kinship Studies,* edited by Sarah Franklin and Susan McKinnon, 147–174. Durham, NC: Duke University Press.

"When Worlds Collide: How Columbus's Voyage Transformed Both East and West." 1991. Columbus Special Issue, *Newsweek* (Fall/Winter).

White, Hayden. 1973. *Metahistory: The Historical Imagination in Nineteenth-Century Europe.* Baltimore: Johns Hopkins University Press.

———. 1976. "The Noble Savage Theme as Fetish." In *First Images of America,* vol. 1, edited by Fredi Chiapelli, Michael J. B. Allen, and Robert L. Benson, 121–135. Berkeley: University of California Press.

White, Richard. 1983. *The Roots of Dependency: Subsistence, Environment, and Social Change among the Choctaws, Pawnees, and Navajos.* Lincoln: University of Nebraska Press.

———. 1993. *"It's Your Misfortune and None of My Own": A New History of the American West.* Norman: University of Oklahoma Press.

White, Richard, and Patricia Limerick. 1994. *The Frontier in American Culture: An Exhibition at the Newberry Library, August 26, 1994–January 7, 1995; Essays by Richard White and Patricia Nelson Limerick,* edited by James R. Grossman. Berkeley: University of California Press.

Whiteley, Peter. 1998. "The End of Anthropology (at Hopi)?" In *Rethinking Hopi Ethnography,* 163–187. Washington, DC: Smithsonian Institution Press.

———. 2004. "Native American Ethnography." In *A Companion to the Anthropology of American Indians,* edited by Thomas Biolsi, 435–471. Malden, MA: Blackwell Publishers.

Wilkins, David E. 1997. *American Indian Sovereignty and the U.S. Supreme Court: The Masking of Justice.* Austin: University of Texas Press.

Wilkins, David E., and Tsianina Lomawaima. 2001. *Uneven Ground: American Indian Sovereignty and Federal Law.* Norman: University of Oklahoma Press.

Wilkins, David E., and Heidi Kiiwetinepinesiik Stark. 2011. *American Indian Politics and the American Political System,* 3rd ed. Lanham, MD: Rowman and Littlefield Publishers.

Wilkinson, Charles. 1987. *American Indians, Time, and the Law: Native Societies in a Modern Constitutional Democracy.* New Haven, CT: Yale University Press.

Wilkinson, Charles, and Eric R. Biggs. 1977. "The Evolution of the Termination Policy." *American Indian Review* 5 (1): 139–184.

Williams, John. 1976 [1707]. *The Redeemed Captive Returning to Zion*, edited by Edward W. Clark. Amherst: University of Massachusetts Press.

Williams, Raymond. 1977. *Marxism and Literature*. Oxford: Oxford University Press.

———. 1983. *Keywords: A Vocabulary of Culture and Society*. New York: Oxford University Press.

Williams, Robert A., Jr. 1990. *The American Indian in Western Legal Thought: The Discourse of Conquest*. Oxford: Oxford University Press.

Williamson, Margaret Holmes. 1992. "Pocahontas and Captain John Smith: Examining a Historical Myth." *History and Anthropology* 5: 365–402.

Willis, Holly. 2012. "Art Sims." New York: AIGA/The Professional Association for Design. http://www.aiga.org/design-journeys-art-sims/.

Wilson, Waziyatawin Angela, and Michael Yellow Bird, eds. 2005. *For Indigenous Eyes Only: A Decolonization Handbook*. Santa Fe: School of American Research.

Wilson, Terry P. 1992. "Blood Quantum: Native American Mixed Bloods." In *Racially Mixed People in America*, edited by Maria P. P. Root, 108–125. Newbury Park, CA: Sage Publications.

Witherspoon, Gary. 1996. *Navajo Kinship and Marriage*. Chicago: University of Chicago Press.

Wolfe, Patrick. 1998. *Settler Colonialism and the Transformation of Anthropology: The Politics and Poetics of an Ethnographic Event*. New York: Continuum.

Wood, Daniel B. 2008. "Where U.S.-Mexico Border Fence Is Tall, Border Crossings Fall." *Christian Science Monitor*, April 1. http://www.csmonitor.com/USA/2008/0401/p01s05-usgn.html.

Woodard, Charles L. 1989. *Ancestral Voice: Conversations with N. Scott Momaday*. Lincoln: University of Nebraska Press.

Wright, Lawrence. 1994. "Annals of Politics: One Drop of Blood." *The New Yorker* 70 (25): 46–55.

Yanagisako, Sylvia. 2005. "Flexible Disciplinarity: Beyond the Americanist Tradition." In *Unwrapping the Sacred Bundle: Essays on the Disciplining of Anthropology Now*, edited by Daniel A. Segal and Sylvia J. Yanagisako, 78–98. Durham, NC: Duke University Press.

Yankowitz, Joan. 1995. *Behind the Scenes of the Indian in the Cupboard*. New York: Scholastic.

Young, Iris. 2001. "Two Concepts of Self-Determination." In *Human Rights: Concepts, Contests, Contingencies*, edited by Austin Sarat and Thomas R. Kearns, 25–44. Ann Arbor: University of Michigan Press.

Young, James E. 1994. *The Texture of Memory: Holocaust Memorials and Meaning*. New Haven, CT: Yale University Press.

Zack, Naomi, ed. 1995. *American Mixed Race: The Culture of Microdiversity*. Lanham, MD: Rowman and Littlefield.

Ziff, Bruce, and Pratima V. Rao. 1997. *Borrowed Power: Essays on Cultural Appropriation*. New Brunswick, NJ: Rutgers University Press.

Zimmerman, Larry. 2004. "Archaeology." In *A Companion to the Anthropology of American Indians*, edited by Thomas Biolsi, 526–541. Malden, MA: Blackwell Publishers.

Zirin, Dave. 2010. "The Resurrection of the Chief." In *The Native American Mascot Controversy: A Handbook*, edited by C. Richard King, 183–185. Lanham, MD: Scarecrow Press.

Zitkala Ša (Gertrude Bonnin). 2003 [1900]. "'The School Days of an Indian Girl' and 'An Indian Teacher among Indians.'" *Atlantic Monthly*. Reprinted in *American Indian Stories, Legends, and Other Writings*, edited by Cathy N. Davidson and Ada Norris. New York: Penguin.

Multimedia Sources (Films, Videos, Scores, CD-ROMs, Podcasts)

1492: Conquest of Paradise. 1992. Directed by Ridley Scott. Paramount Pictures.

Aladdin. 1992. Directed by John Musker. Disney Company.

Atanarjuat (Fast Runner). 2001. Directed by Zacharias Kunuk. Isuma Igloolik Productions.

Bamboozled. 2000. Written and directed by Spike Lee. New Line Cinema.

Beauty and the Beast. 1991. Directed by Kirk Wise. Walt Disney Company.

Box of Treasures. 1983. Directed by Chuck Olin and U'mista Cultural Centre. Documentary Educational Resources.

Christopher Columbus: The Discovery. 1992. Directed by John Glen. Warner Brothers.

"Colors of the Wind." 1995. Music from the Disney animated feature film *Pocahontas*. Music by Alan Menken, lyrics by Stephen Schwartz.

Columbus Day Legacy. 2010. Directed by Bennie Klain. Trickster Films.

Dances with Wolves. 1990. Directed by Kevin Costner. Orion.

Disney's Pocahontas: Illustrated Songbook. 1995. Music by Alan Menken. Lyrics by Stephen Schwartz. Wonderland Music Company, Inc., and Walt Disney Music Company. Distributed by Hal Leonard Corporation.

"Geronimo E-KIA, A Poem by the 1491s." 2011. Written by Ryan Red Corn and Dallas Goldtooth. YouTube. http://www.youtube.com/watch?v=y7vKu7X4aNA.

Imagining Indians. 1992. Written, produced, and directed by Victor Masayesva Jr. Electronic Arts Intermix.

The Indian in the Cupboard. 1995. Directed by Frank Oz. Paramount Pictures and Columbia Pictures in association with Scholastic Books.

The Indian in the Cupboard: A Magical Learning Adventure on CD-ROM. 1995. Viacom New Media. Developed with the cooperation of Scholastic Books and the National Museum of the American Indian, Smithsonian Institution.

In Whose Honor? American Indian Mascots in Sports. 1997. Written and produced by Jay Rosenstein. New Day Films.

Journey: Museums and Community Collaboration. 1996. Science Museum of Minnesota.

"Just Around the Riverbend." 1995. Music from the Disney animated feature film *Pocahontas*. Music by Alan Menken, lyrics by Stephen Schwartz.

The Lion King. 1994. Directed by Roger Allers and Rob Minkoff. Walt Disney Company.

The Little Mermaid. 1989. Directed by John Musker and Ron Clements. Walt Disney Company.

Man of the House. 2005. Directed by Stephen Herek. Sony Pictures.

Nanook of the North. 1922 [DVD, 1999]. Directed by Robert J. Flaherty. Criterion Collection.

Netsilik Eskimo Series. 1967. Produced by National Film Board of Canada. Documentary Educational Resources.

Pocahontas. 1995. Directed by Mike Gabriel and Eric Goldberg. Music by Alan Menken. Lyrics by Stephen Schwartz. Walt Disney Company.

The Return of Navajo Boy. 2000. Directed by Jeff Spitz. Produced by Jeff Spitz and Bennie Klain. Public Broadcasting Service.

The Return of the Sacred Pole. 1988. Directed and produced by Mike Farrell. Nebraska Educational Television.

"Savages." 1995. Music from the Disney animated feature film *Pocahontas.* Music by Alan Menken, lyrics by Stephen Schwartz.

The Searchers. 1956. Directed by John Ford. Based on the novel by Alan Le May. Warner Brothers.

Tununeremiut: The People of Tununak. 1973. Produced by Sarah Elder and Leonard Kamerling. Alaska Native Heritage Film Project.

U.S. Senate Committee on Indian Affairs. 2011. Oversight Hearing on "Stolen Identities: The Impact of Racist Stereotypes on Indigenous People." Podcast. http://indian.senate.gov/hearings/hearing.cfm?hearingID=e655f9e2809e5476862f735da16ba74a.

World Song. 1992. Directed and written by Larry Sulkis. BRC Imagination Arts.

Legislation and Court Cases

American Indian Religious Freedom Act [AIRFA], 1978 (92 US Stat. 469).

Bonnichsen v. US, 2004 (367 F.3d 864—Court of Appeals, 9th Circuit).

Cherokee Nation v. Georgia, 1831 (30 US 5 Pet. 1).

Civil Rights Act, 1964 (78 US Stat. 241).

Dawes Allotment Act, 1887 (24 US Stat. 388).

Ex parte Crow Dog, 1883 (109 US 556).

Harjo v. Pro-Football, Inc., 2009 (130 S. Ct. 631).

Indian Child Welfare Act [ICWA], 1978 (93 US Stat. 3071).

Indian Citizenship Act, 1924 (43 US Stat. 253).

Indian Gaming Regulatory Act [IGRA], 1988 (102 US Stat. 2467).

Indian Reorganization Act [IRA], 1934 (48 US Stat. 984).

Indian Self-Determination and Education Assistance Act, 1975 (88 US Stat. 2203).

Major Crimes Act, 1885 (23 US Stat. 62).

National Museum of the American Indian Act, 1989 (103 US Stat. 1336).

Native American Graves Protection and Repatriation Act [NAGPRA], 1990 (104 US Stat. 3048).

Santa Clara Pueblo v. Martinez, 1978 (436 US 49).

Secure Fence Act, 2006 (120 US Stat. 2638–2640).

Worcester v. Georgia, 1832 (31 US 6 Pet. 515).

SOURCES AND CREDITS

Portions of the following chapters first appeared in the publications listed below; all chapters are revised and updated. Some of the original versions contain more extensive documentation and visual imagery than is found here. Previously published materials are included by permission of the publishers and, in the case of Chapters 2 and 4, the second author.

Chapter 1: "Representational Practices," 341–359 in *A Companion to the Anthropology of North American Indians,* edited by Thomas Biolsi (Malden, MA: Blackwell Publishers, 2004). Chapter 2: (with Barrik Van Winkle) "Tribe and Nation: American Indians and American Nationalism," *Social Analysis: Journal of Cultural and Social Practice* 33 (1993): 9–26. Chapter 3: "Exclusive Labels: Indexing the National 'We' in Commemorative and Oppositional Exhibitions," *Museum Anthropology* 21 (1997): 42–56. Chapter 4: (with Barrik Van Winkle) "'Indian Blood': Reflections on the Reckoning and Refiguring of Native North American Identity," *Cultural Anthropology* 11 (1996): 547–576. Chapter 5: "Captivity in White and Red: Convergent Practice and Colonial Representation on the British-Amerindian Frontier, 1607–1736," 33–104 in *Crossing Cultures: Essays in the Displacement of Western Civilization,* edited by Daniel A. Segal (Tucson: University of Arizona Press, 1992). Chapter 6: "'To Forget Their Tongue, Their Name, and Their Whole Relation': Captivity, Extra-Tribal Adoption, and the American Indian Child Welfare Act," 468–493 in *Relative Values: Reconfiguring Kinship Studies,* edited by Sarah Franklin and Susan McKinnon (Durham, NC: Duke University Press, 2001). Chapter 8: "Cultural Appropriation and the Crafting of Racialized Selves in American Youth Organizations: Towards an Autoethnography," *Cultural Studies/Critical Methodologies*

9 (2009): 197–213. Chapter 9: "Playing Indian in the 1990s: *Pocahontas* and *The Indian in the Cupboard*," 187–205 in *Hollywood's Indian: The Portrayal of the Native American in Film*, edited by Peter C. Rollins and John E. O'Connor (Lexington: University Press of Kentucky, 1998; 2nd edition, 2003). Chapter 10: "The Mascot Slot: Cultural Citizenship, Political Correctness, and Pseudo-Indian Sports Symbols," *Journal of Sport and Social Issues* 28 (2004): 79–87. Chapter 11: "Recent Ethnographic Research on North American Indigenous Peoples," *Annual Review of Anthropology* 34 (2005): 253–268.

Credits for the illustrations are listed in the photo captions.

Index

ABOUT THE AUTHOR

Pauline Turner Strong is Associate Professor of Anthropology and Gender Studies at The University of Texas at Austin, where she also directs the Humanities Institute. She is the author of *Captive Selves, Captivating Others: The Politics and Poetics of Colonial American Captivity Narratives* and the coeditor of *New Perspectives on Native North America: Cultures, Histories, and Representations.*